Rome
2008
WHAT'S NEW | WHAT'S ON | WHAT'S BEST

www.timeout.com/rome

Contents

Don't Miss: 2008

Itineraries

Rome by Area

Essentials

Published by Time Out Guides Ltd
Universal House
251 Tottenham Court Road
London W1T 7AB
Tel: + 44 (0)20 7813 3000
Fax: + 44 (0)20 7813 6001
Email: guides@timeout.com
www.timeout.com

Managing Director Peter Fiennes
Editorial Director Ruth Jarvis
Deputy Series Editor Dominic Earle
Business Manager Gareth Garner
Editorial Manager Holly Pick
Accountant Ija Krasnikova

Time Out Guides is a wholly owned subsidiary of Time Out Group Ltd.

© **Time Out Group Ltd**
Chairman Tony Elliott
Financial Director Richard Waterlow
Time Out Magazine Ltd MD David Pepper
Group General Manager/Director Nichola Coulthard
Managing Director, Time Out International Cathy Runciman
Time Out Communications Ltd MD David Pepper
Production Director Mark Lamond
Group Marketing Director John Luck
Group Art Director John Oakey
Group IT Director Simon Chappell

Time Out and the Time Out logo are trademarks of Time Out Group Ltd.

This edition first published in Great Britain in 2007 by Ebury Publishing
A Random House Group Company
Company information can be found on www.randomhouse.co.uk
10 9 8 7 6 5 4 3 2 1

For further distribution details, see www.timeout.com

ISBN 13: 978184670 0248
ISBN 10: 1-84670-024-8

A CIP catalogue record for this book is available from the British Library

Printed and bound by Firmengruppe APPL, aprinta druck, Wemding, Germany

The Random House Group Limited makes every effort to ensure that the papers used in
our books are made from trees that have been legally sourced from well-managed and
credibly certified forests. Our paper procurement policy can be found on
www.randomhouse.co.uk

Rome Shortlist

The **Time Out Rome Shortlist 2008** is one of a new series of guides that draws on Time Out's background as a magazine publisher to keep you current with what's going on in town. As well as Rome's key sights and the best of its eating, drinking and leisure options, it picks out the most exciting venues to have opened in the last year and gives a full calendar of events from September 2007 to December 2008. It also includes features on the important news, trends and openings, all compiled by locally based editors and writers. Whether you're visiting for the first time in your life or the first time this year, you'll find the *Time Out Rome Shortlist 2008* contains everything you need to know, in a portable and easy-to-use format.

The guide divides central Rome into six areas, each containing listings for Sights & Museums, Eating & Drinking, Shopping, Nightlife and Arts & Leisure, and maps pinpointing their locations. At the front of the book are chapters rounding up these scenes city-wide, and giving a shortlist of our overall picks. We include itineraries for days out, plus essentials such as transport information and hotels.

Our listings give phone numbers as dialled within Italy. Rome's prefix is 06; you must dial this prefix even if you're calling from within the city. The international code for Italy is 39. When calling from outside Italy, do not drop the initial '0' of the Rome prefix. Listed numbers beginning with a '3' are mobiles.

We've noted price categories by using one to four euro signs (€-€€€€), representing budget, moderate, expensive and luxury. Major credit cards are accepted unless otherwise stated. We also indicate when a venue is NEW, and give Event highlights.

All our listings are double-checked, but businesses do sometimes close or change their hours or prices, so it's a good idea to call a venue before visiting. While every effort has been made to ensure accuracy, the publishers cannot accept responsibility for any errors that this guide may contain.

Venues are marked on the maps using symbols numbered according to their order within the chapter and colour-coded according to the type of venue they represent:

❶ Sights & Museums
❶ Eating & Drinking
❶ Shopping
❶ Nightlife
❶ Arts & Leisure

Map key	
Major sight or landmark	
Railway station	
Park	
Area name	TRIDENTE
Metro line	
Hospital	H
Church	

Time Out Rome Shortlist 2008

EDITORIAL
Editor Anne Hanley
Copy Editor John Shandy Watson
Proofreader Gill Harvey

DESIGN
Art Director Scott Moore
Art Editor Pinelope Kourmouzoglou
Senior Designer Henry Elphick
Graphic Designer Gemma Doyle
Junior Graphic Designer Kei Ishimaru
Digital Imaging Simon Foster, Tessa Kar
Ad Make-up Jodi Sher
Picture Editor Jael Marschner
Deputy Picture Editor Tracey Kerrigan
Picture Researcher Helen McFarland

ADVERTISING
Sales Director/Sponsorship Mark Phillips
International Sales Manager Fred Durman
International Sales Consultant
 Ross Canadé
International Sales Executive Charlie Sokol
Advertising Sales Time Out (Rome):
 Margherita Tedone
Advertising Assistant Kate Staddon

MARKETING
Marketing Manager Yvonne Poon
**Sales & Marketing Director, North
America** Lisa Levinson
Marketing Designer Anthony Huggins

PRODUCTION
Production Manager Brendan McKeown
Production Co-ordinator Caroline Bradford
Production Controller Susan Whittaker

CONTRIBUTORS
This guide was researched and written by Anne Hanley, with the exception of Pope-spotting, A Papal Procession, Chasing Caravaggio, Down by the river, Wall to wall, Latin lovers, Vatican tack (Julia Crosse).

PHOTOGRAPHY
All photography by Gianluca Moggi, New Press Photo, except: pages 14, 26, 46, 64, 65, 93, 127, 134, 139, 150, 169, 175, 176 Agnese Sanvito; page 29 Foto D'Annibale/ Maratona della Città di Roma; page 35 (top left) Peter van Hattem; page 35 (top right) Tristram Kenton; page 39 Pietro Pesce; pages 147, 159 Adam Eastland.

The following images were provided by the featured establishments/artists: pages 35 (bottom), 36, 98.

Cover photograph: Colosseum in Rome. Credit: © Paul Hardy/Corbis.

MAPS
LS International Cartography, via Decemviri 8, 20138 Milan, Italy (www.geomaker.com).

Thanks to Fulvio Marsigliani at LS International, Raffaella Malaguti, Julia and Richard Owen, Lee and Clara Marshall, and all contributors to past editions of *Time Out Rome*.

About Time Out

Founded in 1968, Time Out has expanded from humble London beginnings into the leading resource for those wanting to know what's happening in the world's greatest cities. As well as our influential what's-on weeklies in London, New York and Chicago, we publish more than a dozen other listings magazines in cities as varied as Beijing and Mumbai. The magazines established Time Out's trademark style: sharp writing, informed reviewing and bang up-to-date inside knowledge of every scene.

Time Out made the natural leap into travel guides in the 1980s with the City Guide series, which now extends to over 50 destinations around the world. Written and researched by expert local writers and generously illustrated with original photography, the full-size guides cover a larger area than our Shortlist guides and include many more venue reviews, along with additional background features and a full set of maps.

Throughout this rapid growth, the company has remained proudly independent, still owned by Tony Elliott nearly four decades after he started Time Out London as a single fold-out sheet of A5 paper. This independence extends to the editorial content of all our publications, this Shortlist included. No establishment has been featured because it has advertised, and no payment has influenced any of our reviews. And, for our critics, there's definitely no such thing as a free lunch: all restaurants and bars are visited and reviewed anonymously, and Time Out always picks up the bill.
For more about the company, see www.timeout.com.

Don't Miss
2008

The Colosseum

Sights & Museums

History in Rome is not confined to museums and galleries: it tumbles out of everywhere. And though the city is reassuringly compact, this doesn't stop the cultural onslaught from being utterly bewildering and exhausting.

It pays to approach the Eternal City knowing that you won't see everything. Remember, too, that if you shut yourself up in the city's extraordinary collections and sites, you'll miss something equally as important: the urban landscape and its inimitable inhabitants. To best appreciate it, you'll need to walk (bring comfy shoes) and lounge – seating yourself at a pavement café may crank up the price of your *cappuccino*, but a front-row seat at the magnificent spectacle that is Rome is cheap at any price.

Rome today is looking good: many of its historic buildings have been restored and are gorgeously illuminated at night; the Ara Pacis (p84) has a controversial new enclosure; streets and squares have been repaved with traditional basalt cobbles. Parts of the *centro storico* have been pedestrianised; there are clean green electric buses and the metro is being extended.

Ancient sites

The area with the greatest density of remains lies between the Palatine, Capitoline, Esquiline and Quirinal hills. Located here are the Roman Forum (p58), the Colosseum (p55), and ancient Rome's most desirable residential area, the Palatine (p58). But ancient Rome doesn't stop there: the Museo Nazionale Romano group (Palazzo Massimo alle Terme, p104; Palazzo Altemps, p72; Crypta Balbi, p61; and the Baths of Diocletian, p101) houses a mind-boggling collection of ancient statuary, of which there's more in the Vatican and Capitoline museums (p145 and p54). And the Pantheon (p72) is a work of art in itself.

Churches

Down the centuries popes, princes and aristocrats commissioned architects and artists to build and adorn their preferred places of worship, with the result that central Rome is home to more than 400 churches, containing endless artistic treasures.

Churches are places of worship; though only the Vatican imposes its dress code rigidly (both in St Peter's and the Vatican Museums), very short skirts, bare midriffs, over-exposed shoulders and shorts are all frowned upon. Churches ask tourists to refrain from visiting during services. A supply of coins for the meters to light up the most interesting art works is handy, as is a pair of binoculars.

Museums and galleries

Rome has long boasted some of the world's greatest galleries and museums, but the last few years have seen a rash of new permanent exhibits, and new showcases for old ones. The ancient, Renaissance and Baroque dominate, of course; but initiatives such as MACRO and MAXXI (both p99) mean that contemporary art is being increasingly well catered for.

Improved services at major sights means – unfortunately and unforgiveably – that some less-visited museums have suffered: we have indicated where staffing shortages are likely to make opening hours unreliable.

SHORTLIST

Ancient splendour
- Ara Pacis Museum (p84)
- Baths of Caracalla (p120)
- Colosseum (p55)
- Hadrian's Villa (p158)
- Imperial Fora & Trajan's Market (p56)
- Ostia Antica (p157)
- Pantheon (p72)
- Roman Forum (p58)

Ancient collections
- Capitoline Museums (p54)
- Centrale Montemartini (p121)
- Palazzo Altemps (p72)
- Palazzo Massimo alle Terme (p104)
- Vatican Museums (p145)

Churches with digs
- San Clemente (p110)
- San Nicola in Carcere (p59)
- Santa Cecilia in Trastevere (p129)
- Santi Giovanni e Paolo (p112)

Grand masters
- Capitoline Museums (p54)
- Galleria Borghese (p92)
- Galleria Doria Pamphili (p72)
- Palazzo Barberini (p95)

Baroque wonders
- *Baldacchino* and colonnade in St Peter's (p143)
- Four Rivers fountain in piazza Navona (p73)
- San Carlino alle Quattro Fontane (p96)
- Sant'Ivo alla Sapienza (p76)
- *The Ecstasy of St Teresa* in Santa Maria della Vittoria (p96)

Peaceful parks
- Orto Botanico (p129)
- Villa Borghese (p90)
- Villa Pamphili (p138)
- Villa Torlonia (p99)

DON'T MISS: 2008

Tour Schedule

May through November
Tours operate seven days per week
Tour Times 10.00 a.m. and 2.00 p.m.
December through March
Tours available by request and based on availability

Tour Cost: € 75,00 per person

Duration 3 hours
Participants: up to 8 people
Reservation is required
Participant must be at least 13 years old and between 100 and 275 lbs.

Please arrive 15 minutes before your tour time to check in so we can start your training and tour on time.

Tour times, days and locations are subject to change.

Discover Villa Borghese and Roma Antica using the Segway HT

For reservation call +39 06 42014533 or www.iglidetours.com

Ara Pacis Museum p8

Opening hours

Though we have given both winter (*orario invernale*) and summer (*orario estivo*) opening hours, these latter may sometimes be extended significantly, with some major museums and sites keeping doors open as late as 11pm in the high season. Check for current times at information kiosks. Note that many museums – though not churches – are closed on Mondays.

Note that ticket offices at many museums, galleries and ancient sites stop issuing tickets anything up to 75 minutes before gates shut.

Church opening times should be taken as rough guidelines. Whether doors are open or not often depends on anything from priestly whim to the availability of volunteer staff.

Tickets

Entrance to publicly owned sites and museums is free (*gratuito*) or reduced (*ridotto*) for EU citizens (and citizens of other countries with bilateral agreements) aged under 18 or over 65; you must show photo-ID (for children too) at ticket offices to prove that you are eligible. Under-25s in full-time education may also be eligible for discounts, as may journalists, teachers, motoring association members and others. Carry a range of ID just in case.

Many sights have introduced an extra charge for special exhibitions taking place inside; visitors are given no option other than to pay the ticket-plus-exhibition price.

Booking

Booking is mandatory for the Domus Aurea (p101) and Galleria Borghese (p92). It is also a good idea for big one-off shows.

Booking is possible – though really not necessary except for large groups – for many other sites and museums. Note that agencies charge a booking fee that further bumps up the price of tickets.

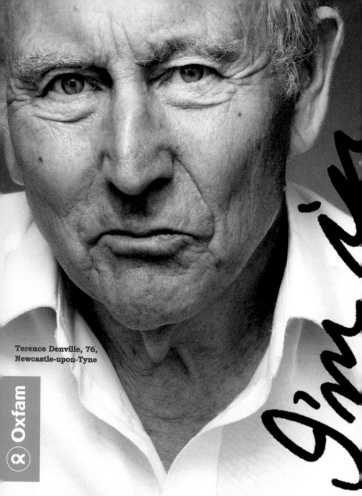

Terence Denville, 76,
Newcastle-upon-Tyne

⊗ Oxfam

Hundreds of thousands of people have said *I'm in* to fight the injustice of poverty. And this kind of pressure
has already made a huge difference. In Ghana, for example, most of the country's debt has been wiped out.
But there's so much more to do: every day, extreme poverty kills 30,000 children. That's unacceptable. Text
'TIMEOUT' and your name to 87099. We'll let you know how to help. We can do this. We *can* end poverty.
Are you in?

I give my support to help end
poverty. and you know what?
things actually get done

Let's end poverty together. Text 'TIMEOUT' and your name to 87099.

The official booking agencies for Rome's major sites are Pierreci (06 3996 7700, www.pierreci.it), which charges a €1.50 booking fee, and Ticketeria (06 32 810, www.ticketeria.it), which charges a €1-€2 booking fee. Both accept MasterCard and Visa.

Discounts and passes

The **Roma Pass** is a multi-entrance card that costs €20 and is valid for three days. It gives free access to any two sights, reduced entry to all others, plus free use of the city's public transport system. For further information, see www.romapass.it.

The **Villa Borghese Card** (€10) lasts 12 months and allows free access to one of the many museums within this park (p90), plus reduced entrance to the others and discounts at bookshops and bars. For further information, see www.villaborghese.it.

The Pantheon p9

The following tickets can be bought (cash only) at any of the museums and archaeological sites involved or at the APT (p187), which charges a €1.50 booking fee.

Appia Card (€6, €3 reductions, valid 7 days) covers the Baths of Caracalla, Tomb of Cecilia Metella and Villa dei Quintili.

Archeologia Card (€20, €10 reductions, valid 7 days) covers the Baths of Caracalla, Baths of Diocletian, Colosseum, Crypta Balbi, Palatine, Palazzo Altemps, Palazzo Massimo alle Terme, Tomb of Cecilia Metella and Villa dei Quintili.

Capitolini Card (€8.50, €6.50 reductions, valid 7 days) covers the Capitoline Museums and Centrale Montemartini.

Museo Nazionale Romano Card (€6.50, €3.50 reductions, valid 3 days) covers the Baths of Diocletian, Crypta Balbi, Palazzo Massimo alle Terme and Palazzo Altemps.

Tours

The Enjoy Rome agency (p187) organises walking tours of the city.

Trambus's 110 Open bus (06 4695 2252) leaves Termini station every 10mins (8.40am-8.30pm). It makes 11 stops on a two-hour circuit. Tours include commentary (in six languages). An all-day stop-and-go ticket costs €13.

The Archeobus passes by the Baths of Caracalla (p120) and along via Appia Antica (Appian Way, p152), leaving Termini station about every 40mins from 9am to 4pm. Stop-and-go tickets cost €8; without stops, the trip takes about two and a half hours.

Tickets for both can be bought at the booth in front of Termini, on board or online (www.trambus open.com). A variety of tickets that combine the tours with museum entrance are also available.

Cinecaffè – Casina delle Rose p94

Eating & Drinking

Romans takes their food and drink very seriously, valuing substance over style: the shabby neighbourhood bar, with its excellent coffee and delicious *cornetti* remains a favourite; and the local trat – where food is hearty and fresh – will always be packed.

But the Eternal City also offers a host of addresses for sipping and dining in style. And if prices have soared since the introduction of the euro – putting Rome on level pegging with many other European cities – the quality and sheer panache of what's on offer here is hard to beat.

Eating

A swathe of designer restaurants opened in Rome around the turn of the millennium, but many have since closed, the survivors being those which offer real culinary excitement, rather than just a few dried twigs in a tall vase and the chance of spotting a once-famous TV starlet.

Trattorie and *osterie*, on the other hand, are going great guns, spurred on by a growing demand for value for money. Some of these are unreconstructed family-run operations that have been serving up the same dishes for generations – but still do them so well that they pack in the punters. Others, however, are newcomers. The big novelty of the last five years or so has been the rise of what might be called the *nuova trattoria* – places that take the trattoria formula then give it a twist by upping the creativity quotient in the kitchen.

But it is the focus on the raw materials that is the real innovation.

Foodie enthusiasm has upped quality no end, the trickle-down effect meaning that even the most basic trat now generally offers decent extra-virgin olive oil with which to dress your salad.

The other positive note is the increasing variety of the Roman dining scene. Once, the choice was between posh restaurant, humble trattoria or pizzeria. Today there are wine bars, salad bars, gastropubs and deli-diners. Even the unchanging pizzeria has been shaken up by the arrival of gourmet pizza emporia. And Rome now has more decent Japanese and Indian restaurants than ever before (see box p125).

Going the course

The standard Italian running order is: *antipasto* (starter), *primo* (usually pasta, sometimes soup), *secondo* (the meat or fish course) with optional *contorno* (vegetables or salad, served separately) and *dolce* (dessert). You're under no obligation to order four courses – few locals do. It's perfectly normal, for example, to order a pasta course followed by a simple *contorno*.

Top-flight restaurants will occasionally offer a special *menu degustazione* (taster menu), but any establishment with a *menu turistico* should usually be avoided.

Drinks

One of the biggest changes over the last decade has been the way even humble eateries have started to get decent wine lists. More and more establishments are now offering a decent selection of wine by the glass (*al bicchiere* or *alla mescita*). In pizzerias, the drink of choice is *birra* (beer) or soft drinks. Mineral water – *acqua minerale* – comes either *gasata* (sparkling) or *naturale* (still) and is usually served by the litre.

DON'T MISS: 2008

S H O R T L I S T

Gourmet delights
- Antico Arco (p138)
- Il Pagliaccio (p69)
- L'Altro Mastai (p78)

Venues with views
- Ar Galletto (p68)
- Ciampini al Café du Jardin (p86)
- Da Giggetto (p68)
- 'Gusto (p86)
- Il Ristoro (p148)
- La Vineria (p69)

Good food, good value
- Cantina Cantarini (p94)
- Gino in Vicolo Rosini (p86)
- Matricianella (p87)
- Osteria dell'Arco (p99)
- Ristoro degli Angeli (p123)

Smart bars for long drinks
- Bartaruga (p68)
- Crudo (p68)
- Etabli (p78)
- Stravinskij Bar (p89)

Great coffee
- Bar Sant'Eustachio (p76)
- Bernasconi (p68)
- Dagnino (p107)

Lunch spots
- Casa Bleve (p77)
- Cinecaffè – Casina delle Rose (p94)
- Enoteca Corsi (p77)

Filling snacks
- Forno Campo de' Fiori (p68)
- Lo Zozzone (p78)
- Paninoteca da Guido (p148)

Perfect pizza
- Da Francesco (p77)
- Dar Poeta (p133)
- Pizza Ciro (p87)
- Remo (p124)

Prices, tipping & times

Places that add service to the bill are still in the minority; if in doubt, ask, *'è incluso il servizio?'* A good rule of thumb is to leave around five per cent in humbler places, or up to ten in smarter eateries. If service has been slack or rude, you should have no qualms about leaving nothing – or checking the bill in detail, as there is still the occasional restaurateur who gets his sums wrong when dealing with foreigners. Most restaurants accept credit cards, but if there is no sticker on the door, ask, *'accettate le carte di credito?'*

Where we have specified '**Meals served**', this is the opening time of the kitchen: the establishment may remain open long after. In the evening, few serious restaurants open before 7.30pm. Pizzerias begin serving earlier, generally by 7pm.

In this guide, we have used the euro (€) symbol to indicate the average price range for a three-course meal without wine for one. € means a meal at €20 or less, €€ is used for anything up to €35, €€€ for up to €50 and €€€€ for over €50. Of course, if three courses prove too challenging, the final bill will be lower.

Children, women & (no) smoking

Taking children into restaurants – even the smartest – is never a problem in Rome. Waiters will usually produce a high chair (*un seggiolone*) and are generally happy to serve youngsters *una mezza porzione* – a half-portion.

Women dining alone will rarely encounter problems, though you have to get used to the local habit of staring frankly. Single diners of either sex can have trouble getting a table in cheaper places at busy times: few proprietors want to waste a table that could hold four.

Smoking is now illegal in all restaurants except where there is a designated smoking area that meets stringent regulations.

Booking is recommended for Friday or Saturday evening or Sunday lunch, even in the more humble-looking places.

Pizza

Traditional Roman pizza is thin; Neapolitan pizza is puffier. Either way, make sure it comes from a wood-fired oven (*forno a legna*).

Pizza toppings are strictly orthodox: don't expect pineapple. Note that pizza is an evening thing – very few places serve it for lunch.

Wine bars & *enoteche*

Neighbourhood *enoteche* (wine shops) and *vini e olii* (wine and oil) outlets have been around in Rome since time immemorial. Recently, a number of upmarket, international-style wine bars have also sprung up, offering snacks and even full meals to go with their wines.

Snacks

The city's snack culture lurks in unlikely places, such as the humble *alimentari* (grocer's) where they'll fill a crusty white roll (*rosetta*), or a slice of *pizza bianca* (pizza base) with ham, salami or cheese. *Pizzerie rustiche* serve pizza by the take-away slab, while most bars have a range of sandwiches and filled rolls.

Vegetarians

Rome has few *bona fide* vegetarian restaurants; but even in traditional trattorias, there's plenty to try – from *penne all'arrabbiata* (pasta in a tomato and chilli sauce) through *tonnarelli cacio e pepe* (thick spaghetti with crumbly sheep's cheese and plenty of black pepper) to *carciofi alla giudia* (deep-fried artichokes). If you are at all unsure about the ingredients of any dish, ask, *'c'è la carne?'*

Pasticcerie & gelaterie

Most *pasticcerie* (cake shops) are bars where freshly baked goodies can be consumed *in situ* with a drink, or taken away.

Many bars have a freezer cabinet with a sign promising *produzione artigianale* (home-made ice-cream). This is often a con: it may mean industrial ice-cream mix whipped up on the premises. While this doesn't necessarily mean the ice-cream will be bad, you'll need to be selective when seeking a truly unique *gelato* experience. If the colours seem too bright to be real, then they aren't. Banana should be creamy-grey, not electric yellow.

As well as the two main choices of *frutta* or *crema* (fruit- or cream-based ice-cream), there's also *sorbetto* or *granita* (water ices). When you've exhausted these, sample a *grattachecca*, a rougher version of water ice.

Drinking

Cafés & bars

The average Roman starts his or her day with a coffee in a local café or bar (in Italy these amount to the same thing since alcohol and coffee are served all day long in both). There'll be snacks, maybe cigarettes and bus tickets, a clean loo and fabulous – and fabulously inexpensive – coffee.

In the touristy *centro storico*, things are different. Standing at the counter like the locals to knock back your tiny cupful is one thing; but occupy a table or, worse, a pavement table, and the bill will double or even treble. Of course there are moments when nothing is more beguiling than sitting at a pavement table; just be aware that you'll pay for the luxury.

Besides the many variations of *caffè* (espresso) and *cappuccino*, most bars offer *cornetti* (croissants),

tramezzini (sandwiches) and *panini* (filled rolls; one is a *panino*). A small bottle of still or sparkling mineral water (*acqua minerale naturale* or *gassata*) costs around €1.

By law, all bars must have a *bagno* (lavatory), which can be used by anyone, whether or not they purchase anything. Bars must also provide dehydrated passers-by with a glass of tap water, free and with no obligation to buy. Smoking is forbidden in all bars and cafés.

Pubs & enoteche

Many of Rome's *enoteche* and *vini e olii* (bottle shops) have recently become charming places to grab a drink and a slice of the *vita romana*. Some of these are chic venues with a *dopocena* (after-dinner) scene and a beautiful, see-and-be-seen crowd.

Rome's pubs are divided between a handful of long-standing UK-style institutions and a host of newer casual joints.

Via Condotti

Shopping

For the visitor, there's something refreshingly old-fashioned about shopping in Rome. There are no huge department stores here; no shopping malls; none of the ubiquitous chains (give or take a Benetton or two) that in many countries make every high street a carbon copy of all the others. Instead, there are corner grocery shops, dark and dusty bottle-lined wine shops, one-off boutiques catering to every imaginable taste… and of course the opulent outlets of Italy's fashion aristocracy.

A local would tell you that this old-worldiness is an illusion. In Rome, as elsewhere, the corner shop is being driven out by big-name inner-city mini-markets; shopping malls are absent only because space restrictions and exhorbitant rents keep them in the outer suburbs; there *are* clothing retail chains – just that they have different names here – and major brands are colonising the Roman high street at a distressing pace.

Traditionalists can draw comfort from the fact that, for now, the tiny boutique and the family-run store are still managing to retain their presence in Rome's retail sector.

Where to shop

As a fashion centre, Rome has long been overshadowed by the *moda* empire that is Milan, but the past few years have seen a blossoming in the Eternal City. The major Italian names in *alta moda* are huddled around piazza di Spagna and via Condotti, in the Tridente. The main streets here are often packed: to avoid the masses, wend your way around the side streets, where smaller boutiques and cafés make for a peaceful and pretty (though often costly) stroll. Slicing through the Tridente from piazza del Popolo to piazza Venezia is via del Corso, home to mid-range outlets for everything from books and music to clothing and shoes.

Further south along via del Corso, the Galleria Alberto Sordi is the biggest recent development on the *centro storico* shopping scene. The former Galleria Colonna, a restored early 20th-century arcade, has fast became one of the city's prime shopping and meeting points. The 20 retail outlets here include bookstore Feltrinelli, teen paradise Jam (trendy togs for rich kids) and a branch of fashion retailer Zara. But there are also a couple of *aperitivo* bars, plus frequent 'happenings' of a musical and artistic nature, all under one beautifully coloured glass roof.

There are more high-street clothing retailers along traffic-clogged via Nazionale; while this street itself is no charmer, the nearby Monti neighbourhood packs unique boutiques and hip originals along its narrow, hilly streets.

Across the river, beneath the Vatican walls in the Prati area, via Cola di Rienzo is a shorter and slightly less crowded version of via del Corso, with major retail chains, and some great food shopping at divine deli Franchi (p151).

For great independent designers and the city's best vintage, on the other hand, head west of piazza Navona to via del Governo Vecchio.

Opening times

Many central-Rome shop owners now forego the sacred siesta in favour of '*no-stop*' opening hours,

SHORTLIST

Treats to take home
- Buccone (wine; p86)
- Franchi (deli; p151)
- Moriondo & Gariglio (chocolate; p80)
- Volpetti (deli; p126)

Books in English
- Almost Corner Bookshop (p136)
- Anglo-American Book (p89)
- The Lion Bookshop (p89)

Pleasant perfumes
- Antica Erboristeria Romana (p79)
- L'Olfattorio (p89)
- Roma – Store (p137)

Independent designers
- Angelo Nepi (p69)
- Arsenale (p79)
- Le Tartarughe (p80)
- Maga Morgana (p80)

Jewels & gems
- Giokeb (p137)
- Laboratorio Marco Aurelio (p70)
- Madò (p80)

Markets
- Campo de' Fiori (fruit & veg; p60)
- ex-Piazza Vittorio (fruit & veg; p107)
- Piazza San Cosimato (fruit & veg; p136)
- Piazza Testaccio (fruit, veg & shoes; p126)
- Porta Portese (flea market; p136)
- Via Sannio (clothes; p113)

Fine footwear
- Borini (p70)
- Loco (p70)
- Piazza Testaccio (p126)

Paper & paint
- Cartoleria Pantheon (p80)
- Ditta G Poggi (p80)

Castel Romano Designer Outlet

More than 100 shops of top brands at prices reduced from 30% to 70% all year round.

Book your shopping shuttle from your hotel! For information and booking please contact hotel reception desk within the day before departure and in any case not later than 11.00 AM of the visit date.

Ask your concierge to phone to 06 37350810; 329 4317686.

The cost of the shuttle is 25€

(deposit at the moment of reservation for the service: 5 €)

If you don't feel like driving there is a **shuttle bus** from Central Rome Piazza della Repubblica to the Castel Romano Designer Outlet on Tuesday, Friday Saturday and Sunday.

Vat Refund point: until 30 June 2007, inside Castel Romano Designer Outlet there is a space where you can claim back Vat immediately. If you made purchases using Tax Free Global Refund, also outside of Castel Romano for example in Rome downtown or other cities in Italy, you are eligible to receive vouchers for an additional 10% value that can be used at all of the shops at Castel Romano Designer Outlet.

(These vouchers are valid only on the same day of purchase).

Via Pontina SS 148 Castel Romano (Rome)

Infoline: 0039 06 5050050
tourism@mcarthurglen.com

mcarthurglen.it

from 9.30 or 10am to 7.30 or 8pm, Monday through Saturday. The occasional independent store still clings to the traditional 1-4pm shutdown. In the centre, more and more stores also open on Sundays.

Times given in this guide are winter opening hours; in summer (approximately June to September), shops that opt for long lunches tend to reopen later, at 5pm or 5.30pm, staying open until 8-8.30pm. Most food stores close on Thursday afternoons in winter, and on Saturday afternoons in summer. The majority of non-food shops are closed Monday mornings. Many shops shut down for at least two weeks each summer (generally in August) and almost all are shut for two or three days around the 15 August public holiday. If you want to avoid finding a particular shop *chiuso per ferie* (closed for holidays), be sure to ring ahead.

Although service is improving, many shop assistants still seem hell-bent on either ignoring or intimidating customers. This is no time for Anglo-Saxon reticence; perfect the essential lines *'mi può aiutare, per favore?'* ('Can you help me please?') and *'volevo solo dare un' occhiata'* ('I'm just looking') and you're ready for any eventuality.

Prices & paying

Whether you're buying a banana, a bus ticket or a bikini, if you last came to Rome with the lira you'll notice that it ain't cheap any more, although home-grown designer names are still a little easier on the wallet here than abroad. Bargaining belongs firmly at the flea-market: in shops, prices are fixed.

In theory you should always be given a *scontrino* (receipt). If you aren't, then ask for it: by law, shops are required to provide one, and they and you are liable for a fine in the (wildly unlikely) event of

your being caught without it. Major credit cards are accepted just about everywhere, although it's worth checking before getting to the till.

The rules on taking purchases back if you have second thoughts are infuriatingly vague. Faulty goods, obviously, must be refunded or replaced. Most shops will also accept unwanted goods that are returned unused with a receipt within seven days of purchase, though this is not obligatory.

Tax rebates

Non-EU residents are entitled to a sales tax (IVA) rebate on purchases of personal goods worth over €155, providing they are exported unused and bought from a shop with the 'Europe Tax Free' sticker. The shop will give you a receipt as well as a 'Tax Free Shopping Cheque', which should be stamped by customs before your departure from Italy.

Micca Club p27

Nightlife

On a national level, arts funding has been falling. Not in Rome, however, where, since he won his first mandate in 2001, jazz- and cinema-loving Mayor Walter Veltroni has promoted arts and culture enthusiastically.

The trickle-down effect on the city's nightlife and music scene is tangible: growing cultural, artistic and musical vibrancy is feeding an ongoing renaissance that is turning the once-sleepy Eternal City into a lively European capital.

Surprisingly, in this hide-bound country, established artists are not the only ones benefitting: young, cutting-edge artistic communities are being given space to bring their innovative entertainment projects out of niches. This flurry of activity seeps into Rome's nightlife, where dancing to the best international DJs and hearing the latest bands is easier than ever. You will, however, need some inside information to avoid the Eurotrash dished out by the plethora of commercial venues.

Where to go, when to go

New compulsory closing times forcing most *centro storico* bars to shut at 2am have cancelled the unwritten 'open until the last punter stumbles out the door' rule that long gave Roman nights their uniquely relaxed feel.

Discos and live venues still stay open until the small hours, though, allowing Romans to keep up their habit of starting the evenings late and ending them even later.

Rome's nightlife venues tend to be concentrated mostly around a few easily accessible areas.

Testaccio is one of the city's liveliest quarters, with nightlife action around Monte Testaccio: you'll be spoilt for choice – just walk around until you find the vibe you're searching for.

The area around via Libetta, off via Ostiense, teems with trendy clubs and is poised to become even more crowded: the city council has slowly begun to develop the whole district as an arts hub.

Fashionistas head for the *centro storico*: spend an evening in the *triangolo della Pace* and you're part of trendy Roman life. The campo de' Fiori area, once another fashionista meeting spot, has become increasingly chaotic and, as the evening progresses, squalid.

San Lorenzo is altogether less pretentious: drinks are cheaper, and there's always something interesting going on.

Trastevere has lovely alleys packed with friendly, crowded bars. If you're longing for conversation but your Italian's non-existent, this is the place for you: English is the lingua franca. Note, though, that around piazza Trilussa, the scene gets seriously seedy in the small hours of the morning.

Clubbing

When picking a club for the night, bear in mind that many of Rome's mainstream venues serve up commercial house or 1980s retro on Fridays and Saturdays. Established places like Goa (p126), La Saponeria (p127) and Micca Club (p114) can be relied upon to offer high-quality DJ sets.

For something alternative try the Brit-pop/punk rock served up by the Beatles-look-alike DJs of Fish & Chips (on Fridays at Radio Café, via Principe Umberto 57, www.radiocaferoma.org) or dance the night away at Screamadelica (at Circolo degli Artisti, p116), where global live acts are topped by DJs playing rock, pop and indie. On Tuesdays, DJ Andrea Esu and international guests spin their electro-house and tech sounds at L-Ektrica (at Akab, p126). Vintage enthusiasts strike gold at Twiggy, Rome's best '60s night, where Italy's top live bands introduce DJs Luzy L and Corry X (one Saturday a month at Metaverso, p127).

Going live

Magnificently eclectic programming at the Auditorium – Parco della Musica (p99) has helped seduce music-shy Romans into making live sounds a regular diary fixture.

But Rome's vocation for live music is also being prodded along by a string of smallish clubs – with the 2005 opening of Casa del Jazz strengthening the city's jazz scene (see box p104) – and by the daring

programme at the cool Teatro Palladium (p127). Moreover, City Hall continues to fund the exciting RomaEuropa Festival (p34), the cutting-edge Enzimi festival (www.enzimi.com), and the occasional free mega-concert in a grand setting.

Until very recently, much of Rome's alternative live action centred on *centri sociali* – disused buildings occupied by dissatisfied youth and transformed into spaces for art, music and politics. With more opportunities elsewhere, their importance has waned, but they still have plenty to offer at bargain prices (admission is usually €5).

Summer in the city

Rome gives its best over the long summer: you'll be spoilt for choice between festivals, concerts, open-air cinema, theatre and discos, most of which come under the EstateRomana (p38) umbrella.

Gay Rome

Gay life in the Italian capital has undoubtedly become more mainstream. Increased visibility is matched by new oganisations, venues and facilities. The historic Mario Mieli (www.mariomieli.org) group, flanked by the newer, hyperactive Di'Gay Project (www.digayproject.org), is doing a superb job of adding more social goodies to the shopping trolley.

Likewise, the gay going-out scene continues to diversify and cater for distinct clienteles, with restaurants, pubs, clubs and bars attracting punters of all ages. A proliferation of mixed one-nighters also mirrors the increasing number of places where men and women can have fun under the same roof. Or, for that matter, in the open air: one of the most notable successes in the Roman calendar is the summer Gay Village (p38).

Many gay venues ask for an Arcigay Card, which costs €15 for annual membership, though a €8 one-month version is available for out-of-towners. The card can be bought at any participating venue.

Getting in

Getting into Rome's fashionable mainstream clubs can be stressful, no matter how elegantly you're dressed. Intimidating bouncers will bar your way, while PR luvvies smirk as they whisk supposed VIPs through the door past lines of frustrated would-be clients. But persistence and patience will get you in eventually.

Clubs and discobars generally charge an entrance fee at weekends but not on weekdays; be aware that you will often have to pay for a *tessera* (membership card) on top of, or sometimes instead of, the entrance fee. Tickets often include a 'free' drink, but you can expect the drinks you buy thereafter to be pricey. Another popular formula is to grant 'free' admission while forcing you to buy a (generally expensive) drink. To get out again you have to hand a stamped drink card to the bouncer, so hold on to whatever piece of paper they give you or you'll be forced to pay twice.

Where we haven't specified a price for entrance, admission is free.

Finding out

For details of upcoming events, consult the listings magazines *Trovaroma* (Thursday with the *La Repubblica* daily), *Roma C'è* (Wednesday) or *Zero6* (a monthly, free in shops and pubs). For an alternative look at Rome's nightlife, check out www.romastyle.info, which is especially good for techno and drum 'n' bass, and www.musica roma.it and www.indierock.it for the latest gigs. Fans of indie and punk rock should take a look at www.myspace.com/romecityrockers and www.pogopop.it.

Casa del Jazz p27

City of Rome Marathon p31

Arts & Leisure

The new millennium brought a centre-left administration that began to channel much-needed funds into Rome's moribund cultural scene. The results are now really beginning to show.

Music

The music panorama is the one in which, arguably, horizons have changed the most: Rome is back on the music-lovers' map of Europe after over a century of neglect.

This is thanks, mainly, to the activity of the Auditorium – Parco della Musica, inaugurated in 2002. The complex of exhibition and concert spaces, designed by Renzo Piano, has been hugely successful, enticing Romans of all tastes with a programme of such extraordinary breadth it is second only to New York's Lincoln Center for the variety of its offerings. This democratic eclecticism has cast its spell over citizens who had never set foot in a classical music venue in their lives: the year 2006 saw a over a million presences. Even more miraculous, in a country where the arts are traditionally a financial black hole, the Auditorium is self-funding and firmly in the black.

But it is not the only venue in Rome for music. Many of the more traditional concert halls and locations have also benefited from the surge of energy and extra funding, and many of them offer high-quality programmes.

So Rome is more or less sorted for 'serious' music, opera being the one exception: despite two glorious locations (Teatro dell'Opera, p108, and the Baths of Caracalla, p120), programmes are constipated and productions are generally mediocre.

One bonus here is that Rome's musical offerings often take place in settings so breathtaking that the quality doesn't always matter. Not that it's always low – for instance, La Stravaganza (06 7707 2842, www.lastravaganzamusica.it) organises delightful chamber music concerts inside the Palazzo Doria Pamphili; during the interval the audience is invited to wander into the adjacent gallery (p72) to enjoy the superb Doria Pamphili art collection. On Sunday mornings, there are noon recitals in the sumptuous Cappella Paolina of the president's residence, Palazzo del Quirinale (www.quirinale.it, p96). At the church of Sant'Anselmo (piazza Cavalieri di Malta 5, www. santanselmo.org) on the Aventine,

Benedictine monks sing Gregorian chant evensong daily at 7.15pm.

Check the local press, and look out for wall posters for other such concerts, many of which are free.

Theatre

The Italian school of drama, with its strong traditions and roots in the *Commedia dell'arte*, and the stiff style imposed by its stuffy dramatic arts academy, is worlds apart from what British, Irish or North American theatre-goers are used to. If you're thinking of an evening at the theatre, don't expect daring performances. You're on safer ground if you stick to big names and classic titles.

One interesting recent project is the Casa dei Teatri (06 4544 0707, www.casadeiteatri.culturaroma.it), in a palazzo in Villa Pamphili. The aim of this new centre is to give a multidisciplinary perspective to drama, integrating performances with workshops and research.

Dance

This Cinderella of Italian arts is allowed out of the kitchen more often nowadays, and features in seasonal programmes and festivals such as RomaEuropa (p34).

Film

Italian dubbers are recognised as the world's best, but that's no consolation if you like to hear films in the original language (*lingua originale* or *versione originale* – VO in newspaper listings). This said, you're better served in Rome than in any other Italian city for original-language films – which generally means English. The historic Pasquino in Trastevere has been closed since 2005 and shows no signs of reopening, but the Nuovo Olimpia (via in Lucina 16B), just off via del Corso, seems to have taken over its role as Rome's

Auditorium – Parco della Musica p29

VO picturehouse. The Metropolitan (via del Corso 7) also has regular VO programming. There are VO screenings at the Alcazar (via Merry del Val 14) and at the Nuovo Sacher (see box p134) on Mondays.

The city-sponsored Casa del Cinema (largo M Mastroianni 1, www.casadelcinema.it) inside Villa Borghese screens an interesting selection of movies for free.

Rome's annual Cinema – Festival Internazionale di Roma (p34) had its debut in October 2006 and is definitely one to watch out for.

Sport

In spite of the sight of thousands running past the city's landmarks in the City of Rome Marathon (p36), most Romans have an aversion to physical activity. But their passionate loyalty as supporters has always distinguished them. Italy's defeat over France in the 2006 World Cup football final was, predictably, an excuse for weeks of city-wide celebration in Rome.

Rome is home to two first-class football clubs: AS Roma (www.asromacalcio.it) and SS Lazio (www.sslazio.it). The two teams share the Stadio Olimpico (p99) in the Foro Italico complex.

In 2007 a spate of stadium violence prompted tough new measures. Tickets can no longer be bought directly from the Stadio Olimpico box office: you must get them online from www.listicket.com or from specialist merchandising outlets. Tickets are personal (you'll need to present photo-ID to get into the stadium) and non-transferable.

Though most Romans reserve their enthusiasm for football, the city also has its rugby fans. Since 2000, the national side has been in the Six Nations' Championship, with home games played at the Stadio Flaminio (viale Tiziano, 06 3685 7309, www.federugby.it).

SHORTLIST

Best overall arts venue
- Auditorium – Parco della Musica (p99)

Pampering
- El Spa (p151)
- L'Albero e la Mano (p138)
- Salus per aquam (p71)

New(-ish) arts experiments
- Casa del Cinema (p93)
- Casa del Jazz (p104)

Arts festivals
- Estate Romana (p38)
- Fotografia (p36)
- RomaEuropa Festival (p34)
- Rome Literature Festival (p36)

Picturesque in summer
- Alexanderplatz's Jazz & Image festival in Villa Celimontana (p151)
- Cosmophonies in the Roman theatre at Ostia Antica (p38)
- Teatro dell'Opera summer season (p38)

Rome & film
- 'Massenzio' open-air screenings during the EstateRomana (p38)
- Cinema – Festa Internazionale di Roma (Rome Film Festival, p34)

Fun for kids
- Bioparco-Zoo (p90)
- Cinema dei Piccoli (p93)
- Explora – Museo dei Bambini di Roma (p90)

Sporting fixtures
- Football at the Stadio Olimpico (p99)
- Jogging around the Baths of Caracalla (p120)
- City of Rome Marathon (p36)
- Rugby at the Stadio Flaminio (p99)
- Show-jumping in piazza di Siena (p38)

timeout.com

Over 50 of the world's greatest
cities reviewed in one site.

Calendar

Natale (Nativity) scene p34

Since time immemorial, the Romans have never needed much of an excuse for a knees-up. Ancient Rome allotted a whopping 150 days every year for R&R. If today's ten annual public holidays seem paltry in comparison, bear in mind that the final total is usually quite a bit more: any holiday that falls midweek is invariably taken as an invitation to *fare il ponte* ('do a bridge') – between the official holiday and the nearest weekend.

Important religious holidays tend to shut down the entire city. Different districts of Rome hold smaller-scale celebrations of their own patron saints in their own way, from calorific blowouts to costume parades, to extravagant fireworks displays.

Rome's mayor, Walter Veltroni, has lavished an embarrassment of cultural riches on the city in recent years, striking a happy balance between small-scale, independent festivals and bigger-budget citywide events that make ample use of Rome's endless supply of photogenic venues.

Keep an eye on local press and wall posters for the occasional huge free concert, and also for major exhibitions, which tend to be announced on short notice. The websites of the cultural heritage ministry (www.beniculturali.it), the Rome city council (www.comune.roma.it) and the Rome tourist board (www.romaturismo.it) are useful sources of information.

Dates highlighted in **bold** are public holidays.

September 2007

7–8 La Notte Bianca
www.lanottebianca.it
Rome's annual all-night party takes place 8 Sept, but some events kick off

the night before. There are street performances throughout the city, plus shops, clubs and museums stay open through the night.

30–27 Nov **RomaEuropa Festival**
Various locations
www.romaeuropa.net
Rome's most prestigious performing arts festival.

October 2007

Ongoing RomaEuropa Festival
(see Sept)

5–6 Jan 2008 **Mark Rothko**
Palazzo delle Esposizioni (p104)
A major retrospective of the American abstract expressionist artist.

5–27 Jan 2008 **Stanley Kubrick**
Palazzo delle Esposizioni (p104)
A tribute to the late filmmaker.

Oct–Jan 2008 **From Cranach to Monet**
Palazzo Ruspoli (p85)
Works from the Perez-Simon collection in Mexico City.

18–27 **Cinema – Festa Internazionale di Roma**
Auditorium-Parco della Musica (p99) and other venues
www.romacinemafest.org
The second edition of Rome's controversial film festival.

24–27 Jan 2008 **This is Pop!**
Scuderie del Quirinale (p96)
Pop art from 1956 to 1968.

28–15 Feb 2008 **Canova**
Galleria Borghese (p92)
An exhibition marking the 250th anniversary of the sculptor's birth.

Late Oct **Mostra dell'Antiquariato**
Via de' Coronari
Antique fair in this street packed with antique dealers.

November 2007

Ongoing RomaEuropa Festival (see Sept), Mark Rothko (see Oct), Stanley Kubrick (see Oct), This is Pop! (see Oct), Canova (see Oct)

1-2 **All Saints/All Souls**
Cimitero del Verano, piazzale del Verano
Romans visit family graves.

December 2007

Ongoing Mark Rothko (see Oct), Stanley Kubrick (see Oct), This is Pop! (see Oct), Canova (see Oct)

8 **Immacolata Concezione**
Piazza di Spagna (p85)
Immaculate Conception. See box p37.

25-26 **Natale & Santo Stefano**
Nativity scenes in churches and on St Peter's square (p143); Christmas fair in piazza Navona. See box p37.

31 **San Silvestro**
Free concert in piazza del Popolo; much street partying.

January 2008

Ongoing Mark Rothko (see Oct), Stanley Kubrick (see Oct), This is Pop! (see Oct), Canova (see Oct)

1 **Capodanno**
New Year's Day.

6 **Epifania – La Befana**
Piazza Navona (p73)
Old witch brings Epiphany treats for all the children.

17 **Sant'Eusebio**
Sant'Eusebio, via Napoleone III
Animal lovers have pets blessed.

26–5 Feb **Carnevale**
Around the city centre
Kids dress up and throw confetti in the run-up to Lent.

February 2008

Ongoing Canova (see Oct), Carnevale (see Jan)

Feb–June **Sebastiano del Piombo**
Palazzo Venezia (p57)
Works by the great Venetian artist.

March 2008

Ongoing Sebastiano del Piombo (see Feb)

RomaEuropa Festival

9 Feast of Santa Francesca Romana
Monastero Oblate di Santa Francesca Romana, via Teatro di Marcello 32 & 40
Rare opportunity to visit this medieval nunnery; Romans have cars blessed at Santa Francesca Romana church in the Roman Forum.

16 Palazzo Massimo alle Colonne
Corso Vittorio Emanuele 141
Once-a-year opening of the patrician palace, 8am-1pm.

16 Maratona della Città di Roma
Around the city centre
www.maratonadiroma.it
There's a 5km fun-run for those not up to the whole 42km Rome Marathon.

16-24 Holy Week & Easter
Vatican (p139), Colosseum (p55)
Palm Sunday mass at St Peter's; pope's Via Crucis at Colosseum on Good Friday. See box p37.

19 Feast of San Giuseppe
Around via Trionfale

Rome's film festival p34

Partying and batter-ball eating marks St Joseph's day.

23-24 Pasqua & Pasquetta
Easter Sunday and Monday.

29-30 Giornate FAI
Various locations
www.fondoambiente.it
For one weekend each spring, private and institutional owners of historic properties reveal their spectacular interiors, usually off-limits to the public.

April 2008

Ongoing Sebastiano del Piombo (see Feb)

Apr–early June **FotoGrafia**
Various locations
www.fotografiafestival.it
International festival of photography.

21 Natale di Roma
Campidoglio (p52)
Rome celebrates its 2,761st birthday with immense fireworks.

25 Liberation Day

Late Apr **Mostra delle Azalee**
Piazza di Spagna (p85)
Some 3,000 vases of azaleas on the Spanish Steps.

May 2008

Ongoing Sebastiano del Piombo (see Feb), FotoGrafia (see Apr)

1 Primo Maggio
Piazza San Giovanni
www.primomaggio.com
Trade unions organise a huge, free rock concert for May Day.

Mid May **Settimana della Cultura**
www.beniculturali.it
For one week, all state-owned museums are free and many otherwise closed sites are open. Note that dates may vary from year to year.

Mid May–late June
Rome Literature Festival
Basilica di Massenzio, Roman Forum (p58)
www.festivaldelleletterature.it
Book launches and readings.

Pope-spotting

The pope gets out and about quite a bit in Rome: he pays pastoral visits to parishes, performs high-profile ceremonies and greets the faithful on 'popemobile' drives around St Peter's square. So if you're set on seeing the Man in White, there's a good chance of picking out his tiny figure in the distance during your Roman stay.

Benedict XVI celebrates mass at St Peter's every Sunday morning – outdoors in good weather – then recites the traditional noon Angelus from his balcony to the vast crowd below. As the weather heats up, the pope retreats to his palace at Castel Gandolfo, east of Rome, and greets Sunday pilgrims in the palace courtyard.

On Wednesdays at 10.30am, you can catch him at a general audience in St Peter's square; you don't need a ticket unless you want to sit. In winter, however, you – and 8,000 others – will have to apply for (free) tickets for the vast Paul VI audience chamber.

For booking details, see p142. Further information about the pope's appointments can be found on www.vatican.va.

Out & about in 2008

1 Jan (New Year's Day) 10am: pope says mass at St Peter's; noon pope's New Year blessing in piazza San Pietro.

6 Jan (Epiphany) 9.30am: pope says Epiphany mass in St Peter's before colourful costumed Three Kings parade from Castel Sant'Angelo to piazza San Pietro.

6 Feb (Ash Wednesday) 5pm: pope says mass and applies ashes at Santa Sabina (p120).

16 Mar (Palm Sunday) 9.30am: procession and papal mass in piazza San Pietro.

20 Mar (Maundy Thursday) 5.30pm: pope says *In cena domini* (Last Supper) mass and performs foot-washing ritual at San Giovanni in Laterano (p110).

21 Mar (Good Friday) 9pm: pope recites the Via Crucis (stations of the cross) in a torch-lit event at the Colosseum (p55).

23 Mar (Easter Sunday) 10.30am: pope says mass in piazza San Pietro. Pope's *urbi et orbi* blessing at noon.

22 May (Corpus domini) 7pm: pope says mass at San Giovanni in Laterano; torchlit procession to Santa Maria Maggiore (p105).

8 Dec (Feast of the Immaculate Conception) 4pm: pope (helped by firemen and a long ladder) oversees placing of a garland on the statue of the Madonna in piazza Mignanelli, at the bottom of the Spanish Steps (p85).

25 Dec (Christmas Day) 10am: pope says mass in St Peter's.

Mid May–late June
Roseto Comunale
Via Valle Murcia/clivo dei Pubblici
Annual opening of Rome's municipal
rose garden.

Late May **Piazza di Siena**
Piazza di Siena, Villa Borghese
(p90)
www.piazzadisiena.com
Rome's ultra-smart four-day show-
jumping event.

May–Sept **Correggio**
Galleria Borghese (p92)
A tribute to the Renaissance master
from Parma.

June 2008

Ongoing Sebastiano del Piombo
(see Feb), Rome Literature Festival
(see May), Roseto Comunale (see
May), Correggio (see May)

Early June–end Sept
Estate Romana
Various locations
www.estateromana.comune.roma.it
Piazze, palazzi and parks come alive
with music, and films are shown on
outdoor screens. Many events are free.

Early June–Aug
Jazz & Image Festival
Villa Celimontana (p108)
www.villacelimontanajazz.com
Jazz concerts beneath the trees of this
lovely park.

Mid June–early Aug
Roma Incontra il Mondo
Villa Ada, via di Ponte Salario
www.villaada.org
World music by the lake in this park in
the northern suburbs.

Mid June–mid Aug **Fiesta!**
Via Appia Nuova 1245
www.fiesta.it
Latin American music fest at the
Capanelle racecourse near Ciampino.

Late June–early Sept **Gay Village**
Venue varies
www.gayvillage.it
A ten-week open-air bonanza with bars,
restaurants, live acts, discos, cinema –
for boys and girls. Venue moves from
year to year: check the website.

Late June–mid Aug **Teatro
dell'Opera Summer Season**
Baths of Caracalla (p120)
Rome's opera company stages grand
performances in these Roman ruins.

Late June–early Sept
Cosmophonies
www.cosmophonies.com
Roman Theatre, Ostia Antica (p157)
World music, light entertainment and
opera amid the ruins.

29 Santi Pietro e Paolo
Basilica di San Paolo fuori
le Mura (p122)
Street fair outside St Paul's basilica and
mass at St Peter's for the feast day of
Rome's patron saints.

July 2008

Ongoing Correggio (see May),
Estate Romana (see June),
Jazz & Image Festival (see
June), Roma Incontra il Mondo
(see June), Fiesta! (see June),
Gay Village (see June), Teatro
dell'Opera Summer Season
(see June), Cosmophonies
(see June)

Mid July **Festa di Noantri**
Piazza Santa Maria in Trastevere,
piazza Mastai
Two weeks of arts events, street performances and fairground attractions.

August 2008

Ongoing Correggio (see May),
Estate Romana (see June),
Jazz & Image Festival (see
June), Roma Incontra il Mondo
(see June), Fiesta! (see June),
Gay Village (see June), Teatro
dell'Opera Summer Season
(see June), Cosmophonies
(see June)

1 Festa delle Catene
San Pietro in Vincoli (p104)
The chains that bound St Peter are
displayed in a special mass.

5 Festa della Madonna della Neve
Santa Maria Maggiore (p105)
A blizzard of rose petals flutters down
on festive mass-goers.

10 Notte di San Lorenzo
San Lorenzo in Panisperna,
via Panisperna 90
Nuns distribute bread and candles on
this, the night of shooting stars.

15 Ferragosto
Rome closes down for the feast of the
Assumption.

September 2008

Ongoing **Correggio** (see May),
Estate Romana (see June),
Gay Village (see June),
Cosmophonies (see June)

Early Sept **La Notte Bianca**
www.lanottebianca.it
Rome's annual all-night party takes
place on a Saturday (though some
events kick off the night before). There
are street performances throughout the
city, plus shops, clubs and museums
stay open through the night.

Sept–Nov **RomaEuropa Festival**
Various locations
www.romaeuropa.net
Rome's most prestigious performing
arts festival.

October 2008

Ongoing **RomaEuropa Festival**
(see Sept)

Late Oct **Mostra dell'Antiquariato**
Via de' Coronari
Antique fair in this collector's mecca.

November 2008

Ongoing **RomaEuropa Festival**
(see Sept)

1-2 All Saints/All Souls
Cimitero del Verano
Romans visit family graves.

December 2008

8 Immacolata Concezione
Piazza di Spagna (p85)
Immaculate Conception. See box p37.

25-26 Natale & Santo Stefano
Nativity scenes in churches; Christmas
fair in piazza Navona. See box p37.

31 San Silvestro
Free concert in piazza del Popolo; much
street partying.

Rome Literature Festival p36

iglide
Tours & Rentals, Srl
ITALIA

Discover Villa Borghese and Roma Antica using the Segway HT

Tour Schedule

May through November
Tours operate seven days per week
Tour Times 10.00 a.m. and 2.00 p.m.
December through March
Tours available by request and based on availability
Tour Cost: € 75,00 per person

Duration 3 hours
Participants: up to 8 people
Reservation is required
Participant must be at least 13 years old and between 100 and 275 lbs.

Please arrive 15 minutes before your tour time to check in so we can start your training and tour on time.

Tour times, days and locations are subject to change.

For reservation call +39 06 42014533 or www.iglidetours.com

Itineraries

Roman Forum p44

A Papal Procession

A full day's stroll along the **via Papalis** – the route followed by newly elected popes for centuries – takes you along the grandest and most important thoroughfare of the medieval city. To get the most out of your own procession, it helps to know a bit of papal history.

As medieval Rome spiralled into lawlessness and decay, things got so bad that even the pope left town: in 1309 Clement V moved the papal court to Avignon, where it remained for nearly a century. Meanwhile, Rome's 17,000 inhabitants (down from one million in Imperial times) camped out in the ruins by the river, while despotic local barons ruled from their medieval towers.

In 1378 Pope Gregory XI bravely decided to give Rome a try again but died almost the moment he returned, causing a schism that led to two rival popes being elected – one who dashed back to Avignon

within the year, the other brazening it out in Rome. Attempts to sort out the unholy mess only resulted in the election in 1409 of a third pope. It took the Council of Constance (1414) to set things to rights, and Martin V of the powerful Roman Colonna family was elected with the mandate of returning the papacy to the Holy City.

At first the popes only surveyed the ruins of the city from their HQ in the old Lateran palace (p110). Then Nicholas V (1447-55) got moving. He restored the aqueduct, bringing clean water back to the city, and moved the papacy across the river to the Vatican palace.

Linking the Lateran and the Vatican was a route known as the via Papalis: after his election and presentation at St Peter's, each pope had to trek (and still does, though now in a comfy limousine) the three miles to take possession of his seat as bishop of Rome – the magnificent cathedral of San Giovanni in Laterano, in a ceremony known as *il possesso*.

Early processions became ever more spectacular with hundreds of bishops, priests, monks and representatives of charitable corporations following ornately decorated allegorical chariots.

For your own procession, make an early start, and factor in lunch and a few detours en route. If you rush along without stops, you could probably complete it in three hours but you'd be missing the point. (Remember that San Giovanni in Laterano is open until 7pm.) Along the way, you'll be seeing the very best of papal Rome, so take your time and prepare to be dazzled.

Start at the steps of **St Peter's** (p143) beneath the balcony from which a newly elected pope still greets the faithful, then walk across the great piazza to look back at the façade: this is not the church that early popes processed from. It was not until 1506 that – after endlessly patching up the original fourth-century basilica – it was decided to demolish the building and start again using the very latest high-tech Renaissance know-how and style. The new St Peter's was not finished until 1626. Another 40 years passed before Bernini put the finishing touches to his dazzlingly theatrical landscaping of the piazza, with its sweeping colonnade.

The broad Fascist-era via della Conciliazione, which leads from the Vatican towards the river, was part of Mussolini's grand urban plan: an entire medieval quarter was swept away to make way for a tricky piece of road widening. The early popes would have trotted (on a white horse, with everyone else on foot) through the narrow tangle of streets, through piazza Scossacavalli ('horse-frightener square'), where

the horses of Emperor Constantine's relic-hunting mother Helena shied, depositing their cartload of relics from the Holy Land.

Straight ahead is the imposing bulk of the medieval **Castel Sant'Angelo** (p142) constructed atop emperor Hadrian's circular mausoleum. The castle is linked to the Vatican by a secret walkway – *il passetto* – along which the popes could rush when trouble loomed.

The castle overlooks the strategic crossing point of the river Tiber: here, popes exacted a toll from the pilgrims crossing this – then the only bridge – to St Peter's. Cross at the traffic lights and walk down via del Banco di Santo Spirito, named after the bank founded by pope Paul V. Renaissance goldsmith and raconteur Benvenuto Cellini wrote about his day job working in these ornate premises of the former *zecca* (mint) of the Papal States, now a branch of the Banca di Roma.

Turn sharp left before the bank into via dei Banchi Nuovi, a cobbled street where bankers, lawyers, notaries, scribes and merchants made and lost fortunes. Now the historic *palazzi* are the ultra-trendy premises of avant-garde dress designers, antique shops and smart wine bars. Banchi Nuovi segues into via del Governo Vecchio, where **Shaki**, housed in a pretty 16th-century building at No.123 (06 6830 8796, open 10am-2am daily), is a good bet for lunch.

At the end of this street (barely a couple of blocks from sensationally beautiful piazza Navona, p73) is an irregular square with a timeworn classical sculpture covered in pieces of inky, handwritten sheets of paper: this is **Pasquino**, the 'talking' statue. Pause for a moment to read the wicked pen-portraits of Italy's rich and powerful, and ponder the sheer delight in anonymous doggerel in a modern democracy.

Continue to the right here, past the **Museo di Roma** (p72), and head towards busy corso Vittorio Emanuele, an artery hammered through the medieval fabric after the unification of Italy in 1870. Campo de' Fiori (p60), with its morning market stalls and great wine bars, lies tantalisingly close, across the other side of the *corso*.

On corso Vittorio, the extremely fine early Renaissance **Palazzo Massimo alle Colonne** (p72) on your left follows the curve of Roman remains beneath the area; the first printing press to reach Italy in 1471 made its owners a fortune when they set up shop at the back of these premises, printing religious tracts and Bibles. The grand domed church on your right is **Sant'Andrea della Valle** (p67) where the first act of Puccini's *Tosca* is set.

Continue into largo di Torre Argentina (p61), where you can peer down into the central archeological area before taking via del Plebiscito. Halfway along this street, the **Gesù** (p66) church is a masterpiece of the Baroque, reflecting the staggering power and wealth of the Company of Jesus (Jesuits) in 17th-century Rome.

Via dell'Aracoeli leads from here to the bottom of Michelangelo's *cordonata* (staircase) up to the **Capitoline** (p52). Take extreme care – and the zebra crossing – to get to it. You may well wonder how the papal steed and the allegorical carts got up the stairs, but a twisting ramp to the right of the *cordonata* still transports VIPs to the mayor's office in Palazzo Senatorio, at the back of the grand piazza. The bronze statue of Marcus Aurelius – enlightened emperor and philosopher – that stands in the square is a hideous copy of the second-century original: to see that, you'll have to enter the **Capitoline Museums** (p54), where the bronze is now housed.

Skirt to the left of Palazzo Senatorio, past Romulus, Remus and the she-wolf on a column, and descend the steps into the **Roman Forum** (p58). Stroll along the ancient via Sacra. Some of the temples have medieval churches foisted upon them, like that of Antoninus and Faustina, now the church of San Lorenzo in Miranda.

At the far end of the Forum stands the **Colosseum** (p55). This 50,000-seater amphitheatre where thousands of Christians met their deaths was consecrated in 1749 by pope Benedict XIV: on Good Friday each year the pope processes around the ruin in a moving torch-lit *Via Crucis* (Stations of the Cross).

It's about a 15-minute walk from here to San Giovanni, but it's worth stopping en route to explore the exquisite church of **San Clemente** (p110) before you proceed up the long, straight via di San Giovanni in Laterano. Alternatively, save your legs and hop on the 117 electric bus, which will take you from the Colosseum to within sight of the end of the *via Papalis* and the benediction loggia of **San Giovanni in Laterano** (p110).

Tourists (unlike pilgrims) rarely discover this basilica – which is rather a pity. The history of the building mirrors that of the city itself. Built on a site donated by Emperor Constantine, it has been transformed over the centuries by the greatest craftsmen and artists of Christendom. Contrast the gleaming expanse of gold leaf and mosaic with the simplicity of the tranquil 12th-century cloisters, and marvel at the ancient octagonal baptistery (legend says Constantine himself was baptised there) and, across the piazza, the extraordinary **Sancta Sanctorum** (p113), where the holiest relics are kept.

San Giovanni in Laterano

Sant'Agostino

Chasing Caravaggio

Michelangelo Merisi da Caravaggio (1571-1610), the iconic Bad Boy of the Baroque, burned through the Roman art world like a dangerous, dazzling meteor. A hard-drinking rebel with an uncontrollable temper and, reputedly, a penchant both for women and boys, Rome's greatest painter ended up on the run after murdering a man in campo de' Fiori in 1606. For the next four years he hid out in Naples, Sicily and Malta, only to die of malaria on a beach in Tuscany while waiting for a pardon from the pope. He was 39.

Of the 50 or so paintings by the master to have survived, 22 of the very best hang in Roman churches and galleries. This two-morning trail takes you to see them, in hidden corners, glorious Baroque churches and the city's finest art galleries. Start reasonably early in the morning since Roman churches

tend to close their doors on the stroke of midday. Don't forget to phone ahead to secure your ticket to the Galleria Borghese (p92).

We call him Caravaggio after the small town in northern Italy where it was long believed Michelangelo Merisi was born. But in 2007 the record of his baptism in the church of Santo Stefano in Brolo in Milan came to light: we now know the artist was born on 29 September – the feast day of St Michael the Archangel – 1571 in Milan.

The moment he realised he had the talent to make the big time, Caravaggio set out for Rome – the city of the popes, the papal court and the juiciest commissions. It was boom time in Rome, then the richest city in Europe: the best architects were summoned to build palaces and churches, the best painters to decorate them. There were fortunes, and reputations, to be made.

Set yourself up with a *gran caffè* at **Bar Sant'Eustachio** (p76) then stroll around the corner into via Dogana Vecchia where sentry boxes hold smart-uniformed *carabinieri* protecting the rear of the Italian Senate in **Palazzo Madama**. On corso Rinascimento, examine the Renaissance façade of this splendid palace, built in 1503 for Giovanni de' Medici, who would later become Pope Leo X. In 1595 this was the residence of Cardinal Francesco del Monte, a cultivated, art-loving millionaire career cardinal, whose live-in staff included Rome's most talented young painters and musicians; Caravaggio lived in a small room on an upper floor. Here, he completed his series of paintings featuring musicians with their lutes, and singers – portraits of fellow palazzo interns. In one composition, a well-known book of madrigals by Francesco de Layolle lies open on the table, painted so meticulously that you could play every note of this 16th-century hit tune. In another version of the work, the madrigal depicted is by French composer Jacques Arcadelt (1515-68), the sexy lyrics 'Vous savez que je vous aime et vous adore… je fus votre' still clearly visible.

It was through Cardinal del Monte that Caravaggio won his first church commission: to decorate a chapel in memory of a cardinal in Rome's French church. Pop back into via Dogana Vecchia, turn left past the magnificent Palazzo Giustiniani, (residence of Vincenzo Giustiniani – another patron of the young artist) and into the ornate **San Luigi dei Francesi** (p73), which contains three of Caravaggio's finest paintings.

Cardinal Matthieu Cointrel (also known as Matteo Contarelli) left behind detailed instructions that the paintings should illustrate particular scenes from the life

of St Matthew: *The Calling* (c1602), where rich tax collector Matthew, shown counting money (note the coin in the brim of Matthew's smart black hat), is called by Jesus; and *The Martyrdom* (c1600), where the saint collapses, watched by a horrified crowd as an angel flies over the executioner's sword. In the central altarpiece (c1602), another angel of extraordinary elegance hovers above the head of the pensive saint.

Outside the church, turn left past the French bookshop and left again on to via delle Coppelle. The beautiful church of **Sant'Agostino** (p75), begun in 1420, had recently been modernised when Caravaggio, flush with his success in the French church, was asked to paint a large altarpiece. His shockingly realistic portrayal of the *Madonna of the Pilgrims* (c1604) caused a storm of controversy, not least because of the dirty feet of the impoverished pilgrims kneeling before the infant Jesus.

Caravaggio left the del Monte household in 1601 to live in the grand palazzo of the Mattei family (now Palazzo Caetani, on via delle Botteghe Oscure) near campo de' Fiori. It was here that he famously lost his temper during a tennis match and killed his opponent.

It might be tempting to cut across piazza Navona to try to work out the dynamics of the crime while you sit in the campo over an early lunch; but instead, set off north along via della Scrofa (which becomes via Ripetta) towards piazza del Popolo: it's a pleasant ten-minute stroll, past the mausoleum of Augustus and the Ara Pacis Museum (p84), to the church of **Santa Maria del Popolo** (p85). Sit in the sun for a moment at **Rosati** (p87) with a restorative cappuccino, but don't linger too long or you'll miss two

ITINERARIES

of Caravaggio's most dramatic canvases: the upside-down *Crucifixion of St Peter* (1601) and the blinding light of the *Conversion of St Paul* (1601) in the Cerasi chapel to the left of the main altar.

If the weather's fine, you could cut down via del Babuino and pick up that picnic basket you ordered from **GiNa** (p86), then stroll up the Spanish Steps into the glorious Villa Borghese park. (If you didn't pre-plan, there are cafés in Villa Borghese that serve snacks.)

On the far side of the park, Cardinal Scipione Borghese's jewel-like summer house, now the **Galleria Borghese** (p92), has no fewer than six Caravaggio masterpieces: the dazzling *Boy with a Basket of Fruit* (c1593), bursting with good health; the greenish *Sick Bacchus* (c1593); a shocking *David with the Head of Goliath* (c1610; the blood-spattered head is a self-portrait); two devotional studies – a wrinkled *St Jerome in his Study* (1605) and a youthful, naked *St John the Baptist* (1606); and the breath-taking *Madonna with Child and St Anne* (1606), painted for St Peter's but rejected by Church authorities.

It's an easy downhill stroll back through the Porta Pinciana and along café-lined via Veneto.

Unless you're a close personal friend of the US president or the ambassador, there is absolutely no chance whatsoever of getting inside the US embassy halfway along via Veneto to inspect the weird frescoes (c1597) Caravaggio painted to decorate the **Casino Ludovisi**. These depict Jupiter, Neptune and Pluto, the sons of Kronos – an earlier ruler of the universe.

At the far end of the street, in the gloomy Cappuchin church of **Santa Maria della Concezione** (p94), is a kneeling, brown-robed *St Francis in Meditation* (c1606), staring intently at a skull like the ones piled in designs of grotesque artistic fantasy in the crypt beneath the church. Scholars disagree about whether this is a work by *il maestro*, or a very good copy.

By now you may be flagging, but if you can summon up the energy, round up your first day of Caravaggio-gazing with a visit to the **Palazzo Barberini** (p95), which towers over piazza Barberini at the bottom of via Veneto. Inspect the hauntingly introspective *Narcissus* (c1599) and the chilling *Decapitation of Holofernes* (c1599), in which a prim, white-smocked Judith calmly saws off her rapist's head with a kitchen knife.

Alternatively (or as part of Day Two), hop on any of the buses going from piazza Barberini via del Corso, and make your way to the **Galleria Doria Pamphili** (p72). Here you can see a variant on the young *St John the Baptist* (c1602); a tender *Penitent Magdalene* (c1597); and one of the finest of all the Rome paintings, *The Rest on the Flight into Egypt* (c1595). This work features another musical score – a 1519 motet, *Quam pulchra es et quam decora*, by Flemish composer Noel Baulduin – played to lull an exhausted Madonna and her baby; Joseph holds up the music for the fiddle-playing angel.

The morning of your second Caravaggio day could be pleasantly spent at the Vatican Museums' **Pinacoteca** (p146), which has a fine *Deposition of Christ* (c1604). From there, you can proceed to the **Capitoline Museums** (p54), which have two Caravaggios: the splendidly sly *Gypsy Fortune Tellers* (c1594) plus a simpering *St John the Baptist* (c1602). Enjoy an alfresco lunch on the terrace of the Café Caffarelli, on the roof of the museum. (If you didn't include the Galleria Doria Pamphili in Day One, this is the time to visit there.)

Freni e Frizioni

Aperitivo, Digestivo

Designer bars come and go in Rome, their fates decided by whether their fashion-conscious owners manage to create a congenial atmosphere as well as a 'look'. Because, for most Romans, style is all very well but substance – here in the form of well-priced drinks and an inviting space to get deep into conversation with friends, preferably while keeping an eye on the surroundings and being seen too – is even more essential.

This walk will take you to some old Roman drinking favourites, and to a couple of new ones that look like they've found the right balance. It will also lead you past some of Rome's most iconic sights, as you meander from Trastevere and through the *centro storico* to the Spanish Steps. What more could you ask of a full night out?

As thirst and peckishness hit, join the young artsy-alternative crowd at **Freni e Frizioni** (p135) on the riverside road in Trastevere.

To be precise, you'll probably join that crowd *outside* Freni e Frizioni because that's where the *habitués* of this new-ish trendy drinking hole hang out. Get your drink at the bar, load up with a pile of whatever you fancy from the huge buffet spread in the next room, then join in the urgent hum of conversation on the pavement: there are no chairs, no tables, no comforts of any sort – just the pleasure of an early-evening get-together with friends.

Now you're ready for a romantic stroll across to the other side of the river: pause on the pedestrianised Ponte Sisto to observe the reflections in the rushing waters of the Tiber.

Follow via dei Pettinari and then via Capo di Ferro to reach piazza Farnese, dominated by magnificent Palazzo Farnese, partly designed by Michelangelo and now the French embassy. Any of the alleys on the north-east side of the square go to **campo de' Fiori** (p60), where the hulking statue of humanist heretic Giordano Bruno (Gordon Brown to local British wits) moodily surveys the evening antics. Later on, this square becomes the realm of drunken, raucous Anglo students on 'programs' and bongo-banging *punkabestie* with mangy dogs on bits of string. But before dinner, the outside tables of long-running **La Vineria** (p69) give a front-row view of (more salubrious) life in this gorgeous square. Stake a claim to one of the hotly-contested tables and order one of the many wines by the glass.

By now you may be ready for dinner. The area between here and piazza Navona is packed with dining options (p68 and p76). Whether you eat before or after, be sure to explore the **triangolo della Pace**, the wedge of streets with its northernmost point at the eastern end of via dei' Coronari, and extending south to piazza Chiesa Nuova on the west and to piazza Navona on the east. Rome's perma-tanned, perma-coiffed and designer-clad Bright Young (and not so young) Things congregate here, in places such as the classic **Bar della Pace** (p76) or the squeaky-new **Etabli** (p78). If the evening's fine, we recommend the outside tables at the former, beneath the swaying ivy. You'll pay over the odds for your drinks but just think of it as a ticket for a great seat at a very unique show.

Make sure your *triangolo* stroll ends in **piazza Navona** (p73), the great Baroque theatre of Rome and stunning when lit up at night. Exit to the east, wiggling through the narrow, reveller-packed streets to piazza della Rotonda, where the Pantheon (p72) looks equally breathtaking in its after-dark guise.

From here, via dei Pastini leads to piazza di Pietra where you can take the weight off your feet by sinking into a deep sofa at **Salotto 42** (p78). This is another more recent addition, but one that has worked from the word go. There are arty books on the shelves and a very cool lounge soundtrack.

You'll be ready now for (a second) dessert. Take via di Pietra, cross via del Corso to via delle Muratte, stop to ogle the Trevi Fountain (p96), then continue on past and take a left into via la Panetteria.

Halfway down this street on the right, **Il Gelato di San Crispino** (p97) makes what may be the world's finest ice-cream – and after your long walk, it will certainly seem that way. Nothing in this exquisite ice-cream is artificial: the ingredients are the finest possible and the whole production process has something religious about it.

Continue along via della Panetteria, cross thundering via del Tritone, and carry on (more or less) straight until you reach piazza di Spagna. It takes nothing short of torrential rain to drive the happy hordes off the Spanish Steps (p85) at any time of the year. There will be guitar strumming, beer-chugging and much merriment, all of it getting in your way as you try to climb this very gracious rococo staircase (though one of Rome's best-kept secrets is the lift that goes from via del Bottino up to the top).

Pause here for a moment to gasp at the view of Rome spread at your feet, then, with your back to the steps, turn left. It's only a few metres to **Ciampini al Café du Jardin** (p86), where you can admire the same superb panorama with a glass in hand – but only from mid-May to mid-September. If Ciampini is closed, drop down via Sistina and take a left into via F Crispi. Where this road meets via Ludovisi is the **Hotel Eden** (p171) where the view from the rooftop bar (open 10.30am-1am daily) is even more spectacular.

Rome by Area

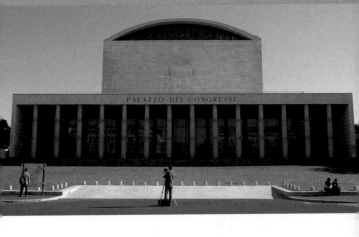

PALAZZO DEI CONGRESSI

Roman Forum p58

Il Centro

Centro archeologico

In the eighth century BC, a tribe built huts on a hill overlooking the Tiber. This settlement grew into the hub of a superpower extending from Spain to Asia Minor.

It was from here that the Republic – and later the Empire – was run and justice administered in grandiose buildings around richly decorated public squares (the **Roman Forum**); that magnificent palaces (the **Palatine**) overlooked the hustle and bustle of life below; that imposing temples dominated the most sacred of Rome's seven hills (the **Capitoline**); and that successive emperors strove to assert their own particular importance and munificence (the **Imperial Fora**). Here, too, emperors kept public discontent at bay with gory diversions and heart-stopping sports (the **Colosseum** and **Circus Maximus**).

The Capitoline (Campidoglio) was the site of two major temples, to Jupiter Capitolinus – chunks of which are visible inside the **Capitoline Museums** – and Juno Moneta ('giver of advice'), where the church of **Santa Maria in Aracoeli** now stands.

The splendid piazza that now tops the Capitoline was designed in the 1530s by Michelangelo; the best approach is via the steps called the *cordonata*, also by Michelangelo, with two giant Roman statues of the mythical twins Castor and Pollux at the top. The building directly opposite is Rome's city hall; on either side are the *palazzi* housing the Capitoline Museums.

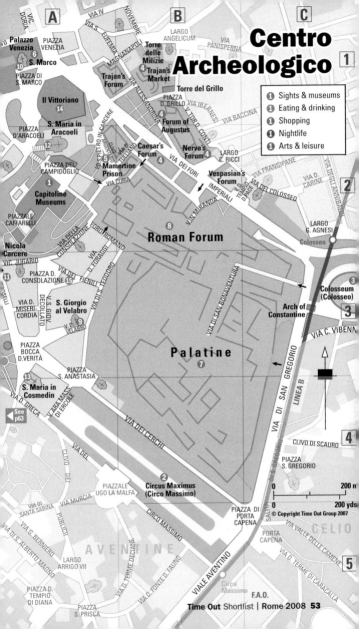

Centro Archeologico

1. **Sights & museums**
1. **Eating & drinking**
1. **Shopping**
1. **Nightlife**
1. **Arts & leisure**

VIC. DORIA

PIAZZA VENEZIA

Palazzo Venezia 6

S. Marco 10

PIAZZA DI S. MARCO

VIA IV NOVEMBRE

VIA S. EUFEMIA

MAGNANAPOLI

LARGO ANGELICUM

VIA PANISPERNA

VIA ALESSANDRINA

Trajan's Forum

Torre delle Milizie 4

Trajan's Market 4

Il Vittoriano 14

S. Maria in Aracoeli

PIAZZA D.GRILLO

Torre del Grillo

VIA IBERNES

VIA BACCINA

PIAZZA D'ARACOELI

Forum of Augustus 4

VIA DEI FORI

Caesar's Forum 4

Nerva's Forum 4

LARGO C. RICCI

VIA FRANGIPANE

VIA D. CARINE

PIAZZA DEL CAMPIDOGLIO

Mamertine Prison

Capitoline Museums

Vespasian's Forum

VIA CURIA

VIA MIRANDA

VIA DEL COLOSSEO

LARGO G. AGNESI

PIAZZALE CAFFARELLI

VIA DELLA CONSOLAZIONE

FORO ROMANO

Roman Forum 8

Colosseo

Nicola Carcere

VIC. JUGARIO

PIAZZA D. CONSOLAZIONE 15

VIA DEI FIENILI

VIA DI S. TEODORO

VIA DI SAN BONAVENTURA

Colosseum (Colosseo) 3

VIA D. MISERICORDIA

S. Giorgio al Velabro 9

V. D. VELABRO

Arch of Constantine

VIA C. VIBENN

PIAZZA BOCCA D.VERITA

Palatine 7

LINEA B

PIAZZA S. ANASTASIA

S. Maria in Cosmedin 13

VIA D. GRECA

V.ABA MASS. DI ERCOLE

See p63

VIA DEI CERCHI

VIA DI SAN GREGORIO

CLIVO DI SCAURO

PIAZZA S. GREGORIO

VIA DEL

CLIVO DEI

VIA DI SANTA SABINA

VIA MURCIA

PIAZZALE UGO LA MALFA

Circus Maximus (Circo Massimo) 2

CIRCO MASSIMO

PIAZZA DI PORTA CAPENA

PORTA CAPENA

VIA VALLE DELLE CAMENE

CELIO

0   200 m

0   200 yds

© Copyright Time Out Group 2007

VIA G. BERNERO

VIA DI S. ALBERTO MAGNO

AVENTINE

LARGO ARRIGO VII

PIAZZA D. TEMPIO DI DIANA

PIAZZA S. PRISCA

VIA D. TERME DECIANE

VIA D. FONTE D. FAUNO

VIALE AVENTINO

Circo Massimo

F.A.O.

VIA D. TERME DI CARACALLA

The equestrian statue of Marcus Aurelius in the centre is a computer-generated copy; the second-century gilded bronze original is inside the museum.

The *cordonata* leads down to piazza Venezia. Dominating this dizzying roundabout is the **Vittoriano**, a piece of nationalistic kitsch that outdoes anything dreamed up by the ancients.

South of the Capitoline, on low ground by the river, was the *velabrum*, the marshy area where Remus and Romulus were, according to Rome's foundation myth, discovered floating in a basket and then suckled by a she-wolf. Two delightful Republican-age temples still stand here, and the area is dotted about with remains of the *forum boarium* and *forum holitorium* (cattle and vegetable markets) that were to later occupy this space.

Sights & museums

Capitoline Museums

Piazza del Campidoglio 1 (06 6710 2475/06 8205 9127/www.musei capitolini.org). **Open** 9am-8pm Tue-Sun. **Admission** €6.50; €4.50 reductions. *Special exhibitions* €1.50 extra. No credit cards. **Map** p53 A2 ❶

Housed in two *palazzi* opposite each other on Michelangelo's piazza del Campidoglio, the Capitoline Museums (Musei capitolini) are the oldest museums in the world, opened to the public in 1734, though the collection was begun in 1471 by Pope Sixtus IV. His successors continued to add ancient scuptures and, later, paintings.

Entry is through the Palazzo dei Conservatori (to the right at the top of the steps). The courtyard contains parts of a colossal statue of Constantine that originally stood in the Basilica of Maxentius in the Roman Forum. Inside, ancient works are mixed with statues by the Baroque genius Gian Lorenzo Bernini.

Capitoline Museums

In a smart new section on the first floor, the second-century statue of Marcus Aurelius has finally been given a suitably grand space. Also here are chunks of the temple of Jupiter. Currently undergoing restoration, Rome's symbol – a much-reproduced fourth-century BC Etruscan she-wolf and suckling twins (added in the Renaissance) – may also end up here.

The upstairs gallery has paintings by greats such as Titian, Tintoretto and Caravaggio. Across the piazza (or via the underground Tabularium, the ancient Capitoline archive building, the Palazzo Nuovo houses one of Europe's greatest collections of ancient sculpture, including the coy *Capitoline Venus*, the *Dying Gaul* and countless portrait busts of emperors and their families.

Circus Maximus

Via del Circo Massimo. **Map** p53 B4 ❷
Little of the actual structure remains at the Circus Maximus, ancient Rome's major chariot-racing venue, but it's still possible to visualise the flat base of the long basin as the racetrack, and the sloping sides as the stands. At the southern end are some brick remains of the original seating (the tower is medieval). The oldest and largest of Rome's ancient arenas, the Circus Maximus hosted chariot races from at least the fourth century BC. It was rebuilt by Julius Caesar to hold as many as 300,000 people. Races involved up to 12 rigs of four horses each; the circus was also flooded for mock sea battles.

Colosseum

Piazza del Colosseo (06 700 5469/ 06 3996 7700). **Open** 9am-sunset daily. **Admission** (incl Palatine) €9; €4.50 reductions. *Special exhibitions* €2 extra. No credit cards. **Map** p53 C3 ❸
Note: If the queue outside the Colosseum is daunting, buy tickets at the Palatine and enter directly.
Built in AD 72 by Emperor Vespasian, il Colosseo hosted gory battles between combinations of gladiators, slaves,

Dreams of empire

Plans to bring more of the ancient city to life.

The project is ambitious, the timescale (for Rome) startling: in April 2007 it was announced that work would begin almost immediately on a new **Museo di Roma** – 30,000 square metres dedicated to the fortunes of the ancient city, from its origins to its decline and fall – in the palazzo surrounding the church of Santa Maria in Cosmedin.

Into the restored premises will go the contents of the Museo della Civiltà Romana (p156) – including giant plaster models of the ancient city – which now languish, under-visited, in EUR. And out from under wraps will come many pieces – including the remaining fragments of the 13-metre by 18-metre marble *Forma Urbis Severiana* map of Republican Rome – that were simply too big to be displayed in spaces available up to now.

This is merely the first step, Mayor Walter Veltroni promised, of what will become a museum complex extending from the Circus Maximus to the Imperial Fora. The long-awaited **Museo dei Fori Imperiali**, centring on Trajan's Market and due to open in October, will become a part.

Talks were under way to secure a lease on Palazzo Rivaldo, sandwiched between the Roman Forum and via dei Fori Imperiali; and negotiations were well advanced to purchase the Torlonia family's (see box p98) superlative collection of ancient statuary to put inside it.

prisoners and wild animals of all descriptions. Properly called the Amphitheatrum Flavium, the building was later known as the Colosseum not because it was big, but because of a gold-plated colossal statue, now lost, that stood alongside. The arena was about 500 metres (a third of a mile) in circumference and could seat over 50,000 people. Nowhere in the world was there a larger setting for mass slaughter. In the 100 days of carnage held to inaugurate the amphitheatre in AD 80, 5,000 beasts perished. Sometimes, animals got to kill people: a common sentence in the Roman criminal justice system was *damnatio ad bestias*, where miscreants were turned loose, unarmed, into the arena. After the fall of the Roman Empire authorities banned games here and the Colosseum became a quarry for stone and marble to build Roman *palazzi*. The pockmarks on the Colosseum's masonry date from the ninth century, when the lead clamps holding the stones together were pillaged. This irreverence didn't stop until the mid-18th century, when the Colosseum was consecrated as a church.

Standing beside the Colosseum, Constantine's triumphal arch was erected in AD 315, shortly before the emperor left the city for Byzantium.

Imperial Fora & Trajan's Market

Visitors' centre *via dei Fori Imperiali* (06 679 7786/06 679 7702). **Open** *Oct-Mar* 8.30am-4.30pm daily. *Apr-Sept* 8.30am-6.30pm daily. **Map** p53 B1 **4**

Trajan's Market *via IV Novembre 94* (06 679 0048/06 679 1620). **Open** (lower site only, access from via Madonna di Loreto) 9am-2pm Tue-Sun. **Admission** €3. No credit cards.

Note: Excavations and restoration work mean that timetables for opening and guided tours of this area can vary from week to week, and parts can be closed off temporarily. However, all the fora and much of Trajan's Market are visible from the pavement of via dei Fori Imperiali.

Excavations carried out in the Imperial Fora in the 1990s opened up massive amounts of archaeological space. The great hemicycle in the upper area of Trajan's Market is earmarked as the new Museo dei Fori Imperiali, a bells-and-whistles multimedia museum.

As existing fora became too small to cope with the growing city, emperors combined philanthropy with propaganda and created new ones of their own, resulting in what is now known collectively as the *Fori imperiali* (Imperial Fora). Along via dei Fori Imperiali (sliced cavalierly through the ruins by Mussolini) are five separate fora, each built by a different emperor.

Most impressive is Trajan's forum, at the piazza Venezia end of via dei Fori Imperiali. Laid out in the early second century AD, it is dominated by Trajan's column (AD 113), with detailed spiralling reliefs showing victories over Dacia (modern-day Romania). The rectangular foundation to the south of Trajan's column, where several imposing granite columns still stand, was the basilica Ulpia, an administrative building.

The most distinctive feature of the forum complex is the multi-storey brick crescent to the south-east of the basilica Ulpia. This great hemicycle, forming part of the *Mercati di Traiano* (Trajan's Market), was built in AD 107. Entering from via IV Novembre, the first room is the Great Hall, a large space possibly used for the corn dole in antiquity. To the south of the Great Hall are the open-air terraces at the top of the great hemicycle. To the east of the Great Hall, stairs lead down to the so-called via Biberatica, an ancient street flanked by well-preserved shops. The shops here were probably *tabernae* (bars), hence the name (*bibere* is Latin for 'to drink'). More stairs lead down through the various layers of the great hemicycle, where most of the 150 shops or offices have remained in perfect condition, many with doorjambs still showing the grooves where shutters slid into place when the working day was over.

Across the road from Trajan's forum, Caesar's forum was the first of the *Fori imperiali*, built in 51 BC by Julius Caesar. Three columns of the Venus Generatrix temple have been rebuilt. Back on the same side as Trajan's forum, Augustus' forum was inaugurated in 2 BC; here, three columns from the temple of Mars Ultor still stand, as does the towering wall that separated the forum from the sprawling Suburra slum behind. Nerva's forum (AD 97) lies mainly beneath via dei Fori Imperiali. On the south side of the road, Vespasian's forum (AD 75) was home to the temple of peace, part of which is now incorporated into the church of Santi Cosma e Damiano. Maps placed on a wall here by Mussolini show how Rome ruled the world.

Mamertine Prison

Clivio Argentario 1 (06 679 2902).
Open *Nov-Mar* 9am-5pm daily.
Apr-Oct 9am-7pm daily **Admission** donation expected. **Map** p53 A2 ⑤
Anyone thought to pose a threat to the security of the ancient Roman state was thrown into the Carcere Mamertino (Mamertine Prison), a dank, underground dungeon between the Roman Forum and present-day via dei Fori Imperiali. The prison's most famous inmates, legend has it, were Saints Peter and Paul; Peter head-butted the wall in the ground-level room leaving his features impressed on the rock, and caused a miraculous well to bubble up.

Museo di Palazzo Venezia

Via del Plebiscito 118 (06 6999 4243).
Open 8.30am-7.30pm Tue-Sun.
Admission *Museum* €4; €2 reductions. *Special exhibitions* varies. No credit cards. **Map** p53 A1 ⑥
This collection contains a hotchpotch of anything from terracotta models (by Baroque sculptor Gian Lorenzo Bernini) for the angels that now grace Ponte Sant'Angelo, to medieval decorative art. Major exhibitions (extra charge applies) are staged regularly here;

these often give access to the huge Sala del Mappamondo, which was used by Mussolini as his office.

NEW Opened in 2006, the *lapidarium* occupies the upper level of the cloister of the 'secret garden of Paul II'. Here are ancient, medieval and Renaissance sarcophagi, coats of arms, funerary monuments and assorted fragments.

Palatine

Via di San Gregorio 30/piazza di Santa Maria Nova 53 (06 699 0110/ 06 3996 7700). **Open** 9am-sunset daily. **Admission** (incl Colosseum) €9; €6.50 reductions. *Special exhibitions* €2 extra. No credit cards. **Map** p53 B3 **7**

Legend relates that a basket holding twin babes Romulus and Remus was found in the swampy area near the Tiber to the west of here. In 753 BC, having murdered his brother, Romulus scaled the Palatine hill and founded Rome. In fact, archaeological evidence shows that proto-Romans had settled on Il Palatino a century – or maybe much more – before that. Later, the Palatine became the Beverly Hills of the ancient city, where the movers and shakers built their palaces. With Rome's decline it became a rural backwater; in the 1540s, much of the hill was bought by Cardinal Alessandro Farnese, who turned it into a pleasure villa and garden. His gardens – the Horti farnesiani – are still a lovely leafy place to wander on a hot day. Beneath the gardens is the Cryptoporticus, a semi-subterranean tunnel built by Nero. South and south-east from the gardens are the remains of vast imperial dwellings, including Emperor Domitian's Domus Augustana, with what may have been a private stadium in the garden. Next door, the Museo Palatino charts the history of the Palatine from the eighth century BC.

Roman Forum

Entrances from via dei Fori Imperiali, piazza del Colosseo & via di San Teodoro (06 700 5469/06 3996 7700). **Open** 9am-1hr before sunset daily. **Admission** free. **Map** p53 B2 **8**

During the early years of the Republic this was an open space with shops and a few temples, and it sufficed; but by the second century BC, ever-conquering Rome needed to give an impression of authority and wealth. Out went the food stalls; in came law courts, offices and immense public buildings with grandiose decorations. The *Foro romano* remained the symbolic heart of the Empire, and emperors continued to embellish it until the fourth century AD. Entering from the Colosseum, the Forum is framed by the Arch of Titus (AD 81), built to celebrate the sack of Jerusalem. To the right are the towering ruins of the basilica di Massenzio, completed in 312. Along the via Sacra, the Forum's high street, are (all on the right) the great columns of the Temple of Antoninus and Faustina; the giant Basilica Emilia – once a bustling place for administration, courts and business; and the Curia, the home of the Senate, begun in 45 BC by Julius Caesar. Straight ahead lies the Arch of Septimius Severus, built in AD 203. Beside the arch are the remains of an Imperial rostra, from where Mark Antony supposedly asked Romans to lend him their ears.

San Giorgio in Velabro

Via del Velabro 19 (06 6920 4534). **Open** 10am-12.30pm, 4-6.30pm daily. **Map** p53 A3 **9**

This austere little church of the fifth century has 16 Roman columns that were pilfered from the Palatine and the Aventine hills in its nave, and pieces of an eighth- or ninth-century choir incorporated into the walls. In the apse is a much-restored 13th-century fresco of St George. Outside, to the left, is the Arco degli Argentari, built in AD 204; it was a gate on the road between the main Forum and the *forum boarium* (cattle market) along which money-changers (*argenteri*) plied their trade.

San Marco

Piazza San Marco (06 679 5205). **Open** 4-7pm Mon; 8.30am-12.30pm, 4-7pm Tue-Sun. **Map** p53 A1 **10**

Campo de' Fiori p60

Founded, tradition says, in 336 on the site of the house where St Mark the Evangelist stayed, this church was rebuilt by Pope Paul II in the 15th century when the neighbouring Palazzo Venezia was constructed, and given its Baroque look in the mid-18th century. Remaining from its earlier manifestations are the 11th-century bell tower, and the ninth-century mosaic of Christ in the apse. In the portico is the gravestone of Vanozza Catanei, mother of the notorious Cesare and Lucrezia Borgia.

San Nicola in Carcere

Via del Teatro di Marcello 46 (06 6830 7198). **Open** 7am-7pm daily. **Map** p63 E5 ⓫

The 12th-century San Nicola was built over three Roman temples, dating from the second and third centuries BC; a guide (donation appreciated) takes you down to these. On the outside of the church, six columns from the Temple of Janus can be seen on the left; the ones on the right are from the Temple of Spes (Hope).

Santa Maria in Aracoeli

Piazza del Campidoglio 4 (06 679 8155). **Open** *Nov-Mar* 9.30am-12.30pm, 2.30-5.30pm daily. *Apr-Oct* 9am-12.30pm, 3-6.30pm daily. **Map** p53 A2 ⓬

Up a daunting flight of steps, the romanesque Aracoeli ('altar of heaven') stands on the site of an ancient temple to Juno Moneta. The current basilica-form church dates from the late 13th century. The first chapel on the right has scenes by Pinturicchio from the life of St Francis of Assisi's helpmate St Bernardino (1486). To the left of the altar, a round chapel contains relics of St Helena, mother of Emperor Constantine. At the back of the transept, the Chapel of the Holy Child contains a much-venerated disease-healing *bambinello*, which is often whisked to the bedside of moribund Romans.

Santa Maria in Cosmedin & the Mouth of Truth

Piazza della Bocca della Verità 18 (06 678 1419). **Open** *Oct-Mar* 9am-5pm daily. *Apr-Sept* 9am-6pm daily. **Map** p53 A4 ⓭

Via Giulia

Built in the sixth century and enlarged in the eighth, Santa Maria was embellished with a glorious Cosmati-work floor, throne and choir in the 11th-13th centuries. The altar is a Roman bathtub; in the sacristy is a fragment of an eighth-century mosaic of the Holy Family, brought here from the original St Peter's. The church is better known as the *bocca della verità* (the mouth of truth), after the great stone mask of a man with a gaping mouth on the portico wall – probably an ancient drain cover. Anyone who lies while their hand is in the mouth will have that hand bitten off, according to legend. It was reportedly used by Roman husbands to determine the fidelity of their wives. On the little green opposite, you can see the first-century BC temples of Hercules (round) and Portunus (square).

Vittoriano

Piazza Venezia (06 699 1718).
Open *Monument* 9.30am-4pm daily.
Museo Centrale del Risorgimento
9.30am-6pm daily. *Complesso del Vittoriano* (06 678 0664; for exhibitions only) 9.30am-7.30pm Mon-Thur; 9.30am-11.30pm Fri-Sat; 9.30am-8.30pm Sun. **Admission** free. *Exhibitions* varies. **Map** p53 A1 ⑭
Variously known as 'the wedding cake' and 'the typewriter', this eyesore of a monument to united Italy, constructed between 1885 and 1911, contains exhibits on the struggle to unify the country and stages good temporary art shows. Best of all, you can climb to the top for a 360° view over Rome from the only spot where the spectacle isn't marred by the Vittoriano itself. There's a café halfway up.

Eating & drinking

San Teodoro

Via dei Fienili 49-51 (06 678 0933).
Meals served 1-3.15pm, 8pm-11.30pm Mon-Sat. Closed 1wk Dec; 2wks Jan; 1wk Easter. **€€€€. Map** p53 A3 ⑮
Of a summer's evening there are few better places in Rome for an alfresco meal than at this seafood-oriented restaurant around the back of the Forum, in the prettiest of residential squares. You'd better come prepared to splash out, though. Some dishes are pure *cucina romana*; others, like the *tonnarelli San Teodoro* (with shrimps, courgettes and cherry tomatoes) are lighter and more creative.

The Ghetto & campo de' Fiori

The area that stretches south from busy corso Vittorio Emanuele (aka corso Vittorio) to the Tiber is one of contrasts: **campo de' Fiori** – with its lively morning market and livelier partying crowds at night – stands next to solemn, dignified piazza Farnese with its grand Palazzo Farnese, partly designed by Michelangelo. Top-end antique dealers in via Giulia rub along with craftsmen plying their trades in streets with names (via dei Leutari – lutemakers; via dei Cappellari – hatmakers) that recall the jobs of their medieval ancestors.

In ancient times, this was the *Campus martius* (field of war), where Roman males did physical jerks to stay fighting fit. Packed with theatres, it was also where ancient Romans headed for low-brow fun. After barbarian hordes rampaged through Rome in the fifth and sixth centuries, the area fell into ruin. By the late Middle Ages, it was densely populated and insalubrious; but when the pope made the Vatican – just across the Tiber river – his main residence in the mid-15th century, the area's fortunes improved. Nowadays, its tightly wedged buildings, narrow cobbled alleys and mixture of graceful Renaissance columns and chunky blocks of ancient travertine form the perfect backdrop to everyday Roman street life.

Towards the south-east, largo Argentina is a polluted transport hub with a chunk of ancient Rome at its heart: when you peer over the railings you're able to spot columns, altars and foundations from four temples, dating from the mid-third century BC to c100 BC.

On the southern side of the square lies the **Ghetto**: the district's picture-postcard winding alleys mask a sorrowful history. Rome's Jews occupy a unique place in the history of the Diaspora, having maintained a presence in the city that's been uninterrupted for over 2,000 years. The Ghetto was walled off from the rest of the city in 1556, and remained that way until the 1870s. In piazza Mattei stands the beautiful, delicate Turtle Fountain, erected overnight in the 1580s, though the turtles may have been an afterthought.

Turtle Fountain

Sights & museums

Crypta Balbi

Via delle Botteghe Oscure 31 (06 678 0167). **Open** 9am-5pm Tue-Sun. **Admission** €7; €3 reductions. *Special exhibitions* €2 extra. No credit cards. **Map** p63 E4 ⑯

This museum displays the Crypta Balbi (an ancient theatre lobby) and combines the best of the ancient with the latest technology: it's packed with displays, maps and models that explain (in English) Rome's evolution from the pre-Imperial era, to early Christian times and on through the dim Middle Ages.

Galleria Spada

Piazza Capo di Ferro 3 (06 687 4896/ www.galleriaborghese.it). **Open** 8.30am-7.30pm Tue-Sun. **Admission** €5; €2.50 reductions. No credit cards. **Map** p62 C4 ⑰

This gem of a palace – alas, showing signs of neglect recently – was acquired by art collector Cardinal Bernardino Spada in 1632; the walls are crammed

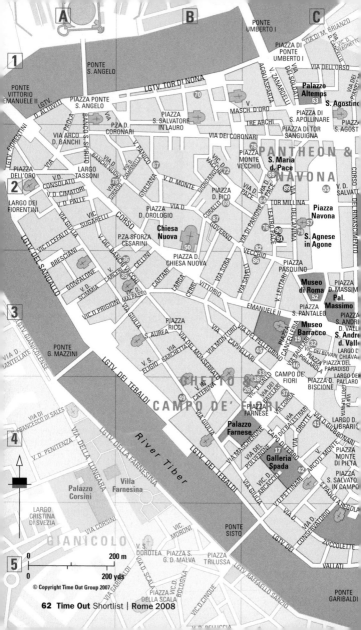

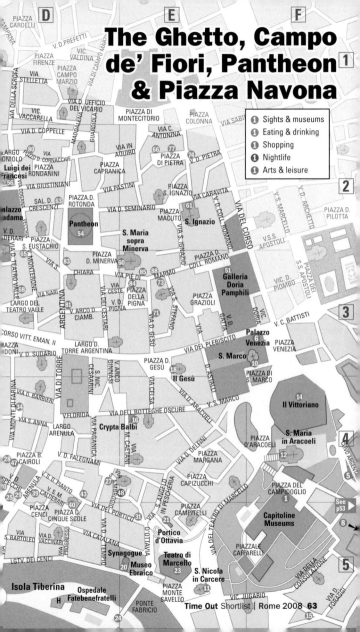

The Ghetto, Campo de' Fiori, Pantheon & Piazza Navona

1 Sights & museums
1 Eating & drinking
1 Shopping
1 Nightlife
1 Arts & leisure

Pantheon
54

S. Maria sopra Minerva

S. Ignazio

Galleria Doria Pamphili

Palazzo Venezia

S. Marco

Il Gesù

Il Vittoriano

S. Maria in Aracoeli

Crypta Balbi

Capitoline Museums

Portico d'Ottavia

Teatro di Marcello

Synagogue

Museo Ebraico

S. Nicola in Carcere

Isola Tiberina

Ospedale Fatebenefratelli

Down by the river

Once upon a time, Romans used their river – washing in, boating on and even drinking from its far-from-clean waters. But Old Father Tiber repaid this affection with regular floods. So when 'modernisers' moved in after Italian Unification in the 1870s, massive *banchine* (embankments) were built.

Ever since, Romans shunned their walled-off waterway. They blame the steep flights of uneven stone steps for discouraging all but the fittest from struggling down to the towpath, but it's a feeble excuse. And it's also a pity. The noble old Tiber could be an important leisure zone – a fact city hall is now trying to drum home.

Rent a bike to explore the towpath-cycle track and you'll find a surprisingly peaceful world: there are cormorants, bubbling fish and ratty-looking coypu (plus groups of homeless bivouacking beneath bridges). Alternatively, take one of the **Battelli di Roma** river boats.

Most of the year, you'll have the riverbanks to yourself. In summer, however, locals are being enticed down by a host of initiatives. A fully-equipped 'beach' materialises beneath Castel Sant'Angelo: **Portal-Tevere Village** has sun beds, umbrellas, juice bars, sand and a sparkling blue swimming pool. Movies are screened in alfresco cinemas – on the towpath, and on the Tiber Island – on hot summer evenings.

To remove Romans' chief excuse for refusing to make the descent, a €1.2 million scheme has been approved to install lifts linking the high embankment with the towpaths. Work is due to start in January 2008.

Also planned for 2008 is a cycle path from the delightful Villa Sciarra, across Ponte Sublicio, to an archaeological area beneath the Aventine hill, where another lift will transport people and bikes up to the Parco degli Aranci, with its spectacular view over the city.

And last but not least, €8 million has been earmarked for cleaning up the river. No one has written a song called *The Blue Tiber* yet, but it can only be a matter of time.

■ www.battellidiroma.it
■ www.portalestate.com
■ www.estateromana.
comune.roma.it

with paintings. There are impressive names here: Domenichino, Guido Reni, Guercino plus the father-daughter Gentileschi duo, Orazio and Artemisia. The main attraction of the museum, however, is the 'Borromini Perspective', where visual trickery makes a 9m-long colonnade look much longer.

Il Gesù

Piazza del Gesù (06 697 001). **Open** *Church* 6am-12.30pm, 4-8pm daily. *Loyola's rooms* 4-6pm Mon-Sat; 10am-noon Sun. **Map** p63 E4 ⓙ

The Gesù, built in 1568-84, is the flagship church of the Jesuits, and was designed to involve the congregation as closely as possible in services, with a nave unobstructed by aisles. One of Rome's great Baroque masterpieces – *Triumph in the Name of Jesus* by Il Baciccia (1676-79) – decorates the ceiling of the nave. On the left is the ornate chapel of Sant'Ignazio (1696). Above the altar is what was long believed to be the biggest lump of lapis lazuli in the world; in fact, it's covered concrete. Outside the church, you can visit St Ignatius' rooms.

Museo Barracco

Corso Vittorio 166 (06 687 5657). **Open** 9am-7pm Tue-Sun. **Admission** €3; €1.50 reductions. No credit cards. **Map** p62 C3 ⓙ

This compact collection of mainly pre-Roman art was amassed in the first half of the 20th century. Don't miss the copy of the *Wounded Bitch* by the fourth-century BC sculptor Lysippus, on the second floor.

Museo Ebraica di Roma

Lungotevere Cenci (06 6840 0661/www. museoebraico.roma.it). **Open** *Oct-May* 10am-5pm Mon-Thur, Sun; 9am-2pm Fri. *June-Sept* 10am-7pm Mon-Thur, Sun; 9am-4pm Fri. Closed Jewish holidays. **Admission** €7.50; €3 reductions. No credit cards. **Map** p63 E5 ⓙ

As well as luxurious crowns, Torah mantles and silverware, this museum presents vivid reminders of the persecution suffered by Rome's Jews at various times in history: copies of the 16th-century papal edicts that banned Jews from many activities, and heart-rending relics from the concentration

Designed in 1524 by Giacomo della Porta, this church was handed over to Carlo Maderno, who stretched the design upward, creating a dome that is the highest in Rome after St Peter's. Puccini set the opening act of *Tosca* in the chapel on the left.

Teatro di Marcello

Via Teatro di Marcello.
Map p63 E5 ㉓
This is one of the strangest and most impressive sights in the Eternal City – a Renaissance palace grafted on to an ancient theatre. Julius Caesar began building the theatre, but it was finished in 11 BC by Augustus, who named it after his favourite nephew. Originally it comprised three tiers and seated as many as 20,000 people. Abandoned in the fourth century AD, it was turned into a fortress in the 12th century and then into a palazzo in the 16th by the Savelli family.

Tiber Island & Ponte Rotto

Map p63 D5 ㉔
When the last Etruscan king was driven from Rome, the Romans uprooted the wheat from his fields and threw it in baskets into the river. Silt accumulated and formed an island where Aesculapius, the Roman god of medicine, founded a sanctuary in the third century BC. That's what the legend says, and the island has always had a vocation for public health. Today a hospital occupies the north end. The church of San Bartolomeo is built over the original sanctuary; the columns in the nave are from that earlier building. Remains of the ancient building can also be seen from the riverside footpath, from where there's also a fine view over the *ponte rotto* (broken bridge). This stands on the site of the Pons aemilius, Rome's first stone bridge, built in 142 BC. It was rebuilt many times before 1598, when they gave up trying. To the east of the bridge is a tunnel in the embankment: the gaping mouth of the city's great Cloaca Maxima sewer, built in the sixth century BC.

camps. Recently refurbished, the museum displays exquisite carvings from long-gone Roman synagogues.

Portico d'Ottavia

Via Portico D'Ottavia. **Map** p63 E5 ㉑
Great ancient columns and a marble frontispiece, held together with rusting iron braces, now form part of the church of Sant'Angelo in Pescheria, but they were originally the entrance of a massive colonnaded square (portico) containing temples and libraries, built in the first century AD by Emperor Augustus and dedicated to his sister Octavia. A walkway (open 9am-6pm daily) has been opened through the *forum piscarium* – the ancient fish market; it continues past a graveyard of broken columns and capitals to the Teatro di Marcello, passing by three towering columns that were part of the Temple of Apollo (433 BC).

Sant'Andrea della Valle

Corso Vittorio 6 (06 686 1339). **Open** 7.30am-12.30pm, 4.30-7.30pm daily.
Map p62 C3 ㉒

Eating & drinking

See also Casa Bleve (p77).

Alberto Pica

Via della Seggiola 12 (06 686 8405).
Open *Jan-Mar, Oct, Nov* 8.30am-
2am Mon-Sat. *Apr-Sept, Dec* 8.30am-
2am Mon-Sat; 4.30pm-2am Sun.
Closed 2wks Aug. No credit cards.
Map p63 D4 **㉕**

Horrendous neon lighting, surly staff
and some of Rome's most delicious
ice-cream are the hallmarks of this long-
running bar. The rice specialities stand
out: imagine eating frozen, partially
cooked rice pudding and you'll get the
picture. *Riso alla cannella* (cinnamon
rice) is particularly delicious.

Ar Galletto

Piazza Farnese 102 (06 686 1714).
Meals served 12.15-3pm, 7.15-11pm
Mon-Sat. Closed 10 days Aug. €€€.
Map p62 C4 **㉖**

You don't need to pay the inflated
prices charged by other restaurants
around here for a ringside view of
piazza Farnese. Humbler than the competition, Ar Galletto has tables on the
square in summer. The food is firmly
in the local tradition, but dishes like
penne all'arrabbiata or *spaghetti alle
vongole* are appetising and – for the
location – well priced.

Bartaruga

*Piazza Mattuga 7 (06 689 2299/
www.bartaruga.it).* **Open** 6pm-
midnight Mon-Thur; 6pm-2am Fri,
Sat; 6pm-1pm Sun. No credit cards.
Map p63 D4 **㉗**

This baroque *locale* – decorated in
peach and midnight blue, with divans
and candelabra – is the haunt of the
beautiful, the eccentric and those too
entranced by the lovely square outside
to move on elsewhere.

Bernasconi

Piazza Cairoli 16 (06 6880 6264).
Open 7am-8.30pm Tue-Sun. Closed
Aug. No credit cards. **Map** p63 D4 **㉘**
It's well worth fighting your way inside
this cramped, inconspicuous bar to sam-
ple unbeatable chewy, yeasty *cornetti*.

Bruschetteria degli Angeli

Piazza B Cairoli 2A (06 6880 5789).
Open 12.30-3.30pm, 7.30pm-1.30am
daily. Closed 1wk Aug. €.
Map p63 D4 **㉙**
The star turns here are the heavenly
house *bruschette* (average €8) with
various toppings ranging from red
chicory and bacon to grilled courgettes and mozzarella. There's also
pasta, grilled steaks and a good choice
of draught beers.

Crudo

NEW *Via degli Specchi (06 683 8989/
www.crudoroma.it).* **Open** 7.30pm-2am
daily. **Map** p63 D4 **㉚**
With a dazzling designer interior
complemented by art installations,
plasma screens and DJs, Crudo offers
some of the best *aperitivi* in town, plus
glamorous dining (€€€).

Da Giggetto

*Via Portico d'Ottavia 21A-22 (06
686 1105/www.giggettoalportico.com).*
Meals served 12.30-3pm, 7.30-11pm
Tue-Sun. Closed 2wks July. €€€.
Map p63 E5 **㉛**
This old standby in the Ghetto serves
up decent versions of Roman-Jewish
classics like *carciofi alla giudia* (fried
artichokes) and fried *baccalà* (salt cod).
The atmosphere is warm and bustling,
with large tables of tourists enjoying
the ambience and plentiful helpings.

Ditirambo

*Piazza della Cancelleria 74 (06 687
1626/www.ristoranteditirambo.it).*
Meals served 7.30-11.30pm Mon;
1-3pm, 7.30-11.30pm Tue-Sun. Closed
3wks Aug. €€€. **Map** p62 C3 **㉜**
This funky trattoria serves up good-
value dishes based on fresh, mainly
organic ingredients. They specialise in
traditional fare with a creative kick, as
in the excellent baby squid with a purée
of *cicerchie* beans or the *girello di vitello*
(veal silverside) braised in coffee.

Forno Campo de' Fiori

Vicolo del Gallo 14 (06 6880 6662).
Open 7.30am-2.30pm, 5-8pm Mon-Sat.
No credit cards. **Map** p62 C3 **㉝**

This little bakery dishes out the best takeaway sliced pizza in the campo de' Fiori area by far. Their plain *pizza bianca* base is delicious in itself, but check out the one with *fiori di zucca* (courgette flowers) too.

Gloss

Via del Monte della Farina 43 (06 6813 5345/www.glossroma.it). **Open** 6.30-10.30pm Mon; 6.30pm-2am Tue-Sat. No credit cards. **Map** p63 D4 ③④

This inviting bar offers an *aperitivo*-hour buffet (from 7pm) and a wide range of cultural offerings, including ever-changing art displays. Music comes live, or courtesy of DJs.

Il Goccetto

Via dei Banchi Vecchi 14 (06 686 4268). **Open** 11.30am-2pm, 6.30pm-midnight Mon-Sat. Closed 1wk Jan; 3wks Aug. **Map** p62 B3 ③⑤

One of the more serious *centro storico* wine bars, with dark wood-clad walls and a cosy, private-club feel. Wine is the main point here, with a satisfying range by the glass from €2.50.

Il Pagliaccio

Via dei Banchi Vecchi 129A (06 6880 9595/www.ristoranteilpagliaccio.it). **Meals served** 8-10pm Mon, Tue; 1-2pm, 8-10pm Wed-Sat. Closed 1wk Jan; 2wks Aug. €€€€. **Map** p62 B3 ③⑥

Though its first Michelin star in 2007 has pushed prices up somewhat, Anthony Genovese's *centro storico* restaurant still offers one of the best-value gourmet dinners in Rome. The chef's risk-taking approach is clearly illustrated in an antipasto of grilled scallops with teriyaki-marinated beef and caramel zabaione. But his skill is equally evident in less pyrotechnic dishes like the gnocchi with lamb and two varieties of wild mushroom. Leave space for the excellent desserts.

La Vineria

Campo de' Fiori 15 (06 6880 3268). **Open** 8.30am-2am Mon-Sat. Closed 2wks Aug. **Map** p62 C4 ③⑦

The longest-running wine bar on the campo, La Vineria is where Romans flock to chat and plan the evening ahead over good wines by the (very small) glass, starting at just €1.50.

Le Piramidi

Vicolo del Gallo 11 (06 687 9061). **Open** 10am-12.30am Tue-Sun. Closed Aug. €. No credit cards. **Map** p62 C4 ③⑧

Le Piramidi makes for a welcome change from pizza if you're just in the mood for a quick snack. The range of Middle Eastern takeaway fare is small, but it's all fresh, cheap and tasty.

Mad Jack's

Via Arenula 20 (06 6880 8223). **Open** *Sept-July* 11am-2am daily. *Aug* 10am-2am Mon-Thur, Sun; 10am-3am Fri, Sat. Closed 1wk Aug. **Map** p63 D4 ③⑨

This formulaic but reliable Irish pub is packed at night and at weekends with crowds of young Italians and Anglos spilling out on to the pavement. The beverages of choice are beer and cider but there's also an array of wines and cocktails.

Sora Margherita

Piazza delle Cinque Scole 30 (06 687 4216). **Meals served** *Oct-Mar* 12.45-2.45pm, 8-11.30pm Tue-Thur; 8-11.30pm Fri, Sat. *Apr-Sept* 12.45-2.45pm, 8-11pm Mon-Thur; 8-11.30pm Fri. Closed Aug. €€. No credit cards. **Map** p63 D5 ④⓪

This rustic hole-in-the-wall trattoria is not for health freaks, but no one argues with serious Roman Jewish cooking at these prices. The classic pasta and meat dishes on offer include a superlative *pasta e fagioli* (with beans), *tonnarelli cacio e pepe* (pasta with cheese and pepper) and ossobuco washed down with the rough-and-ready house wine.

Shopping

Angelo Nepi

Via dei Giubbonari 28 (06 689 3006). **Open** noon-7.30pm Mon; 9.30am-7.30pm Tue-Sat. **Map** p62 C4 ④①

This Roman designer's clothes for women come in rich, exotic colours and fabrics, sometimes with beaded details.

ROME BY AREA

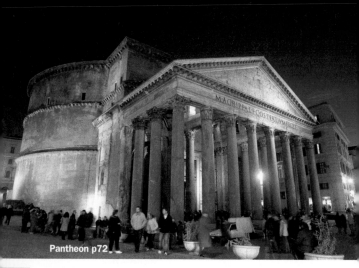

Pantheon p72

Borini

Via dei Pettinari 86 (06 687 5670).
Open 3.30-7.30pm Mon; 9am-1pm,
3.30-7.30pm Tue-Sat. Closed 3wks Aug.
Map p62 C4 ❷

Franco Borini's shop is chaotic, with
piles of shoes inside peeling walls. His
elegant but durable footware follows
fashion trends religiously and comes at
prices that won't make you gasp.

Forno del Ghetto

Via Portico d'Ottavia 1 (06 687 8637).
Open 7am-2pm, 3.30-7.30pm Mon-
Thur; 8am-2pm Fri; 7.30am-5pm Sun.
Closed 3wks Aug & Jewish holidays.
No credit cards. **Map** p63 D4 ❸

This tiny shop has no sign but is
immediately recognisable by the line
of slavering regulars outside. Among
other goodies, they come for the unfor-
gettable damson and ricotta tarts.

Ibiz

Via dei Chiavari 39 (06 6830 7297).
Open 9.30am-7.30pm Mon-Sat. Closed
2wks Aug. **Map** p62 C4 ❹

Ibiz bags are made by hand in the
on-site workshop: look on as you mull
over which of the handbags, briefcases,
backpacks and leather accessories you
want to take home.

Laboratorio Marco Aurelio

*Via del Pellegrino 48 (06 686 5570/
www.marcoaurelio.it).* **Open** 11am-
2pm, 5-9pm Tue-Sat. **Map** p62 C3 ❺

This jewellery designer creates stunning and often unconventional pieces in
hammered and wrought silver, on site.
Sizable stones and intricate patterns
recall ancient Rome: after all, this is
Marcus Aurelius we're talking about…

Loco

Via dei Baullari 22 (06 6880 8216).
Open 3.30-8.30pm Mon; 10.30am-
8.30pm Tue-Sat. Closed 2wks Aug.
Map p62 C3 ❻

If you like your shoes avant-garde, this
small copper and wood decorated store
is the place for you. From classy to wild
and eccentric, its pieces are always one
step ahead of the flock.

Momento

Piazza Cairoli 9 (06 6880 8157). **Open**
10.30am-7.30pm daily. **Map** p63 D4 ⓴
The poshest of princesses and her boho
cousin will be equally awed by the collection of clothes and accessories at this
treasure trove for the fearless and
colourful, at very approachable prices.

Nightlife

Rialtosantambrogio

*Via Sant'Ambrogio 4 (06 6813 3640/
www.rialtosantambrogio.org).* **Open**
times & days vary. Closed Aug.
Admission free-€5. No credit cards.
Map p63 E4 ⓳
This *centro sociale* (squat) in the Ghetto
hosts performances, art exhibitions,
live music and disco evenings with
cutting-edge electronica DJs and VJs,
especially at the weekend. A meeting
point for a radical crowd.

Arts & leisure

Salus per Aquam

Via Giulia 4 (06 687 7449). **Open**
9am-7.30pm Mon-Sat. Closed 3wks
Aug. **Map** p62 B4 ⓴
This gorgeous spa frequented by
Rome's beautiful offers a mouth-
watering range of massage and beauty
treatments for men and women, plus
a hammam and hairdressing. By
appointment only.

The Pantheon & Piazza Navona

This area of picturesque alleys
in the loop of the river north of
corso Vittorio Emanuele was part
of the ancient *Campus martius*,
where Roman manhood drilled
for war then retired to luxurious
bathhouses to wash off the sweat,
to theatres for entertainment and
to grand temples to dwell on
notions of empire.

After the Empire fell, the *Campus*
was prime construction territory
and every medieval wall tells a tale

Bernini's Elephant p76

of primitive recycling: grand
palazzi were built from stolen
marble; humbler souls constructed
their little houses among the ruins.
It's still a democratic area, where
mink-coated contessas mingle
with pensioners, craftsmen and
tradesmen. After dark, smart
restaurants and hip bars fill
to bursting, especially around
Santa Maria della Pace.

Two squares – both living
links to ancient Rome – dominate
the district: piazza della Rotonda
– home to the **Pantheon** – and
magnificent **piazza Navona**.

West of piazza Navona, piazza
Pasquino is home to a truncated
classical statue; for centuries,
Romans have let off steam by
pinning scraps of satirical verse
(*pasquinate*) to this sculpture.
Further north, elegant, antique-
shop-lined via dei Coronari was
once the haunt of pilgrim-fleecing
rosary-makers (*coronari*).

ROME BY AREA

When corso Vittorio was hacked through the medieval fabric in the 1870s, only the most grandiose of homes were spared: Palazzo Massimo at number 141, with its curved façade following the stands in Domitian's odeon (small theatre), is one notable example.

To the east of the Pantheon, on the other hand, **Galleria Doria Pamphilj** contains one of Rome's finest art collections, while the charmingly rococo piazza Sant' Ignazio looks like a stage set. In neighbouring piazza di Pietra, the columns of the Temple of Hadrian can be seen embedded in the walls of Rome's ex-stock exchange.

Sights & museums

Chiesa Nuova/Santa Maria in Vallicella

Piazza della Chiesa Nuova (06 687 5289/www.chiesanuova.net). **Open** Nov-Mar 8am-1pm, 4-7.30pm daily. Apr-Oct 8am-1pm, 4.30-7.30pm daily. **Map** p62 B2 ⑤⓪
Filippo Neri (1515-95) was a wealthy Florentine who abandoned commerce to live among the poor in Rome. He founded the Oratorian order in 1544. In 1575 work began on the order's headquarters, the Chiesa Nuova. Neri wanted a large, simple building; the walls were covered with the exuberant frescoes and multicoloured marbles only after his death. Pietro da Cortona painted the *Assumption of the Virgin* (1650) in the apse, Rubens the *Virgin and Child* (1608) over the altar.

Galleria Doria Pamphilj

Piazza del Collegio Romano 2 (06 679 7323/www.doriapamphilj.it). **Open** 10am-5pm Mon-Wed, Fri-Sun. **Admission** €8; €5.70 reductions. No credit cards. **Map** p63 E3 ⑤①
The entrance to this magnificent private gallery is through state apartments planned in the mid-16th century. The main galleries are around the central courtyard. Velázquez's portrait of the Pamphili Pope Innocent X is the

highlight of the collection; there's a splendid bust by Bernini of the same pontiff next to it. At the end of the Galleria degli Specchi are four small rooms ordered by century. In the 17th-century room, Caravaggio is represented by the *Rest on the Flight into Egypt* and the *Penitent Magdalene*; the 16th-century room includes Titian's shameless *Salome* and Raphael's *Portrait of Two Men*.

Museo di Roma

Palazzo Braschi, via di San Pantaleo 10 (06 6710 8346/www.museodiroma. comune.roma.it). **Open** 9am-7pm Tue-Sun. **Admission** €6.50; €3 reductions. *Special exhibitions* €1.50 extra. No credit cards. **Map** p62 C3 ⑤②
The rotating collection here recounts the evolution of the city from the Middle Ages to the early 20th century. Sculpture, clothing, furniture and photographs help to put the city's monuments in a human context.

Palazzo Altemps

Piazza Sant'Apollinare 48 (06 687 2719). **Open** 9am-7.45pm Tue-Sun. **Admission** €6.50; €3.50 reductions. *Special exhibitions* €2.50 extra. No credit cards. **Map** p62 C1 ⑤③
The 15th- to 16th-century Palazzo Altemps houses part of the state-owned stock of Roman treasures: gems of classical statuary purchased from the Boncompagni-Ludovisi, Altemps and Mattei families. The Ludovisis liked 'fixing' statues: an *Athena with Serpent* (room 9) was revamped in the 17th century by Alessandro Algardi, who also 'improved' the *Hermes Loghios* in room 19. Room 21 has the *Ludovisi Throne*, the museum's greatest treasure, a fifth-century BC work from Magna Grecia… though some believe it to be a fake.

Pantheon

Piazza della Rotonda (06 6830 0230). **Open** 8.30am-7.30pm Mon-Sat; 9am-6pm Sun; 9am-1pm public holidays. **Map** p63 D2 ⑤④
The Pantheon was built by Hadrian in AD 119-128 as a temple to the most important deities; the inscription on the

Piazza Navona

pediment records a Pantheon built 100 years before by General Marcus Agrippa (which confused historians for centuries). Its fine state of preservation is due to the building's conversion to a church in 608, though its bronze cladding was purloined over the centuries: part is now in Bernini's *baldacchino* in St Peter's. The bronze doors are the original Roman ones. Inside, the Pantheon's glory lies in its dimensions. The diameter of the hemispherical dome is exactly equal to the height of the building. At the centre of the dome is the oculus, a circular hole 9m (30ft) in diameter, a symbolic link between the temple and the heavens. Until the 18th century the portico was used as a market: supports for the stalls were inserted into the notches still visible in the columns.

Piazza Navona

Map p62 C2 ⑤⑤

This tremendous theatrical space owes its shape to an ancient athletics stadium, built in AD 86 by Emperor Domitian. Just north of the piazza, at piazza di Tor Sanguigna 16, remains of the original arena are visible from the street. The piazza acquired its current form in the mid-17th century. The central fountain of the *Four Rivers*, finished in 1651, is one of the most extravagant masterpieces designed by Bernini. Its main figures represent the longest rivers of the four continents known at the time; Ganges of Asia, Nile of Africa, Danube of Europe and Plata of the Americas, all embellished with appropriate flora. The figure of the Nile is veiled, because its source was unknown.

San Luigi dei Francesi

Piazza San Luigi dei Francesi (06 688 271/www.saintlouis-rome.org). **Open** 8.30am-12.30pm, 3.30-7pm Mon-Wed, Fri-Sun; 8.30am-12.30pm Thur. **Map** p63 D2 ⑤⑥

Completed in 1589, San Luigi (St Louis) is the church of Rome's French community. In the fifth chapel on the left are Caravaggio's spectacular scenes from the life of St Matthew (1600-02). But don't overlook lovely frescoes of St Cecilia by Domenichino (1615-17), in the second chapel on the right.

To get to the other side

Crossing the road is a risky proposition in Rome.

You can tell recent arrivals in the Eternal City at a glance: they're the ones hesistating on the kerb, their goal in sight on the other side of thundering traffic, a look of terror in their eyes.

Terror turns to disbelief as they notice locals and old hands striding nonchalantly into the flow. It's all about eye contact and attitude, they'll tell you. But should Romans be so confident?

Between July 2004 and June 2005, 186 people died in accidents on Rome's roads; of these, 63 were pedestrians. A Eurostat survey of road safety in 14 EU capitals named Rome the most dangerous city, with 8.37 dead and injured in accidents per 1,000 population, making second-placed Copenhagen's 1.47 per 1,000 look paltry.

The problem, in part, is the sheer number of vehicles on the roads: around 950 per 1,000 population, three times that of London. Of these, 2,580,000 are private cars; two-wheelers number over 366,000, more than any other Italian city. But resistance to public transport doesn't help, with only 30 per cent of Rome's population making use of a comparatively modern fleet. These buses, however, ply routes covering just 163.2 kilometres per 100 square kilometres – placing Rome 60th for bus services among Italian towns and cities.

So what can visitors do to ensure they don't end up as a road safety statistic, yet still reach that tantalising sight on the other side of the road? Well, first of all, stick to the *centro storico* where the 700-hectare ZTL (*zona a traffico limitato*) is Italy's largest: here, at least, the concentration of cars is less daunting. And seek out the many pedestrianised zones (second only to Venice), though watch out for mad *motorino* riders who whip through them anyway. Finally, work on the attitude and remember: establishing eye contact with the driver bearing down on you is fundamental.

Sant'Agnese in Agone

Piazza Navona (06 6819 2134/www. santagneseinagone.org). **Open** 9am-noon, 4-7pm Tue-Sat; 9am-1pm, 4-8pm Sun. **Map** p62 C2 ⑤⑦

Legend says that teenage St Agnes was cast naked into the stadium of Domitian around AD 304 when she refused to renounce Christ and marry a powerful local. Her pagan persecutors chopped her head off (the implausibly small skull is still here), supposedly on the exact spot where the church now stands. Begun in 1652 the church was given its splendidly fluid concave façade by Borromini.

Sant'Agostino

Piazza Sant'Agostino (06 6880 1962). **Open** 7.45am-noon, 4-7.30pm daily. **Map** p62 C1 ⑤⑧

This 15th-century church has one of the earliest Renaissance façades in Rome, made of travertine filched from the Colosseum. Inside, the third column on the left bears a fresco of *Isaiah* by Raphael (1512). In the first chapel on the left is Caravaggio's depiction of the grubbiest pilgrims ever to present themselves at the feet of the startlingly beautiful *Madonna of the Pilgrims* (1604).

Santa Maria della Pace

Arco della Pace 5 (06 686 1156). **Open** 10am-noon, 4-6pm Mon-Sat; 10am-noon Sun. **Map** p62 C2 ⑤⑨

Built in 1482, Santa Maria della Pace was given its theatrical Baroque façade by Pietro da Cortona in 1656. Just inside the door is Raphael's *Sybils* (1514). There's a beautifully harmonious cloister by Bramante, his first work after arriving in Rome in the early 16th century; exhibitions are often held here; for information, see www.chiostrodelbramante.it).

Santa Maria sopra Minerva

Piazza della Minerva 42 (06 679 3926/ www.basilicaminerva.it). **Open** 8am-7pm daily. **Map** p63 E3 ⑥⓪

Rome's only Gothic church was built on the site of an ancient temple of Minerva in 1280. Its best works of art are Renaissance: on the right of the transept is the Carafa chapel, with frescoes by Filippino Lippi (1457-1504). Also here is the tomb of the Carafa Pope Paul IV (1555-59), famous for enclosing the Jewish Ghetto and having loincloths painted on the nudes of

L'Altro Mastai p78

Michelangelo's *Last Judgment* in the Sistine Chapel. A bronze loincloth was also ordered to cover Christ's genitals on a work here by Michelangelo, a Christ holding up a cross. The *Madonna and Child*, an earlier work believed by some to be by Fra Angelico, is in the chapel to the left of the altar, close to the artistic monk's own tomb. The father of modern astronomy, Galileo Galilei, who dared suggest that the earth revolved around the sun, was tried for heresy in the adjoining monastery in 1633. In the square in front of the church is a charming marble elephant bearing an obelisk on its back, by Bernini.

Sant'Ignazio di Loyola

Piazza Sant'Ignazio (06 679 4406/ www.chiesasantignazio.org). **Open** 8am-12.15pm, 3-7.15pm daily. **Map** p63 E2 ⑥⑴

Sant'Ignazio was begun in 1626 to commemorate the canonisation of St Ignatius, founder of the Jesuits. Trompe l'oeil columns soar above the nave, and architraves by Andrea Pozzo open to a cloudy heaven. When the monks next door claimed that a dome would rob them of light, Pozzo simply painted a dome on the ceiling. The illusion is fairly convincing if you stand on the disc set in the floor of the nave. Walk away, however, and it collapses.

Sant'Ivo alla Sapienza

Corso Rinascimento 40 (06 686 4987). **Open** 10am-noon Sun. **Map** p63 D3 ⑥⑵

In this crowning glory of Borromini's tortured imagination, the concave façade is countered by the convex bulk of the dome, which terminates in a bizarre corkscrew spire. Inside, the concave and concave surfaces on the walls and up into the dome leave you feeling like someone spiked your cappuccino.

Eating & drinking

Armando al Pantheon

Salita de' Crescenzi 31 (06 6880 3034). **Meals served** 12.30-3pm, 7.15-11pm Mon-Fri; 12.30-3pm Sat. Closed Aug. **€€. Map** p63 D2 ⑥⑶

Armando is a simple, no-frills trattoria: a rare find given it's just a few yards from the Pantheon. It serves classics like *fettucine all'Armando* (with peas, mushrooms and tomatoes) and ossobuco. The only concessions to changing times are some vegetarian dishes.

Bar della Pace

Via della Pace 3-7 (06 686 1216). **Open** 4pm-3am Mon; 8.30am-3am Tue-Sun. **Map** p62 C2 ⑥⑷

Eternally *à la mode*, this bar has warm, antiques- and flower-filled rooms for the colder months and (pricey) pavement tables beneath the trademark ivy-clad facade.

Bar Sant'Eustachio

Piazza Sant'Eustachio 82 (06 6880 2048). **Open** 8.30am-1am Mon-Thur, Sun; 8.30am-1.20am Fri, Sat. No credit cards. **Map** p63 D3 ⑥⑸

Sant'Eustachio is one of the city's most famous coffee bars and its walls are plastered with celebrity testimonials. The coffee is quite extraordinary, if expensive. Try the *gran caffè*: the *schiuma* (froth) can be slurped off afterwards with spoon or fingers. Unless you specify (*amaro* means 'no sugar'), it comes very sweet.

Caffè Fandango

🆕 *Piazza di Pietra 32-33 (06 4547 2913/www.fandango.it).* **Open** 11am-midnight Tue-Thur; 11am-1am Fri, Sat; 11am-9pm Sun. **Map** p63 E2 ⑥⑹

Owned by one of the country's leading independent film distributors, this café is distinctly movie-themed, with scattered memorabilia plus film-related books and DVDs on sale. There are film and docu presentations, art exhibits and live music.

Capricci Siciliani

🆕 *Via di Panico 83 (06 687 3666/ www.capriccisiciliani.com).* **Meals served** noon-3.30pm, 7-11.30pm Tue-Sat. Closed Aug. **€€€. Map** p62 B2 ⑥⑺

Housed in the cellars of the imposing Palazzo Taverna, Capricci Siciliani is stridently Sicilian, producing good ver-

ROME BY AREA

Casa Bleve

sions of regional classics, from *pasta con le sarde* (pasta with sardines and pine-nuts) to *involtini di pesce spada* (swordfish roulades).

Casa Bleve

Via del Teatro Valle 48-49 (06 686 5970). **Meals served** 1-3pm, 7.30-10pm Tue, Sat; 1-3pm, 7-10pm Wed-Fri. **€€€. Map** p63 D3 ⑱

The main room of this elegant wine bar is a huge colonnaded roofed-in courtyard in a palazzo near the Pantheon. The buffet offers a vast choice of cheese, cured meat, smoked fish and salad, and there's an impressive selection of wines. The original Bleve *enoteca* in the Ghetto (via Santa Maria del Pianto 9-11, open 8am-8pm Mon-Sat) is more intimate.

Da Francesco

Piazza del Fico 29 (06 686 4009). **Meals served** 11.50am-3pm, 7pm-12.30am Mon, Wed-Sun; 7pm-12.30am Tue. **€€.** No credit cards. **Map** p62 B2 ⑲

Da Francesco is the genuine *centro storico* pizzeria article. You'll get tasty pizzas; a warm, traditional ambience;

brisk but friendly service; and a range of competent, classic *primi* and *secondi*. Bookings often go astray.

Da Vezio

NEW *Via Tor di Nona 37 (06 683 2951).* **Open** 7am-8pm Mon-Sat. No credit cards. **Map** p62 B1 ⑳

Vezio Bagazzini's legendary neighbourhood bar in the Ghetto is no longer; but this dyed-in-the-wool Communist has moved his Marxist-Leninist souvenirs and photos to new premises in pretty, artsy via Tor di Nona. Best not to ask for a Coke.

Enoteca Corsi

Via del Gesù 87-88 (06 679 0821). **Meals served** noon-3.30pm Mon-Sat. **€. Map** p63 E3 ㉑

This 1940s wine shop was the first in Rome to begin serving lunch. The daily-changing menu is written up on the board at the entrance. Dishes follow the traditional Roman culinary calendar – potato gnocchi on Thursdays and stewed *baccalà* (salt cod) on Fridays. No bookings are taken, so get there early or be prepared to queue.

Etabli

NEW *Vicolo delle Vacche 9 (06 687 1499/www.etabli.it).* **Open** 9am-2am Tue-Sun. **Map** p62 B2 ⑫

This brand new locale in the super-chic *triangolo della pace* area is already drawing Rome's bright young things with its minimalist decor, twiddly chandeliers and deep armchairs around the fireplace. The welcome is suave-warm, the feeling intimate. In one room light meals are served at appropriate times.

Green T

Via Pie' di Marmo 28 (06 679 8628/ www.green-tea.it). **Open** 11am-midnight Mon-Sat. **€€**. **Map** p63 E3 ⑬

Stylish pared-back design and a light touch in its cooking set this Chinese tea house and restaurant (with boutique and bookshop) apart from its competitors. Standards can be somewhat hit-and-miss, especially at lunch time, but the atmosphere is unfailingly laid-back and welcoming.

La Caffettiera

Piazza di Pietra 65 (06 679 8147). **Open** 7am-9pm Mon-Sat; 8am-9pm Sun. **Map** p63 E2 ⑭

Politicians and mandarins from the nearby parliament buildings lounge in the sumptuous tearoom of this temple to Neapolitan goodies, while lesser mortals bolt coffees at the bar. The rum baba reigns supreme, but ricotta lovers rave over the crunchy *sfogliatella*, delicately flavoured with cinnamon and orange peel.

L'Altro Mastai

Via Giraud 53 (06 6830 1296/ www.laltromastai.it). **Meals served** 7.30-11.30pm Tue-Sat. Closed Aug. **€€€€**. **Map** p62 A2 ⑮

At this creative Italian restaurant with elegant neo-Pompeiian decor, chef Fabio Baldassare prepares an ever-changing menu that is well worth splashing out for – not a place for a quick snack, but if you have the time, budget and appetite, you're in for a treat. The wine list is satisfyingly vast, the desserts are to die for.

Cartoleria Pantheon p80

Lo Zozzone

Via del Teatro Pace 32 (06 6880 8575). **Open** *Oct-Mar* 9am-9pm Mon-Fri; 9am-11pm Sat. *Apr-Sept* 9am-9pm Mon-Fri; 9am-11pm Sat, Sun. Closed Aug. **€**. No credit cards. **Map** p62 C2 ⑯

The 'dirty old man' serves Rome's best *pizza bianca ripiena* – which, as a sign explains, is 'White Pizza With Any Thing You Like Inside'. Fillings range from classics like prosciutto and mozzarella to exotic combinations. Pay at the till for a standard slab (€3); then join the receipt-waving hordes to get served.

Salotto 42

Piazza di Pietra 42 (06 678 5804/ www.salotto42.it). **Open** 10am-2am Tue-Sat; 10am-midnight Sun. **Map** p63 E2 ⑰

Incredibly comfortable chairs and sofas give a cosy feel during the day, when a smörgåsbord of nibbles is available. By night, the sleek room becomes a gorgeous cocktail bar with a great soundtrack, excellent mixed drinks and a selection of books on fashion, art and design.

Société Lutèce

Piazza di Montevecchio 17 (06 6830 1472). **Open** 6pm-2am daily. Closed 2wks Aug. **Map** p62 C2 78

Popular with eclectic Roman hipsters, this bar's cramped quarters cause a spill-over into the small piazza. The *aperitivo* buffet (from 6.30pm) is plentiful and the vibe is decidedly laid back.

Stardust

NEW *Via dell'Anima 52 (06 686 8986).* **Open** noon-2am daily. No credit cards. **Map** p62 C2 79

This stalwart of Trastevere's nightlife scene has promised to stick to its old formula in these new premises near piazza Navona: tearoom until 7pm, bistro from 7 to 10pm and a raucous bar/pub thereafter, with bartenders blasting anything from Cuban jazz to Euro-rap and Czech polkas. There's also an 'international' brunch on Sunday afternoons (noon-5pm).

Trattoria

Via del Pozzo delle Cornacchie 25 (06 6830 1427). **Meals served** 12.30-3pm, 7.30-11.30pm Mon-Sat. Closed 2wks Aug. €€€. **Map** p63 D2 80

Ebullient Sicilian chef Filippo La Mantia takes standards from home like *caponata* or *pasta alla Norma* and gives them his own creative twist. There's a €15-a-shot lunchtime cous-cous bar (noon-3pm Mon-Sat).

Shopping

Antica Erboristeria Romana

Via di Torre Argentina 15 (06 687 9493/www.anticaerboristeria romana.com). **Open** 8.30am-7.30pm Mon-Fri; 9am-7.30pm Sat. Closed 1wk Aug. **Map** p63 D3 81

Visit this charming 18th-century apothecary-style shop if only to admire the carved wood ceilings and banks of tiny wooden drawers – some etched with skull and crossbones – in which herbal remedies are hidden away.

Arsenale

Via del Governo Vecchio 64 (06 686 1380). **Open** 3.30-7.30pm Mon; 10am-7.30pm Tue-Sat. Closed 2wks Aug. **Map** p62 C2 82

Patrizia Pieroni's wonderful garments make for great window displays – not

ROME BY AREA

to mention successful party conversation pieces – and have been going down well with the Roman boho-chic luvvy crowd for a decade.

Cartoleria Pantheon

Via della Rotonda 15 (06 687 5313). **Open** 10.30am-7.30pm Mon-Sat; 1-7.30pm Sun. Closed 1wk Aug. **Map** p63 D3 ⓬

Bring out your literary soul with some lovely leather-bound notebooks, hand-painted Florentine stationery and rare paper from Amalfi. Nearly everything for sale has been handcrafted.

Ditta G Poggi

Via del Gesù 74-75 (06 678 4477/ www.poggi1825.it). **Open** 9am-1pm, 4-7.30pm Mon-Sat. Closed 2wks Aug. **Map** p63 E3 ⓮

This wonderfully old-fashioned shop has been selling paints, brushes, canvases and artists' supplies of every description since 1825.

Le Tartarughe

Via Pie' di Marmo 17 (06 679 2240). **Open** 3.30-7.30pm Mon; 10am-7.30pm Tue-Sat. **Map** p63 E3 ⓯

Designer Susanna Liso's sumptuous classic-with-a-twist creations range from cocktail dresses to elegant workwear, all in eye-catching colours. For gorgeous accessories to accompany them, head across the road to no.33.

Madò

Via del Governo Vecchio 89A (no phone). **Open** 11am-7.30pm Mon-Sat. **Map** p62 C3 ⓰

With a glittering collection of oriental-inspired clothing and accessories, this shop feel like an exotic aunt's closet. There's a fabulous range of ethnic jewellery from the 1920s.

Maga Morgana

Via del Governo Vecchio 27 (06 687 9995). **Open** 10am-8pm Mon-Sat. **Map** p62 B2 ⓱

Designer Luciana Iannace's quirky one-of-a-kind women's clothes include hand-knitted sweaters, skirts and dresses. More knitted and woollen items are sold down the road at no.98.

Moriondo & Gariglio

Via del Piè di Marmo 21 (06 699 0856). **Open** 9am-1pm, 3.30-7.30pm Mon-Sat. Closed Aug. **Map** p63 E3 ⓰

This fairytale chocolate shop with beautiful gift-boxes is especially lovely close to Christmas, when you will have to fight to get your hands on the excellent *marron glacé*. It usually closes on Saturday afternoons in June and July.

Nightlife

See also Salotto 42 (p78), Société Lutèce and Stardust (both p79).

Anima

Via Santa Maria dell'Anima 57 (347 850 9256). **Open** 6pm-4am daily. **Map** p62 C2 ⓰

With improbably baroque gilded mouldings, this small venue has a buzzing atmosphere and good drinks, and caters for a mixed crowd of all ages. Music includes hip hop, R&B, funk, soul and reggae. There's an aperitivo evening on Sundays.

Bloom

Via del Teatro Pace 30 (06 6880 2039). **Open** 7pm-3am Mon, Tue, Thur-Sat. Closed July & Aug. **Map** p62 C2 ⓰

A restaurant, bar and disco (generally on Friday and Saturday), Bloom is cooler than ice: eat sushi, sip a cocktail, dance or simply relax and join your fashionable fellow guests checking out each others' outfits.

La Maison

Vicolo dei Granari 4 (06 683 3312/ www.lamaisonroma.it). **Open** 11pm-4am Wed-Sat. Closed June-Sept. **Map** p62 C2 ⓰

One of the clubs of choice of Rome's fashion-victims, La Maison is dressed to impress… but elegantly. Huge chandeliers, dark red walls and curvy sofas give it an opulent, courtly feeling. Surprisingly, the place is not snobbish, and the music on offer is not banal and the atmosphere is truly buzzing. Doormen can be picky.

Ara Pacis Museum p84

Tridente, Trevi & Borghese

The Tridente

Though Federico Fellini set
La dolce vita around via Veneto,
he hung out elsewhere with his
A-list hipster friends: in the area
known as the Tridente.

This super-chic wedge of streets
has long been familiar with jet-set
attention: in the 18th century, the
dolce vita here was called the
Grand Tour. Thousands of English
'milords' took lodgings in piazza
di Spagna and strayed nowhere
without a trusted guide. Even
today there are visitors who never
make it further than the plethora
of glorious fashion retailers here.

The whole area was built as a
showpiece. At the head of the wedge

is Rome's most elegant square,
piazza del Popolo. It was given
its oval form by architect Giuseppe
Valadier in the early 19th century.

Leading out centrally from the
square is the Tridente's principal
thoroughfare, via del Corso,
which passes high-street clothing
retailers en route to the towering
column of Marcus Aurelius (piazza
Colonna) – which was built between
AD 180 and 196 to commemorate
the victories on the battlefield of
that most intellectual of Roman
emperors – and piazza Venezia.

Via Ripetta veers off down the
riverside, leading to Augustus'
mausoleum and the **Ara Pacis**.

The third street, chic via del
Babuino, runs past a series of

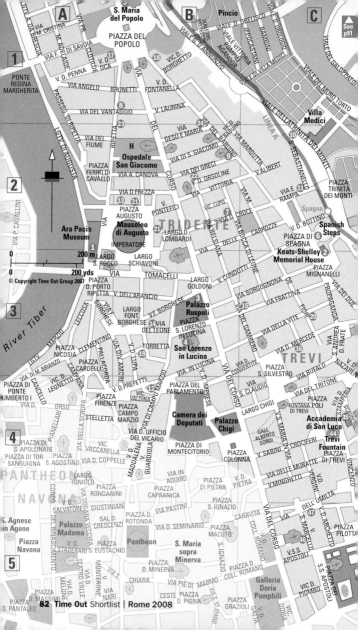

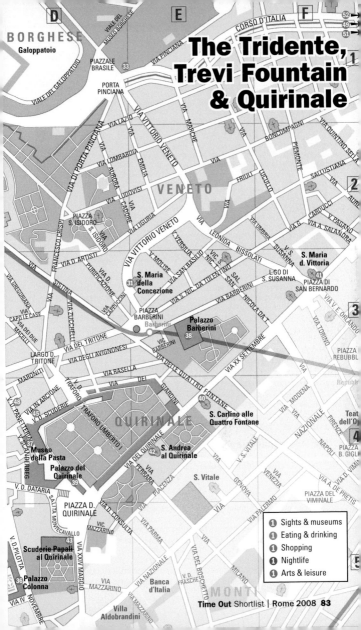

The Tridente, Trevi Fountain & Quirinale

D **E** **F**

CORSO D'ITALIA

BORGHESE
Galoppatoio

VIALE DEL MUSEO BORGHESE

PIAZZALE BRASILE 33

PORTA PINCIANA

VIA DEL GALOPPATOIO

VIALE DI PORTA PINCIANA

PIAZZA S. ISIDORO

VIA FRANCESCO CRISPI

VIA D. ARTISTI

VIA DI PORTA PINCIANA

VIA LOMBARDIA

VIA AURORA

VIA LUDOVISI

VIA LAZIO

VIA EMILIA

VIA VITTORIO VENETO

VIA MARCHE

VIA PIACENTINI

BONCOMPAGNI

PIEMONTE

VIA QUINTINO SELLA

SALLUSTIANA

VENETO

VIA FRIULI

VIA LUCULLO

VIA G. CARDUCCI

V. PAGANO

VIA A. SALANDRA

VIA GREGORIANA

VIA SISTINA

VIA CAPO LE CASE

VIA DUE MACELLI

VIA D. PURIFICAZIONE

VIA D. CAPPUCCINI

VIA LIGURIA

VIA S. ISIDORO

VIA D

VIA LEONIDA BISSOLATI

VIA UMBRIA

VIA S. S. SUSANNA

S. Maria d. Vittoria

41

S. Maria della Concezione 31

Barberini

PIAZZA BARBERINI

VIA V. MOLISE

VIA DEI TORINO

VIA VERSILIA

VIA SAN BASILIO

VIA NIC. S.

VIA S. NIC. DA TOLENTINO

SAL

L.GO DI S. SUSANNA

PIAZZA DI SAN BERNARDO

VIA BARBERINI

NICOLA DA T.

VIA E. ORLANDO

VIA TORINO

PIAZZA REBUBBL

Repub

Palazzo Barberini 38

VIA DEL TRITONE

VIA ZUCCHELLI

VIA DEGLI AVIGNONESI

VIC. BARBERINI

VIA DELLE QUATTRO FONTANE

VIA XX SETTEMBRE

LARGO D. TRITONE

MARONITI

VIA RASELLA

VIA DEI

VIA MODENA

VIA IN ARCIONE

VIA DEI GIARDINI

VIA NAZIONALE

VIA FIRENZE

Teat dell'O

VIA T. TRAFORO UMBERTO I

48

45

SCUDERIE

QUIRINALE

S. Carlino alle Quattro Fontane

40

VIA NAPOLI

PIAZZA B. BIGLI

37

Museo della Pasta

VIA D. PANETTERIA

VIA STAUDERBERG

TRAFORO UMBERTO I

S. Andrea al Quirinale 42

VIA DEL QUIRINALE

VIA FERRARA

VIA PIACENZA

S. Vitale

VIA S. VITALE

VIA V. S. VITALE

VIA VENEZIA

VIA A. DE PRETIS

Palazzo del Quirinale 39

V. D. DATARIA

SALITA MONTECAVALLO

PIAZZA D. QUIRINALE

VIA GENOVA

PIAZZA DEL VIMINALE

VIA PALERMO

VIC. MAZZARINO

VIA D. CONSULTA

Scuderie Papali al Quirinale 43

VIA XXIV MAGGIO

VIA MAZZARINO

Banca d'Italia

VIA PARMA

VIA DEL BOSCHETTO

VIA MILANO

MONTI

V. D. PILOTTA

Palazzo Colonna 36

VIA IV NOVEMBRE

VIA NAZIONALE

V. D. FRASCHETTO

Villa Aldobrandini

❶ Sights & museums
❶ Eating & drinking
❶ Shopping
❶ Nightlife
❶ Arts & leisure

Spanish Steps

tempting antique and designer stores to the **Spanish Steps**.

Parallel to via del Babuino, tucked right below the Pincio hill, is via Margutta, fondly remembered as the focus of the 1960s art scene and 'home' to Gregory Peck in the 1953 classic *Roman Holiday*. Fellini, too, lived on this artsy alley.

Criss-crossing the three main arteries are streets such as via Condotti that have given Rome its reputation as a major fashion centre.

Sights & museums

Ara Pacis Museum

NEW *Via Ripetta/lungotevere in Augusta (06 6710 6756/06 3600 4399/www. arapacis.it)*. **Open** 9am-7pm Tue-Sun. **Map** p82 A2 ❶

The Ara Pacis Augustae ('Augustan Altar of Peace') was inaugurated in 9 BC to celebrate the security that the Emperor Augustus' victories had brought. The altar was rebuilt in the early 20th century from fragments amassed through a long dig and a trawl through the world's museums. The altar itself sits inside an enclosure

carved with delicately realistic reliefs. The upper band shows the ceremonies surrounding the dedication of the altar. The carved faces of Augustus and his family have all been identified. The monument now resides in a container designed by Richard Meier, inaugurated to much fanfare and even more controversy in 2006.

The forlorn brick cylinder next door in piazza Augusto Imperatore was originally a mausoleum covered with marble pillars and statues, begun in 28 BC. Augustus was laid to rest in the central chamber on his death in AD 14.

Keats-Shelley Memorial House

Piazza di Spagna 26 (06 678 4235/ www.keats-shelley-house.org). **Open** 9am-1pm, 3-6pm Mon-Fri; 11am-2pm, 3-6pm Sat. Closed 1wk Dec. **Admission** €3.50. No credit cards. **Map** p82 C3 ❷

The house at the bottom of the Spanish Steps where the 25-year-old John Keats died of tuberculosis in 1821 is crammed with mementos: a lock of Keats' hair and his death mask, an urn holding tiny pieces of Shelley's charred skeleton, and copies of documents and letters.

GiNa p86

Palazzo Ruspoli-Fondazione Memmo

Via del Corso 418 (06 6830 7344/ www.fondazionememmo.com).
Open times vary. **Admission** varies.
No credit cards. **Map** p82 B3 ❸

The palace of one of Rome's old noble families is used for touring exhibitions of art, archaeology and history. The basement rooms often host photo exhibitions. Admission is sometimes free.
Event highlights From Cranach to Monet: masterpieces from the Perez Simon collection (Oct 2007-Jan 2008).

San Lorenzo in Lucina

Piazza San Lorenzo in Lucina 16A (06 687 1494). **Open** 9am-8pm daily.
Map p82 B3 ❹

This 12th-century church – built on the site of an early Christian place of worship – incorporates Roman columns into its exterior. The 17th-century interior has Bernini portrait busts, a kitsch 17th-century *Crucifixion* by Guido Reni and a monument to French artist Nicolas Poussin, who died in Rome in 1665. In the first chapel on the right is a grill, reputed to be the one on which St Lawrence was roasted to death.

Santa Maria del Popolo

Piazza del Popolo 12 (06 361 0836).
Open 7am-noon, 4-7pm Mon-Sat; 7.30am-1.45pm, 4.30-7.30pm Sun.
Map p82 B1 ❺

According to legend, Santa Maria del Popolo occupies the site where the hated emperor Nero was buried. In 1099 Pope Paschal II built a chapel here to dispel demons still believed to haunt the spot. In 1472, Pope Sixtus IV rebuilt the chapel as a church. In the apse are Rome's first stained-glass windows (1509). The apse was designed by Bramante, while the choir ceiling and first and third chapels in the right aisle were frescoed by Pinturicchio. The Chigi Chapel was designed by Raphael for wealthy banker Agostino Chigi, and features Chigi's horoscope. The church's most-gawped-at possessions, however, are the two masterpieces by Caravaggio to the left of the main altar, showing the stories of Saints Peter and Paul.

Spanish Steps & Piazza di Spagna

Map p82 C2 ❻

Piazza di Spagna has been considered a compulsory stop for visitors to Rome since the 18th century. The square takes its name from the Spanish Embassy, but is most famous for the Spanish Steps (Scalinata di Trinità dei Monti), an elegant cascade down from the church of Trinità dei Monti. The steps (completed in 1725) were, in fact, funded by a French diplomat. At the foot of the stairs is a boat-shaped fountain, the *barcaccia*, designed in 1627 by either Gian Lorenzo Bernini or his less-famous father Pietro.

Eating & drinking

Antica Enoteca di Via della Croce
Via della Croce 76B (06 679 0896). **Open** 11.30am-1am daily. **€€.** Closed 1wk Aug. **Map** p82 B2 ❼
A tasteful revamp of this historic wine bar has retained most of the original 1842 fittings, including the marble wine vats and a venerable wooden cash desk. There's a cold antipasto buffet at the bar, and a restaurant with tables in the long back room. It also operates as an off-licence.

Buccone
Via Ripetta 19-20 (06 361 2154/ www.enotecabuccone.com). **Open** *Shop* 9am-8.30pm Mon-Thur; 9am-midnight Fri, Sat. **Meals served** 12.30-3pm, 7.30-10.30pm Mon-Sat. Closed 3wks Aug. **€€. Map** p82 B1 ❽
Originally – and still – a bottle shop, Buccone squeezes tables between its high wooden shelves at meal times. The fare – a few pasta dishes, meaty seconds and creative salads – is simple but good, the prices very reasonable.

Caffè Canova-Tadolini
Via del Babuino 150A (06 3211 0702). **Open** 8am-8.30pm Mon-Sat. **Map** p82 B2 ❾
Once the studio of 19th-century sculptor Antonio Canova, this café has tables among its sculpture models and a refined and elegant old-world feel.

Ciampini al Café du Jardin
Viale Trinità dei Monti (06 678 5678). **Open** *Apr-mid May, mid Sept-mid Oct*

8am-8pm daily. *Mid May-mid Sept* 8am-1am Mon, Tue, Thur-Sun. Closed mid Oct-Mar. **Map** p82 C2 ❿
This open-air café near the top of the Spanish Steps is surrounded by lovely creeper-curtained trellises, with a pond in the centre. There's a spectacular view, especially at sunset.

GiNa
Via San Sebastianello 7A (06 678 0251/www.ginaroma.com). **Open** 11am-5pm Mon; 11am-11pm Tue-Sat; 11am-8pm Sun. Closed 2wks Aug. **Map** p82 C2 ⓫
This bright and artsy light-lunch and dinner bar is a rather good option for snacking by the Spanish Steps. The menu is homely: a couple of soups, four or five daily pasta dishes, a range of creative and gourmet salads, wine by the glass or bottle. You can also order a gourmet picnic hamper.

Gino in vicolo Rosini
Vicolo Rosini 4 (06 687 3434). **Meals served** 1-2.45pm, 8-10.45pm Mon-Sat. Closed Aug. **€€.** No credit cards. **Map** p82 B4 ⓬
In a hard-to-find lane just off piazza del Parlamento, this neighbourhood *osteria* champions the lighter side of the local tradition in dishes like *tonnarelli alla ciociara* (pasta with mushrooms and tomatoes), and pasta and chickpeas in ray sauce; desserts include an excellent tiramisù.

'Gusto
Piazza Augusto Imperatore 9 (06 322 6273/www.gusto.it). **Open** *Wine bar* 11.30am-2am daily. **Meals served** *Pizzeria* 12.30-3.30pm, 7.30pm-1am daily. *Restaurant* 12.30-3pm, 7.30pm-11.30pm daily. **€€-€€€. Map** p82 B2 ⓭
'Gusto is a multi-purpose, split-level pizzeria, restaurant and wine bar, with a kitchen shop and bookshop next door. The ground-floor pizza and salad bar is always packed; upstairs, the more expensive restaurant applies oriental techniques to Italian models, though not always convincingly. The wine bar out back is buzzing and stylish,

L'Olfattorio – Bar à Parfums p89

with a good selection of wines by the glass and nibbles. Around the corner at via della Frezza 16, the mod-*osteria* L'Osteria is part of the same outfit.

Matricianella

Via del Leone 3-4 (06 683 2100/www. matricianella.it). **Meals served** 12.30-3pm, 7.30-11pm Mon-Sat. Closed 3wks Aug. €€€. **Map** p82 B3 ⑭

This is a friendly, bustling place with great prices. The Roman imprint is most evident in classics such as the *bucatini all'amatriciana* (pasta with spicy sausage sauce) or *abbacchio a scottadito* (thin strips of lamb), but there are plenty of more creative options. The well-chosen wine list is a model of honest pricing. Book ahead.

Palatium

Via Frattina 94 (06 6920 2132). **Open** noon-midnight Mon-Sat. Closed 2wks Aug. €€. **Map** p82 C3 ⑮

Though it's backed by the Lazio regional government, this wine bar and eaterie is more than a PR exercise. It gives punters the chance to go beyond the Castelli romani clichés to explore lesser-known local vintages such as Cesanese or Aleatico. There's a generous *aperitivo* buffet from 3 to 7.30pm, after which Palatium switches into restaurant mode, offering light creative dishes made with local ingredients.

Pizza Ciro

Via della Mercede 43 (06 678 6015). **Meals served** 11am-2am daily. €. **Map** p82 C3 ⑯

From the outside this looks like a modest, touristy pizza parlour. But Ciro is in fact one enormous eating factory. The pizzas – of the high-crust Neapolitan variety – are not at all bad, and *primi* such as *tubetti alla Ciro* (pasta with rocket and mussels) provide a decent alternative.

Rosati

Piazza del Popolo 5 (06 322 5859). **Open** 7am-11pm daily. **Map** p82 A1 ⑰

Frequented by Calvino and Pasolini, this bar's art nouveau interior has remained unchanged since its opening in 1922. Try the *Sogni romani* cocktail: orange juice with four kinds of liqueur in red and yellow – the colours of the city.

Stravinskij Bar

Via del Babuino 9 (06 689 1694).
Open 9am-1am daily. **Map** p82 B1 ⑱
Inside the swanky De Russie hotel, this
chic bar has an inside area with comfy
armchairs and a fabulous patio where
tables are surrounded by orange trees.

Vic's

*Vicolo della Torretta 60 (06 687
1445).* **Meals served** 7.30-11pm
Mon; 12.30-3pm, 7.30-11pm Tue-Sat.
Closed 2wks Aug. **€.** No credit cards.
Map p82 B3 ⑲
This wine and salad bar offers a range
of creative salads such as radicchio, pine
nuts, sultanas and parmesan. Pared-
back Roman *osteria* decor, friendly
service and a fairly priced wine list.

Shopping

The Tridente is Rome's chic
shopping area *per eccellenza*.
In this wedge you'll find the big
names of Italian fashion: Prada,
Fendi, Gucci, Dolce & Gabbana…

Anglo-American Book Co

*Via della Vite 102 (06 679 5222/
www.aab.it).* **Open** 3.30-7.30pm Mon;
10am-7.30pm Tue-Sat. Closed 2wks
Aug. **Map** p82 C3 ⑳
A good selection of books in English.

La Soffitta Sotto i Portici

*Piazza Augusto Imperatore (06 3600
5345).* **Open** 9am-sunset 1st & 3rd Sun
of mth. Closed Aug. **Map** p82 B2 ㉑
Street market with collectables of all
kinds, ranging from magazines to
jewellery, at non-bargain prices.

The Lion Bookshop

*Via dei Greci 33 (06 3265 4007/www.
thelionbookshop.com).* **Open** 3.30-
7.30pm Mon; 10am-7.30pm Tue-Sun.
Map p82 B2 ㉒
This friendly shop is a great place for
contemporary fiction and children's
books. There's also a nice café, which
doubles as a gallery space.

L'Olfattorio –
Bar à Parfums

*Via Ripetta 34 (06 361 123/www.
olfattorio.it).* **Open** 11am-7.30pm
Tue-Sun. **Map** p82 B1 ㉓
'Bartender' Maria will awaken your
olfactory organs and guide you
towards your perfect scent. Paradise
for perfume lovers.

TAD

*Via del Babuino 155A (06 3269 5122/
www.taditaly.com).* **Open** noon-7.30pm
Mon, Sun; 10.30am-7.30pm Tue-Fri;
10.30am-8pm Sat. Closed 2wks Aug.
Map p82 B1 ㉔

ROME BY AREA

Fontana del Tritone p90

The concept behind this 'concept store' is that you can shop for clothes, shoes, flowers, household accessories, CDs, mags and perfumes, get your hair done, eat fusion Thai-Italian and drink – all in one super-cool place.

Villa Borghese & Via Veneto

From the days of Republican Rome until the late 1800s, gardens, villas and monasteries filled the area to the north and north-east of the settlement by the Tiber. Since the Renaissance, noble Roman families embellished their sprawling estates here.

When Rome became the capital of Italy in 1871, most of the local greenery was carved up to build pompous *palazzi*. Only the Villa Borghese was saved from post-Unification property speculators.

It is now the city's most central public park, with one of Rome's great art repositories – the superb **Galleria Borghese** – at its heart, and one of Rome's greatest views – from the Pincio, over piazza del Popolo to the dome of St Peter's – from its western flank.

Descending south from the park, via Vittorio Veneto (known simply as via Veneto) was the haunt of the famous and glamorous in the *dolce vita* years of the 1950s and '60s. These days, it's home to insurance companies, luxury hotels and visitors wondering where the sweet life went.

At the southern end of via Veneto is piazza Barberini. In ancient times, erotic dances were performed here to mark the coming of spring. The square's magnificent centrepiece, Bernini's Fontana del Tritone, was once in open countryside. Now he sits – his two fish-tail legs tucked beneath him on a shell supported by four dolphins, blowing on a conch shell – amid thundering traffic. The bees around him are the Barberini family emblem.

Sights & museums

Bioparco-Zoo
Piazzale del Giardino Zoologico 1 (06 360 8211/www.bioparco.it). **Open** 9.30am-5pm daily. **Admission** €8.50; €6.50 reductions. **Map** p91 D1 ㉕
Slightly more sprightly since its makeover from 'zoo' to 'Biopark', this will keep your kids happy for an afternoon. Next door – and accessible through the zoo – is the Museo Civico di Zoologia di Roma, with sections on biodiversity and extreme habitats.

Explora – Museo dei Bambini di Roma
Via Flaminia 82 (06 361 3776/www. mdbr.it). **Open** sessions at 10am, noon, 3pm, 5pm Tue-Sun. **Admission** €6; €7 3-12s. **Map** p91 A2 ㉖

Villa Borghese

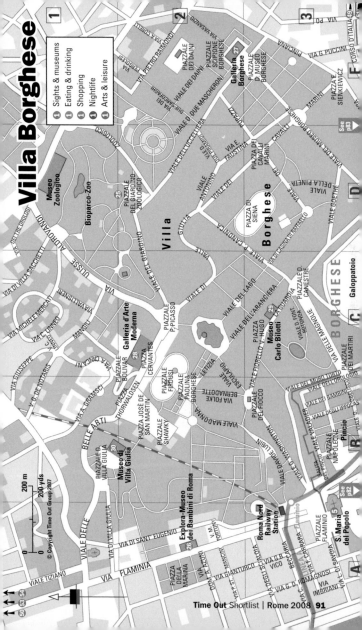

Villa Borghese

1	Sights & museums	
1	Eating & drinking	
1	Shopping	
1	Nightlife	
1	Arts & leisure	

Museo Zoologico

Bioparco-Zoo

PIAZZALE DEL GIARDINO ZOOLOGICO

Galleria Borghese 27

PIAZZALE SCIPIONE BORGHESE

PIAZZALE DEI DAINI

Villa

Borghese

PIAZZA DI SIENA

PIAZZA DE' CAVALLI MARINI

See p83 ▶

Galleria d'Arte Moderna

PIAZZALE P.PICASSO

PIAZZALE BOLIVAR

PIAZZA CERVANTES

PIAZZALE FIRDUSI

PIAZZALE PAOLINA BORGHESE

Museo Carlo Bilotti 29

PIAZZA FIORELLO V. HUGO

Galoppatoio

BORGHESE

PIAZZA DI SIENA

Museo di Villa Giulia 30

PIAZZALE DI VILLA GIULIA

PIAZZA JOSE DE SAN MARTIN

PIAZZA THORWALDSEN

PIAZZALE SHAWKY

BELLE ARTI

Explora-Museo dei Bambini di Roma 26

Roma Nord Railway Station

PIAZZALE NAPOLEONE

Pincio

See p82 ▶

S. Maria del Popolo 5

PIAZZALE FLAMINIO

PIAZZA DELLA MARINA

VIALE TIZIANO

© Copyright Time Out Group 2007

200 m
200 yds

This children's museum provides good educational fun for under-12s. The 3pm and 5pm sessions on Thursday afternoon cost €5 for all. Booking essential.

Galleria Borghese

Piazzale Scipione Borghese 5 (06 32 810/www.galleriaborghese.it). **Open** 9am-7pm Tue-Sun. **Admission** €8.50; €5.25 reductions. **Map** p91 E2 ㉗
Note: Booking is obligatory.

Begun in 1608, the Casino Borghese was designed to house the art collection of Cardinal Scipione Borghese, Bernini's greatest patron. The interior decoration (1775-90) was restored in the 1990s. A curved double staircase leads to the imposing entrance salon, with fourth-century AD floor mosaics showing gladiators fighting wild animals. In Room 1 is Antonio Canova's 1808 waxed marble figure of Pauline, sister of Napoleon and wife of Prince Camillo Borghese, as a topless *Venus*; Prince Camillo thought the work so provocative that he forbade even the artist from seeing it after completion. Rooms 2-4 contain some spectacular sculptures by Gian Lorenzo Bernini: the *David* (1624) in room 2 is a self-portrait of the artist; room 3 houses his *Apollo and Daphne* (1625); room 4 his *Rape of Proserpine* (1622). Room 5 contains important pieces of classical sculpture, including a Roman copy of a Greek dancing faun and a sleeping hermaphrodite. Bernini's *Aeneas and Anchises* (1620) dominates room 6, while room 7 has an Egyptian theme: included among the classical statues is a second-century Isis. The six Caravaggios in room 8 include the *Boy with a Basket of Fruit* (c1594) and the *Sick Bacchus* (c1593), believed to be a self-portrait.

Upstairs, the picture gallery holds a surfeit of masterpieces. Look out for: Raphael's *Deposition* and Pinturicchio's *Crucifixion with Saints Jerome and Christopher* (room 9); Lucas Cranach's *Venus and Cupid with Honeycomb* (room 10); and Rubens' spectacular *Pietà* and *Susanna and the Elders* (room 18). Titian's *Venus Blindfolding*

Cupid and *Sacred and Profane Love*, recently restored but still difficult to interpret, are the stars of room 20, which also contains a stunning *Portrait of a Man* by Antonello da Messina.
Event highlights 'Canova', an exhibition marking the 250th anniversary of the sculptor's birth, runs from 28 Oct 2007 to 15 Feb 2008.

Galleria Nazionale d'Arte Moderna e Contemporanea

Viale delle Belle Arti 131 (06 322 981/ 06 3229 8301/www.gnam.arti. beniculturali.it). **Open** 8.30am-7.30pm Tue-Sun. **Admission** €6.50; €3.25 reductions. *Special exhibitions* €2.50 extra. No credit cards. **Map** p91 C2 ㉘
This collection begins with the 19th century: an enormous statue of *Hercules* by Canova dominates room 4 of the left wing; in the Palizzi room are views of Rome before the dramatic changes to the urban landscape in the late 19th century. The 20th-century component includes works by de Chirico, Modigliani, Morandi and Marini. International stars include *The Three Ages* by Klimt and *The Gardener* and *Madame Ginoux* by Van Gogh. Cézanne, Braque, Rodin and Henry Moore are also represented.

Museo Carlo Bilotti

NEW *Viale Fiorello La Guardia (06 8205 9127/www.museocarlobilotti.it).* **Open** 9am-7pm Tue-Sun. **Admission** €4.50; €2.50 reductions. No credit cards. **Map** p91 C3 ㉙
Opened in 2006, this museum houses the collection of billionaire art tycoon Carlo Bilotti: Giorgio de Chirico, Larry Rivers, Jean Dubuffet and Andy Warhol all feature.

Museo Nazionale di Villa Giulia

Piazzale di Villa Giulia 9 (06 322 6571). **Open** 8.30am-7.30pm Tue-Sun. **Admission** €4; €2 reductions. No credit cards. **Map** p91 B1 ㉚
This collection, in a villa designed by Michelangelo and Vignola for Pope Julius III in the mid-1500s, records the pre-Roman peoples of central Italy, and

In the park: Villa Borghese

Museo Carlo Bilotti

In the early 17th century Cardinal Scipione Borghese made the villa-estate that bears his name into an art-packed pleasure park. In the early 21st century, Rome's city council continues to take that vocation very seriously.

Of course, with much of the collection begun by Scipione still in place in the **Galleria Borghese**, this 'art park' was off to an impressive start. The modern art collection in the **Galleria Nazionale d'Arte Moderna** and the Etruscan museum at **Villa Giulia** on the park's fringes helped too.

But the menu of goodies on offer continues to expand: in 2006, the **Museo Carlo Bilotti** opened in Villa Borghese's 16th-century orangery, displaying the 22 works from the private collection of this Florida tycoon. There are works by Bilotti's friend Giorgio de Chirico, Bilotti family portraits by Larry Rivers and Andy Warhol and a bronze cardinal by Giacomo Manzù, among others.

Children can make art of their own at the *ludoteca*, opened in 2006 in the converted **Casino di Raffaello** (booking obligatory on 06 8205 9127, closed Monday). Or they can explore celluloid art at the **Cinema dei Piccoli** (children's cinema), the world's smallest movie theatre.

There's more film on offer at the **Casa del Cinema** (house of cinema), with its screening rooms and film library, where the chic new **Cinecaffè** and bookshop make a visit even more enticing.

If that weren't enough, the Villa Borghese management has brought the many cultural academies on the fringes of the villa into the Borghese fold: the institutes of Britain, France, Japan, Belgium, Egypt and many more organise activities that branch out into this extraordinary park.

The **Villa Pass** initiative, launched in 2007, gives reductions at the Villa's museums, cafés and shops. But before paying €10 for it, check out the Roma Pass (p13): you may find it's a better deal.

■ www.villaborghese.it

the sophisticated, mysterious Etruscans in particular. The Etruscans went well prepared to their graves, and most of the collection comes from excavations of tombs: the museum has hundreds of vases, pieces of furniture and models of buildings made to accompany the dead. In the courtyard, stairs descend to the nymphaeum; in an adjacent room is the sixth-century BC terracotta *Apollo of Veio*. In the garden there is a reconstruction of an Etruscan temple and a pleasant café.

Santa Maria della Concezione

Via Vittorio Veneto 27 (06 487 1185). **Open** *Church* 7am-noon, 3-7pm daily. *Crypt* 9am-noon, 3-6pm Mon-Sat; 9am-noon, 3-7pm Sun. **Admission** *Crypt* donation expected. **Map** p83 E3 ㉛
Commonly known as *i cappuccini* (the Capuchins) after the long-bearded, brown-clad Franciscan sub-order to which it belongs, this Baroque church's attraction lies in the crypt: the skeletons of over 4,000 monks have been dismantled and arranged in swirls and curlicues through four chapels. Ribs hang from the ceiling in the form of chandeliers, and inverted pelvic bones make the shape of hour-glasses – a reminder (as a notice states) that 'you will be what we now are'.

Eating & drinking

Cantina Cantarini

Piazza Sallustio 12 (06 485 528/06 474 3341). **Meals served** noon-3pm, 7.30-11pm Mon-Sat. Closed 3wks Aug; 2wks Dec-Jan. **€€€**. **Map** off p83 F2 ㉜
This good-value high-quality trattoria is meat-based for the first part of the week, then turns fishy thereafter. The atmosphere is as *allegro* as seating is tight – though outside tables take off some of the pressure in summer.

Cinecaffè – Casina delle Rose

NEW *Largo M Mastroianni 1 (06 4201 6224/www.cinecaffe.it).* **Open** 10am-7pm Mon, Sun; 10am-midnight Tue-Sat. **Map** p83 D1 ㉝
This ultra-civilised café at the via Veneto end of Villa Borghese serves excellent coffee, drinks and wallet-friendly light lunches to office workers, tourists and cinema afficionados.

Nightlife

Gregory's

Via Gregoriana 54 (06 679 6386/ www.gregorysjazzclub.com). **Open** 6pm-3.30am Tue-Sun. Closed Aug. **Map** p82 C3 ㉞
This cosy little venue oozes jazz culture from every pore: top live acts from Tuesday to Saturday.

Trevi Fountain & Quirinale

A tangle of medieval streets all seem in the end to lead to the **Trevi Fountain**, fed by the *acqua vergine*. This is said to be the best water in Rome: Grand Tourists used it to brew their tea. Today's tourists hurl coins into it.

This whole area is a homage to water, from the fabulous fountain itself to the 'miraculous' well in the church of Santa Maria in Via (via Mortaro 24), from where plastic cupfuls of healing liquid are still dispensed, and the Città d'Acqua (vicolo del Puttarello 25) where the *acqua vergine* can be heard rushing below a recently excavated ancient Roman street.

The Trevi district was a service area for the **Quirinal palace**, home to popes, kings and now the Italian president: here were the printing presses, bureaucratic departments and service industries that oiled the machinery of the Papal States. Aristocratic families, such as the influential Barberinis and Colonnas, built their palaces close by; their art collections are now on view to the public.

Sharing the Quirinal hill with the president's palace are two of Rome's finest small Baroque churches – **San Carlino** and **San Andrea** – and a crossroads (between *vie* del Quirinale and Quattro Fontane) adorned with four fountains (1593) representing river gods.

Sights & museums

Accademia di San Luca

Piazza dell'Accademia 77 (06 679 8859/www.accademiasanluca.it). Closed for restoration; due to reopen in 2008. **Map** p82 C4 ㉟
Until the academy's gallery – containing charming images of Rome through the ages – reopens after undergoing a lengthy restoration, you'll have to settle for a peep at Borromini's glorious spiralling staircase in the courtyard.

Galleria Colonna

Via della Pilotta 17 (06 678 4350/ www.galleriacolonna.it). **Open** 9am-1pm Sat. Closed Aug. **Admission** €7; €5.50 reductions. No credit cards. **Map** p83 D5 ㊱

Sant'Andrea al Quirinale p96

This splendid six-room gallery was completed in 1703 for the Colonna family, whose descendants still live in the palace. The immense frescoed ceiling of the mirrored Great Hall pays tribute to family hero Marcantonio Colonna, who led the papal fleet to victory against the Turks in the battle of Lepanto in 1571. The gallery's most famous picture is Annibale Caracci's earthy peasant *Bean Eater*, but don't miss Bronzino's wonderfully sensuous *Venus and Cupid*.

Museo Nazionale delle Paste Alimentari

Piazza Scanderbeg 117 (06 699 1120/www.pastainmuseum.it). **Open** 9.30am-5.30pm daily. **Admission** €10; €7 reductions. No credit cards. **Map** p83 D4 ㊲
This museum is dedicated to pasta-making: rolling and cutting techniques, the equipment, and the selection of ingredients. There's a gift shop with all kinds of pasta-related items.

Palazzo Barberini – Galleria Nazionale d'Arte Antica

Via delle Quattro Fontane 13/via Barberini 18 (06 481 4591/bookings 06 32 810/www.galleriaborghese.it). **Open** 8.30am-7.30pm Tue-Sun. **Admission** €5; €2.50 reductions. No credit cards. **Map** p83 E3 ㊳
This vast Baroque palace, built by the Barberini Pope Urban VIII, houses one of Rome's most important art collections. Top architects like Maderno, Bernini and Borromini queued up to work on this pile, which was completed in just five years (1627-33). Highlights of the collection include Filippo Lippi's *Madonna* (with possibly the ugliest Christ-child ever painted); a recently restored, enigmatic portrait by Raphael of a courtesan traditionally believed to be his mistress; a *Nativity* and *Baptism of Christ* by El Greco; Tintoretto's dramatic *Christ and the Woman taken in Adultery*; Titian's *Venus and Adonis*; two Caravaggios, one of them showing Judith rather gingerly cutting off

Holofernes' head; a Holbein portrait, *Henry VIII Dressed for his Wedding to Anne of Cleves*; a Bernini bust and painted portrait of Pope Urban VIII; and a self-assured self-portrait by Artemisia Gentileschi.

Palazzo del Quirinale

Piazza del Quirinale (06 46 991/www. quirinale.it). **Open** 8.30am-noon Sun. Closed late June-early Sept. **Admission** €5. No credit cards. **Map** p83 D4 ③

The popes still hadn't finished the new St Peter's when (in 1574) they started building a summer palace on the highest of Rome's seven hills. In case an elderly pope died on his hols and had to be replaced, the Quirinale's Cappella Paolina was built as a faithful replica of the Vatican's Sistine Chapel, minus the Michelangelos. On Sunday mornings, when parts of the presidential palace open to the public, you may be fortunate enough to catch one of the midday concerts held in this chapel.

San Carlino alle Quattro Fontane

Via del Quirinale 23 (06 488 3261/ www.sancarlino-borromini.it). **Open** 10am-1pm, 3-6pm Mon-Fri, Sun; 10am-1pm Sat. **Map** p83 E4 ④

This was Carlo Borromini's first solo composition (1631-41), and the one he was most proud of. The dizzying oval dome is remarkable: its geometrical coffers decrease in size towards the lantern to give the illusion of additional height; hidden windows make the dome appear to float in mid-air.

Santa Maria della Vittoria

Via XX Settembre (06 4274 0571). **Open** 8.30am-noon, 3.30-6pm Mon-Sat; 3.30-6pm Sun. **Map** p83 F3 ④

This modest-looking Baroque church holds one of Bernini's most famous works. *The Ecstasy of St Teresa*, in the Cornaro chapel (fourth on the left), shows the Spanish mystic floating on a cloud in a supposedly spiritual trance after an androgynous angel has pierced her with a burning arrow. The result is more than a little ambiguous.

Sant'Andrea al Quirinale

Via del Quirinale 29 (06 474 4872). **Open** 8.30am-noon, 3-7pm Mon-Fri; 3.30-7pm Sat, Sun. **Map** p83 E4 ④

Pope Alexander VII (1655-67) was so pleased with Bernini's design for this dazzling little church, built out of pale pink marble, that it became in effect the palace chapel. It is cunningly designed to create a sense of grandeur in such a tiny space. The star turn is a plaster St Andrew floating through a broken pediment on his way to heaven.

Scuderie Papali al Quirinale

Via XXIV Maggio 16 (06 696 270/ www.scuderiequirinale.it). **Open** times vary. **Admission** varies. **Map** p83 D5 ④

The former stables of the Quirinal palace, this large exhibition space was magnificently reworked by architect Gae Aulenti, who took care to preserve original features like the brickwork ramp to the upper floors. There is a breathtaking view of Rome's skyline glimpsed from the rear staircase as you leave. Credit cards accepted for phone bookings only.

Trevi Fountain

Piazza di Trevi. **Map** p82 C4 ④

Anita Ekberg made this fountain famous when she plunged in wearing a strapless black evening dress (and a pair of waders – but you don't notice those) in Federico Fellini's classic *La dolce vita*. Now, wading is strictly forbidden. Moreover, the sparkling water is full of chlorine (there's a chlorine-free spout hidden at the back of the fountain to the right). The *acqua vergine* was the finest water in the city, brought by Emperor Agrippa's 25km (15.5-mile) aqueduct to the foot of the Quirinal hill. The fountain as we know it (the name Trevi comes from *tre vie* – 'three roads' – though more than that meet here now) was designed by Nicolo Salvi in 1762. It's a rococo extravaganza of sea horses, conch-blowing tritons, craggy rocks and flimsy trees. Nobody can quite remember when the custom

Scuderie Papali al Quirinale

started of tossing coins in to ensure one's return to the Eternal City. The money goes to the Red Cross.

Eating & drinking

Al Presidente
Via in Arcione 94-95 (06 679 7342/ www.alpresidente.it). **Meals served** 1-3.30pm, 8-11pm Tue-Sun. Closed 3wks Jan; 3wks Aug. **€€€€. Map** p83 D4 ㊺
This restaurant under the walls of the Quirinal palace is one of the few really reliable addresses in the largely *menu turistico*-dominated Trevi Fountain area. The creative Italian menu is strong on fish: among the *primi* is a deliciously creamy asparagus and squid soup, while one of the highlights of the *secondi* is the fish and vegetable millefeuille. Outside tables.

Antica Birreria Peroni
Via di San Marcello 19 (06 679 5310). **Meals served** noon-midnight Mon-Sat. Closed 2wks Aug. **€. Map** p82 C5 ㊻
This long-running *birreria* is the perfect place for a quick lunch or dinner. Service is rough-and-Roman but friendly, and the food is good and relatively cheap. Sausage is the main act, with three types of German-style *wurstel* on offer.

Da Michele
Via dell'Umiltà 31 (349 252 5347). **Open** *Oct-Mar* 8am-6pm Mon-Fri, Sun. *Apr-Sept* 8am-10pm Mon-Fri, Sun. Closed Jewish holidays; 10 days Pesach (usually Apr). No credit cards. **Map** p82 C5 ㊼
Recently relocated from the Ghetto, Da Michele (ex-Zi' Fenizia) does over 40 flavours of takeaway pizza, all kosher, and all dairy-free.

Il Gelato di San Crispino
Via della Panetteria 42 (06 679 3924/ www.ilgelatodisancrispino.com). **Open** 11am-12.30am Mon, Wed-Sun. No credit cards. **Map** p83 D4 ㊸
Il Gelato di San Crispino serves what many consider to be the best ice-cream in Rome – some would say in the world. Flavours change according to what's in season – in summer the *lampone* (raspberry) and *susine* (yellow plum) are fabulous. No cones here – only tubs are allowed.

Heading north

North from Villa Borghese, well-heeled suburbs fill the area that stretches between the **Villa**

In the park: Villa Torlonia

For Romans, the name 'Torlonia' is synonymous with 'meteoric rise' – which makes the long-tailed comet on this family's coat of arms particularly fitting. But there's been nothing meteoric, about the restoration of **Villa Torlonia**.

Since the city council bought the dilapidated property 30 years ago, it's been *in restauro*. But now, as more and more of this lush green lung is opened up to the public, people are beginning to feel the wait has (almost) been worthwhile.

Marin Tourlonias arrived in Rome from France in the mid 18th century; he was servant to a cardinal who left him a nest egg that he hatched carefully. Fifty years later, the Torlonias were bankers to the cash-strapped Roman aristocracy. As those families struggled, the Torlonias snapped up their properties and artworks at knock-down prices.

No rich Roman family, however nouveau, could do without a suburban villa: in 1797 Giovanni Torlonia purchased the ancient Colonna family's digs. He brought in the most fashionable architect of the age, Giuseppe Valadier, to overhaul the 16th-century house. And he and his descendents went to work on the park and the many buildings dotted around it.

In 1923 a later Giovanni Torlonia allowed the Mussolini family to make the main villa – the *Casino nobile* – their home, a move that enhanced Torlonia's standing with the Fascists. *Il Duce* stayed until 1943, when Allied troops moved in and trashed this gracious palace and its gorgeous park.

First to be revamped was the Gothick/Swiss folly, the *Casina delle civette*, with its collection of art nouveau stained glass and *boiseries*. In 2006 the *Casino nobile* reopened, its frescoes and plaster mouldings restored to their original glory. The *Casino dei principi* houses exhibitions, the *Limonaia* (where citrus trees were kept in winter) is a pleasant tea room, and the faux-medieval villa houses **Technotown** (06 8205 9127, www.technotown.it, open 4-7pm Tue-Fri, 2-7pm Sat, 9am-7pm Sun, admission €5), a science and technology activity centre for teenagers.

■ www.museivillatorlonia.it

Torlonia and Villa Ada public parks. Down by the river, a vibrant sport and arts hub is springing to life: rugby is played in the Stadio Flaminio, and football across the Tiber at the **Stadio Olimpico**; while the new, Renzo Piano-designed **Auditorium** seethes with music-related activity.

Sights & museums

MACRO

Via Reggio Emilia 54 (06 6710 70400/www.macro.roma.museum). **Open** 9am-6.30pm Tue-Sun. **Admission** €1. No credit cards. **Map** off p83 F1 ㊾

Rome's contemporary art scene was given a shot in the arm in the 1990s with the opening of this municipal gallery in a striking converted brewery outside the walls west of Villa Borghese. This space will grow to cover 10,000 sq m (107,500 sq ft), thanks to an extension designed by architect Odile Decq, due for completion in summer 2008. Shows spill over into the Mattatoio (p120) in Testaccio.

MAXXI

NEW *Via Guido Reni 10 (06 321 0181/ www.maxximuseo.org).* **Open** (exhibitions only) 11am-7pm Tue-Sun. No credit cards. **Map** off p91 A1 ㊿

Works to transform this enormous former army barracks into the *Museo delle arti del XXI secolo* (MAXXI), to a striking design by Zaha Hadid, have been very stop-go. For the time being, it hosts occasional temporary shows, often on architectural themes.

Villa Torlonia

NEW *Via Nomentana 70 (06 8205 9127/www.museivillatorlonia.it).* **Open** *Park* dawn-sunset daily. *Museums & sights* Nov-Feb 9am-4.30pm Tue-Sun; Mar, Oct 9am-5.30pm Tue-Sun; Apr-Sept 9am-7pm Tue-Sun. **Admission** €6.50; €3 reductions. No credit cards. **Map** off p83 F1 ㊿

The makeover of this lushly green park in Rome's northern suburbs is nearing completion. See box p98.

Eating & Drinking

Osteria dell'Arco

Via G Pagliari 11 (06 854 8438). **Meals served** noon-3pm, 7.30-11pm Mon-Fri; 7.30-11pm Sat. Closed Aug. **€€€. Map** off p83 F1 ㊿

This nouveau-rustic wine-oriented *osteria* serves creative Italian cuisine at excellent prices. Follow up a smoked tuna and swordfish starter with pasta with cuttlefish and broccoli, or anglerfish fillets with artichoke. Handy for the MACRO gallery.

Arts & leisure

Auditorium – Parco della Musica

Via P de Coubertin 15 (06 80 242/ box office 06 808 2058/www. auditorium.com). **Map** off p91 A1 ㊿

Rome's huge new performing arts centre is a buzzing success, thanks to an eclectic programme and very reasonable ticket prices. Guided tours of the Renzo Piano-designed complex cost €10 (€5 reductions; no credit cards): times change frequently so call ahead or check the website.

Event highlights Rome's Film Festival will be held here and at venues around the city on 18-27 Oct 2007.

Foro Italico & Stadio Olimpico

Piazza de Bosis/via del Foro Italico. **Map** off p91 A1 ㊿

A marble obelisk, 36m (120ft) high, with the words *Mussolini Dux* carved on it, greets visitors to the Foro Italico, a sports complex conceived in the late 1920s. The avenue leading west of the obelisk is paved with black-and-white mosaics of good Fascists doing sporty Fascist things. It's amazingly well preserved considering the tens of thousands of feet that trample the tiles every weekend on their way to the Stadio Olimpico beyond (built in the 1950s but modified for the 1990 World Cup), where the AS Roma and SS Lazio football teams both play. Tickets cost €10-€100 (no credit cards).

ROME BY AREA

Coming Out p114

Esquilino, Celio & San Lorenzo

Monti & Esquilino

The area covered by the *rioni* (districts) of Monti and Esquilino was always one of contrasts: on the higher, more salubrious Esquiline hill the wealthy and powerful had their gardens and villas. Below, present-day Monti was the giant Suburra slum where streets ran with effluent and inhabitants died of insomnia.

Nowadays, Monti's twisting alleyways – north-east of the Forum, between *vie* Nazionale and Cavour – are noisy and as full of cosmopolitan bustle as they were 2,000 years ago, the only difference being that this area is seriously hip.

Up on the Esquiline hill, on the other hand, the solid, soulless *palazzi* built after Italy was unified in the 1870s look as if they have seen better days. Via Nazionale is a traffic artery lined by carbon-copy high street shops; halfway down, the huge **Palazzo delle Esposizioni** showcase was due to reopen in late 2007 after lengthy restoration; the pretty Villa Aldbrandini park, up a flight of steps at the south-western end, is a green haven with wonderful views over the city.

If you've come to Rome on a budget package, chances are you'll end up in a hotel on the Esquilino, around Termini railway station. It may come as a shock. For despite heroic efforts by the municipal authorities to convince us that a 'renaissance' is under way here, the Esquilino's grimy *palazzi* and questionable after-dark denizens may not be what you expected of the Eternal City. Don't despair: there are charms and attractions. Piazza Vittorio Emanuele II – the city's biggest square and known simply as piazza Vittorio – was given a new lease of life in the 1980s by a revamp of the central gardens and the arrival of a multi-ethnic community, which injected life and colour; the food market recently moved from the piazza into a nearby ex-barracks and bursts with exuberant life. Then there are vast basilicas (**Santa Maria Maggiore**), intimate mosaic-crusted churches (**Santa Prassede**), Roman artefacts (**Palazzo Massimo**) and a magnificent post-war railway station building at Termini.

To the south, on Colle Oppio, Nero fiddled in his **Domus Aurea** entertaining his guests with his Imperial twanging. Nowadays this stretch of green is peopled by Roman mums and their offspring during the day, and some very dubious characters after dark.

Sights & museums

Baths of Diocletian

Via Enrico De Nicola 79 (06 3996 7700). **Open** 9am-7.45pm Tue-Sun. **Admission** €7; €3.50 reductions. *Special exhibitions* €2 extra. No credit cards. **Map** p102 C1 ❶
Officially the 'Museo Nazionale Romano – Terme di Diocleziano', Diocletian's baths were the largest in Rome when they were built in AD 298-306, covering over a hectare (2.5 acres) and able to accommodate 3,000 people. (Round the corner in via Romita, the Aula Ottagona, with its tasteful sprinkling of large classical sculptures, was part of the structure.) A convent complex

was built around the largest surviving chunk of the baths by Michelangelo in the 1560s. It now contains a collection of stone inscriptions that is sufficiently low-key to allow you to focus on the massive bath buildings themselves and on Michelangelo's 16th-century restoration of the place, including its magnificent central cloister.

Domus Aurea

Via della Domus Aurea (06 3996 7700). **Open** (guided tours; by appointment only) 10am-4pm Tue-Fri. **Map** p102 B3 ❷
Note: Though crumbling masonry shut the Domus down in 2005, free guided tours now allow visitors to view the frescoes and plaster mouldings from restorers' scaffolding. The monument was due to reopen fully in 2008.
In summer AD 64, fire devastated a large part of central Rome. Afterwards, anything unsinged east of the Forum was knocked down to make way for Emperor Nero's Domus Aurea (Golden House). A three-storey structure, its main façade faced south and was entirely clad in gold; inside, every inch not faced with mother-of-pearl or inlaid with gems was frescoed by Nero's pet aesthete Fabullus. The moment Nero died in AD 68, however, work was begun to eradicate every vestige of the hated tyrant. So thorough was the cover-up job that for decades after its frescoes were rediscovered in 1480, no one realised it was the Domus Aurea that they had stumbled across.

Museo Nazionale d'Arte Orientale

Via Merulana 248 (06 469 748). **Open** 8.30am-2pm Mon, Wed, Fri, Sat; 9am-7pm Tue, Thur, Sun. Closed 1st & 3rd Mon of mth. **Admission** €4; €2 reductions. No credit cards. **Map** p102 C3 ❸
This impressive collection of oriental art includes artefacts from the Near East – pottery, gold, votive offerings; some from the third millennium BC – 11th- to 18th-century painted fans from Tibet, sacred sculptures, and some Chinese pottery from the 15th century.

ROME BY AREA

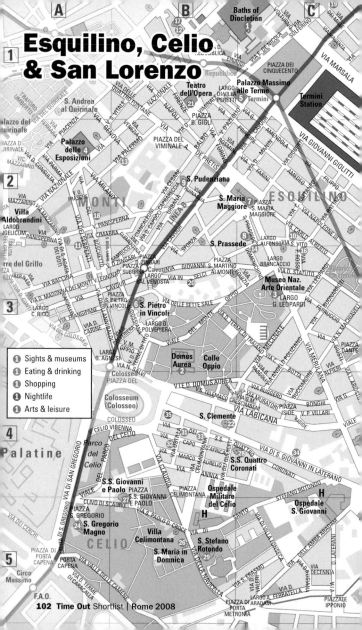

Esquilino, Celio & San Lorenzo

Sights & museums
Eating & drinking
Shopping
Nightlife
Arts & leisure

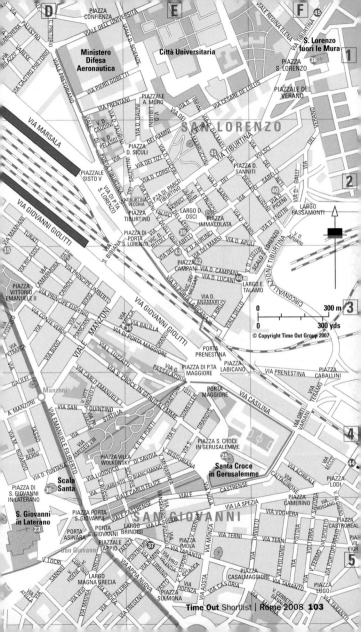

Jazzing up Rome

The Eternal City's appetite for jazz has grown steadily over the past decade, culminating in the 2005 opening of the charming **Casa del Jazz** (viale di Porta Ardeatina 55, 06 704 731, www.casajazz.it) in a 1930s villa close to the Baths of Caracalla.

A project sponsored by the jazz-loving mayor of Rome, Walter Veltroni, this 'Home of Jazz' focuses on the Italian scene, but also hosts a range of international stars. There's a 150-seat auditorium, a garden, a café and a restaurant.

For something more central, check out **Gregory's** (p94), around the corner from the Spanish steps, or **Big Mama** (p137) in Trastevere. Meanwhile in Testaccio, jazz is on the menu at **BeBop Jazz & Blues Live Club** (via Giulietti 14, 06 5728 8959, www.bebopmusicclub.it) and the nearby **Classico Village** (p126).

In Prati, beneath the shadow of St Peter's, **The Place** and the legendary **Alexanderplatz** (both p151) each offer jam sessions and concerts.

Alexanderplatz moves outdoors from early June for the delightful **Jazz & Image** festival (www.villacelimontanajazz.com) in leafy Villa Celimontana. There's also al fresco jazz at the **La Palma** club (p116).

Italian jazz has several excellent names to watch out for, including Antonello Salis, Roberto Gatto, Paolo Fresu, Enrico Pieranunzi, Rosario Giuliani, Stefano di Battista and singer Ada Montellanico.

Palazzo delle Esposizioni

Via Nazionale 194 (06 489 411/ www.palaexpo.it). Closed at the time of writing; due to reopen Sept 2007. **Map** p102 A2 ❹

This imposing 19th-century exhibition space was due to reopen for the 2007 Notte Bianca (p33) after a series of major restoration works.

Palazzo Massimo alle Terme

Largo di Villa Peretti 1 (06 480 201/ bookings 06 3996 7700). **Open** 9am-7pm Tue-Sun. **Admission** €7; €3.50 reductions. *Special exhibitions* €2 extra. No credit cards. **Map** p102 C1 ❺

In the basement of Palazzo Massimo – home to a large chunk of the Museo Nazionale Romano collection – is an extensive collection of coins, Roman luxuries, descriptions of trade routes and audio-visual displays. On the ground and first floors are busts of emperors – including a magnificent Augustus in Room 5 – and lesser mortals. The first floor begins with the age of Vespasian (AD 69-79): his pugilistic portrait bust is in Room 1; room 5 has a gracefully crouching *Aphrodite* from Hadrian's Villa (p158); in room 7 is a peacefully sleeping hermaphrodite, a second-century AD copy of a Greek original. Upstairs, rare wall paintings from assorted villas have been reassembled. Room 10 contains Botero-like, larger-than-life (megalographic) paintings, and room 11 has dazzlingly bright marble intarsio works.

San Pietro in Vincoli

Piazza di San Pietro in Vincoli 4A (06 9784 4952). **Open** 8am-noon, 3-6pm daily. **Map** p102 B3 ❻

Built in the fifth century but reworked many times since, this church is dominated by the monument to Pope Julius II, with Michelangelo's imposing *Moses* (1515). Julius was hoping for a much grander tomb but died too soon to oversee it; his successors were less ambitious. As a result, the mighty Moses (in a bad translation of the Old Testament, the Hebrew word for

Fresco in Palazzo Massimo alle Terme

'radiant' was mistaken for 'horned') is wildly out of proportion, and infinitely better than the rest, by Michelangelo's students. Pilgrims come here for the chains: Eudoxia, wife of Emperor Valentinian III (445-55), was given a set of chains said to have been used to shackle St Peter in Jerusalem; with others used on the saint in the Mamertine prison, they are now conserved in a reliquary on the main altar.

Santa Maria Maggiore

Piazza Santa Maria Maggiore
(06 483 195/museum 06 483 058).
Open *Church* 7am-7pm daily. *Museum* 9am-6pm daily. *Loggia* (guided tours only) 9am & 1pm daily. **Admission** *Church* free. *Museum* €4. *Loggia* €3. No credit cards. **Map** p102 C2 **7**

Local tradition says a church was built on this spot in c366. The church was extended in the 13th and 18th centuries. Inside, above the columns of the nave, heavily restored fifth-century mosaics show scenes from the Old Testament. In the apse, 13th-century mosaics show Christ crowning Mary Queen of Heaven. The Virgin theme continues in fifth-century mosaics on the triumphal

arch. The ceiling in the main nave is said to have been made from the first shipment of gold from the Americas. In the 16th and 17th centuries two flamboyant chapels were added: the first was the Cappella Sistina (last chapel on the right of the nave), designed by Domenico Fontana for Sixtus V (1585-90); directly opposite is the Cappella Paolina, an even gaudier Greek-cross chapel, designed in 1611 by Flaminio Ponzio for Paul V to house a ninth- (or possibly 12th-) century icon of the Madonna on its altar. To the right of the main altar, a plaque marks the burial place of Baroque genius Gian Lorenzo Bernini. In the loggia, high up on the front of the church (tours leave from the baptistry; call ahead to check they're taking place), are glorious 13th-century mosaics that decorated the façade of the old basilica, showing the legend of the foundation of Santa Maria Maggiore.

Santa Prassede

Via Santa Prassede 9A (06 488 2456).
Open 7.30am-noon, 4-6.30pm Mon-Sat; 8am-noon, 4-6.30pm Sun.
Map p102 C2 **8**

Playground on via Claudia

This church is a ninth-century scale copy of the original St Peter's. Artists from Byzantium made the rich, exotic mosaics. In the apse, Christ is being introduced to St Praxedes by St Paul on the right, while St Peter is doing the honours on the left for her sister St Pudenziana. The mosaic on the triumphal arch shows the heavenly Jerusalem, with palm-toting martyrs heading for glory. Off the right-hand side of the nave is the chapel of San Zeno, a dazzling swirl of blue and gold mosaics, punctuated with saints, animals and depictions of Christ and his mother. The wall and ceiling mosaics are ninth-century; the jolly Mary in the niche above the altar is 13th century. In a room to the right is a portion of column said to be the one that Jesus was tied to for scourging.

Santa Pudenziana
Via Urbana 160 (06 481 4622). **Open** 8am-noon, 3-6pm Mon-Sat; 9am-noon, 3-6pm Sun. **Map** p102 B2 ❾

The mosaic in the apse of Santa Pudenziana dates from the fourth century (although it was hacked about in a brutal restoration in the 16th), and is a remarkable example of the continuity between pagan and Christian art, depicting Christ and the apostles as wealthy Roman citizens wearing togas, against an ancient Roman cityscape.

Eating & drinking

Agata e Romeo
Via Carlo Alberto 45 (06 446 6115/ www.agataeromeo.it). **Meals served** 12.30-3pm, 7.30-10.30pm Mon-Fri. Closed 2wks Jan; 2wks Aug. €€€€. **Map** p102 C2 ❿

Agata Parisella was the first chef to demonstrate that Roman cuisine could be refined without sacrificing its wholesome essence. Among the *primi*, the terrine of *coda alla vaccinara* (p189) is an affectionate tribute to a legendary Roman dish. Agata's husband, Romeo Caraccio, presides over the dining room

Doozo

NEW *Via Palermo 51 (06 481 5655).*
Meals served 12.30-3pm, 8-11pm
Tue-Sat. **€€€. Map** p102 B2 ⑬
This Japanese newcomer on a quiet
street parallel to via Nazionale is spacious and cultured, with tables spilling
into gallery, bookshop and a lovely little Zen garden. There's good sushi,
sashimi, tempura and karaage chicken
served in bento boxes.

Hang Zhou

*Via San Martino ai Monti 33C (06
487 2732).* **Meals served** noon-3pm,
7pm-midnight daily. Closed Aug. **€€.**
Map p102 C3 ⑭
Hang Zhou rises above most of Rome's
Chinese eateries not so much for the
food – which is quite acceptable – but
because it's colourful, friendly, theatrical and incredibly good value. No bookings are taken, so be prepared to queue.

Indian Fast Food

Via Mamiani 11 (06 446 0792).
Open 11am-4pm, 5-10.30pm Mon-Sat;
noon-4pm, 5-10.30pm Sun. **€.** No credit
cards. **Map** p103 D3 ⑮
This Indian takeaway is located just
off piazza Vittorio. You can eat in too,
accompanied by Indian music videos.

Trattoria Monti

Via di San Vito 13A (06 446 6573).
Meals served 12.45-2.45pm, 7.45-
11pm Tue-Sat. Closed 1wk Easter;
3wks Aug; 1wk Sept. **€€€.**
Map p102 C3 ⑯
The cuisine, like the family that runs
the place, is from the Marches – so
meat, fish and game all feature on the
menu. Vegetarians are well served by
a range of *tortini* (pastryless pies).
Make sure you book in the evening.

Shopping

The Monday to Saturday morning
food market once known simply
as 'piazza Vittorio' has now moved
into more salubrious premises in a
former barracks in via Lamarmora:
stalls stock the usual Italian fresh
produce, cheese and meats, and also

and extensive wine list. The service is
friendly but professional; the decor
elegant but welcoming; the bill is steep.

Al Vino al Vino

Via dei Serpenti 19 (06 485 803).
Open 10.30am-2.30pm, 5pm-1am daily.
Closed 2wks Aug. **Map** p102 A3 ⑪
This friendly hostelry offers more than
500 wines, with more than 25 available
by the glass. But its speciality is *distil-
lati*: grappas, whiskeys and other
strong spirits. There's Sicilian-inspired
food to soak it all up.

Dagnino

*Galleria Esedra, via VE Orlando
75 (06 481 8660/www.pasticceria
dagnino.com).* **Open** 7am-11pm
daily. **Map** p102 B1 ⑫
Genuine 1950s decor sets the scene for
this café-*pasticceria* that is a corner of
Sicily in Rome. If it's Sicilian and edi-
ble, it's here: ice-cream in buns, crisp
cannoli siciliani filled with ricotta
cheese, and shiny green-iced cassata.

pulses, halal meat and spices, as well as some exotic fabrics and household goods.

Feltrinelli International

Via VE Orlando 84 (06 482 7878). **Open** 9am-8pm Mon-Sat; 10.30am-1.30pm, 4-8pm Sun. **Map** p102 B1 ⓱
Stocks an excellent range of fiction, non-fiction, magazines and guidebooks in English and other languages.

Le Gallinelle

Via del Boschetto 76 (06 488 1017). **Open** 3.30-7.30pm Mon; 10am-1pm, 3.30-7.30pm Tue-Sat. Closed 2wks Aug. **Map** p102 A2 ⓲
Vintage and ethnic garments are reworked by Wilma Silvestri and her daughter Giorgia in their funky shop. There are also classic linen suits for men and women.

Trimani

Via Goito 20 (06 446 9661). **Open** 9am-1.30pm, 3.30-8.30pm Mon-Sat. Closed 1wk Aug. **Map** off p102 C1 ⓳
Trimani is Rome's oldest and best-stocked wine shop. Purchases can be shipped anywhere.

Nightlife

Hangar

Via in Selci 69A (06 488 1397/www. hangaronline.it). **Open** 10.30pm-2.30 am Mon, Wed-Sun. Closed 3wks Aug. No credit cards. **Map** p102 B3 ⓴
American John Moss has been at the helm of Rome's oldest gay bar since it opened over two decades ago. Hangar maintains its friendly but sexy atmosphere whether half full or packed (at weekends and for porn-video Monday and striptease Thursday). The venue also boasts a small dark area.

Arts & leisure

Teatro dell'Opera di Roma – Teatro Costanzi

Piazza B Gigli 1 (06 4816 0255/www. operaroma.it). **Map** p102 B1 ㉑
The lavish late 19th-century *teatro all'italiana* interior is quite a surprise

after the Mussolini-era angular grey façade and its esplanade with tacky potted palms. The acoustics vary greatly: the higher (cheaper) seats are unsatisfactory, so splash out on a box.

Celio & San Giovanni

It was in these little-visited neighbourhoods of Rome that western Christianity was born.

Now lush and unkempt, the Celio in ancient times was for an elite of a bucolic bent. The district gives a glimpse of what early Christian and medieval Rome were like. From the remains of Imperial aqueducts near the verdant and lovely Villa Celimontana park (open daily, dawn to dusk), to frescoes of stretched and boiled martyrs in the church of **Santo Stefano Rotondo**, this area has a bit of everything.

Around Villa Celimontana is a slew of ancient churches, including **Santi Giovanni e Paolo**, with its excavated Roman houses beneath.

The streets south-east of the Colosseum conceal the fascinating church of **San Clemente**, and **Santi Quattro Coronati**, with its extraordinary frescoes.

Further east, amid traffic, smog and drab post-Unification apartment buildings are some of Christianity's most important churches and a host of fascinating minor ancient remains.

Emperor Constantine was clearly hedging his bets when he chose to build **San Giovanni in Laterano**, the first Christian basilica, in this (then) far-from-central spot. To the south of the basilica are the sunken brick remains of the Porta Asinaria, an ancient gate in the third-century AD Aurelian Wall. A park follows the ancient wall north to **Santa Croce in Gerusalemme**, which is surrounded by a panoply of easily visible Roman ruins: through

Wall to wall

Aurelian Wall

You're on your way into the city from the airport. 'Inside the walls or out?' the taxi driver will ask. As you sit there, map in hand, trying to work out if your hotel lies within this medieval catchment area, remember that the right answer – inside – will save you a €10 surcharge on the fare. The logic being, we suspect, why bother to come all the way to Rome and stay *outside* the walls anyway?

Rome is girdled by impressive defences known as the *mura aureliane* (Aurelian Walls). Emperor Aurelian had his *muratori* and slaves throw up an astonishing 19 kilometres of eight-metre-high walls, with watchtowers every 100 Roman feet, in just five years, from AD 271. Subsequent bits of DIY bumped up the number of towers to 383; 116 latrines were bolted on; and a few extra crenellated metres were added in a desperate, vain sixth-century attempt to keep barbarians out.

If fortifications are your thing, it is possible (with a great deal of perseverance) to trek round the whole ring. And you can add the Vatican's magnificent ninth-century Leonine Walls, and the 17th-century *mura gianicolensi* (around the Gianicolo) to your list.

Alternatively, limit yourself to a closer look at these spectacularly preserved sections: the Muro Torto bordering Villa Borghese (p90); the stretch by the Baths of Caracalla (p120); and the great eastern gates of Porta San Giovanni/Porta Asinara (p108), Porta San Paolo (containing the Museum of Via Ostiense, p121), and the Porta San Sebastiano, which houses the **Museo delle Mura** (via Porta San Sebastiano 18, 06 7047 5284, www.museo dellemuraroma.it, open 9am-2pm Tue-Sat, admission €3, €1.50 reductions). Here you can play centurion, marching along the top of the stretch running to the west.

If appreciating this feat of engineering is tricky today, in the not-too-distant future you will be able to walk or cycle round the circuit (or laze on the grass while musing on the rise and fall of walls and empires). December 2007 was the scheduled starting date for the creation of a car-free city park, the uncatchily named **Integrated Linear Park of the Aurelian Walls**.

Work was to begin between Porta Metronio and Porta Latina; three more sections will follow, around the Castro Pretorio, between San Lorenzo and Termini station, and then the wonderful line of wall cresting the leafy Gianicolo hill down to St Peter's.

ROME BY AREA

the opening in the Aurelian Wall to the right of the church is the Amphitheatrum Castrum, and part of the Circus Varianus; the Baths of Helena, of which you can see only the cistern; and the monumental travertine archway built by Emperor Claudius in the first century AD to mark the triumphal entrance of the aqueducts into the city. The well-preserved oven-shaped Tomb of Eurysaces, an ancient Roman baker, lies to the east.

Sights & museums

San Clemente

Via San Giovanni in Laterano (06 774 0021). **Open** 9am-12.30pm, 3-6pm Mon-Sat; noon-6pm Sun. **Admission** *Church* free. *Excavations* €5. No credit cards. **Map** p102 B4 ㉒

This 12th-century basilica is a 3D time line. In the main church, the *schola cantorum* (choir), with its carving and mosaics, survives from the fourth century. The apse mosaic is 12th century: from the drops of Christ's blood springs the vine representing the Church, Doctors of the Church and a host of animals. In the chapel of St Catherine of Alexandria, frescoes by Masolino show the saint praying as her torturers prepare the wheel on which she was stretched to death. From the sacristy, steps lead down to the fourth-century basilica. From there, a stairway descends to an ancient Roman alley. On one side is a second-century Roman insula (apartment building) containing a site where the Persian god Mithras was worshipped. On the other side of the lane are rooms used for meetings by early Christians.

San Giovanni in Laterano

Piazza San Giovanni in Laterano 4 (06 6988 6433). **Open** *Church* 7am-6.30pm daily. *Baptistry* 8am-noon,

Santi Giovanni e Paolo p112

4-7pm daily. *Cloister* 9am-6pm daily. *Lateran Museum* 9am-noon Mon-Sat. **Admission** *Church* free. *Cloister* €2. *Museum* €4. No credit cards. **Map** p103 D5 ㉓

Until the move across the river to the Vatican in the 15th century, the papal headquarters were at San Giovanni and the Lateran palace. Constantine gave the plot of land to Pope Melchiades to build the church in 313 but little remains of the original basilica. The interior was revamped by Borromini in 1646. The façade, with its huge statues of Christ, the two Johns (Baptist and Evangelist) and Doctors of the Church, was added in 1735. A few treasures from earlier times survive: a 13th-century mosaic in the apse, a fragment of a fresco attributed to Giotto (behind the first column on the right) showing Pope Boniface VIII announcing the first Holy Year in 1300, and the Gothic *baldacchino* over the main altar. Off the left aisle is the 13th-century cloister; a small museum off the cloister contains vestments and some original manuscripts of music by Palestrina. The north façade was designed in 1586 by Domenico Fontana, who also placed Rome's tallest Egyptian obelisk outside. Also on this side is the octagonal baptistry that Constantine had built. The four chapels surrounding the font have mosaics from the fifth and seventh centuries; the bronze doors come from the Baths of Caracalla.

San Gregorio Magno

Piazza di San Gregorio Magno 1 (06 700 8227). **Open** 8.30am-1pm, 3.30-7pm daily. **Map** p102 A5 ㉔

This Baroque church stands on the site of the home of one of the most remarkable popes, Gregory I (the Great; 590-604), who spent his 14-year pontificate vigorously reorganising the Church. In a chapel on the right is a marble chair dating from the first century BC, said to have been used by Gregory as his papal throne. Also here is the tomb of Tudor diplomat Sir Edward Carne, who travelled to Rome several times to persuade the pope to annul the marriage of Henry VIII and Catherine of Aragon, so that the king could marry Anne Boleyn. Outside stand three small chapels (closed in August), behind which are the remains of shops that lined an ancient road, the Clivus Scauri.

Santa Croce in Gerusalemme

Piazza Santa Croce in Gerusalemme 12 (06 701 4769/www.basilicasanta croce.it). **Open** *Church* 7am-12.45pm, 2.30-7pm Mon-Sat; 8am-12.45pm, 2.30-7pm Sun. *Chapel of the Relics* 8am-12.30pm, 2.30-6.30pm daily. **Map** p103 E4 ㉕

Founded in 320 by St Helena, mother of Emperor Constantine (who legalised Christianity in 313), this church was rebuilt in the 12th century, and again in the mid-18th century. Helena had her church constructed to house the relics that she brought back from the Holy Land: three chunks of Christ's cross, a nail, two thorns from his crown and the finger of St Thomas – allegedly the very one that the doubting saint stuck into Christ's wound. All of these are displayed in a chapel at the end of a Fascist-era hall at the left side of the nave. Outside, the gorgeous vegetable garden, kept by the monks of the adjoining monastery, can be visited by appointment.

Santa Maria in Domnica

Via della Navicella 10 (06 7720 2685). **Open** 8.30am-12.30pm, 4.30-7pm daily. **Map** p102 B5 ㉖

The carved wood ceiling and porticoed façade may date from the 16th century but Santa Maria in Domnica – known locally as the Navicella (little ship), after the Roman statue that stands outside – is a ninth-century structure containing one of Rome's most charming apse mosaics. What sets this lovely design in rich colours apart is that Mary and Jesus appear positively cheerful: the cherry-red daubs of blush on their cheeks give them a ruddy, healthy glow.

A little less 'action!'

Cinecittà studios were opened by the Fascists in 1937 on what had been virgin farmland southeast of Rome. But even before that, the fledgling film industry had been fascinated with Rome as backdrop. And through the glory years of Hollywood on the Tiber, to more recent filming here of such films as *Ocean's Twelve* (2004) and the HBO-BBC TV series *Rome* (2005), the Eternal City has continued to be a star in its own right. On an average day in 2006, 41 film crews were out on the streets.

Topping the list of sought-after locations is the Colosseum and the nearby Celio district, where, in 2005, one day in every four saw this small grid of narrow streets fill up with trucks, trailers, and light and sound units, not to mention curious onlookers hoping to catch a glimpse of film and TV heroes. In an area where parking is a Herculean task, the interlopers met with growing hostility until pressure groups forced city hall to call a moratorium on shooting in the Celio.

Elsewhere, however, the outside-unit invasion continues unabated. Piazza Navona, via dei Fori Imperiali, piazza di Spagna and the Trevi Fountain are all up there in the list of desired cinematic locations.

Less iconic areas of the city, too, are ringing to cries of 'Action!': the presence of Nicole Kidman, shooting an ad for Sky TV in 2006, brought Testaccio grinding to a halt.

Santi Giovanni e Paolo

Piazza Santi Giovanni e Paolo 13 (church 06 700 5745/excavations 06 7045 4544/www.caseromane.it). **Open** *Church* 8.30am-noon, 3.30-6pm daily. *Excavations* 10am-1pm, 3-6pm Mon, Thur-Sun. **Admission** *Church* free. *Excavations* €6; €4 reductions. No credit cards. **Map** p102 B5 ㉗

Traces of the original fourth-century church can still be seen in the 12th-century façade on piazza Santi Giovanni e Paolo, which is overlooked by a bell tower from roughly the same period. A revamp in the 18th century left the interior of the church looking like a luxury banqueting hall. Outside and around the corner in clivo Scauro is a door leading to an area of labyrinthine excavations: occupying four different buildings – including the house of fourth-century martyrs John and Paul – and dating from the first century AD onwards, the 20-odd excavated rooms include some that were evidently used for secret Christian worship. Be sure to call ahead if you want to arrange a tour conducted in English.

Santi Quattro Coronati

Via dei Santi Quattro 20 (06 7047 5427). **Open** *Church & cloister* 9.30-11.50am, 4-5.30pm Mon-Sat; 9.30-10.30am, 4-5.50pm Sun. *Oratory* 9.30am-noon, 3.30-6pm daily. **Map** p102 C4 ㉓

A fourth-century church here was rebuilt as a fortified monastery in the 11th century; the outsize apse is from the original church. Santi Quattro Coronati has an upper-level matronium, where women sat during religious functions. There is also a beautiful cloister dating from the first half of the 13th century. In the oratory next to the church (you have to ring the bell and ask for the key) are several frescoes, painted in the 13th century as a defence of the popes' temporal power. They show a pox-ridden Constantine being healed by Pope Sylvester, who is crowning him with a tiara and giving him a cap to symbolise the pope's spiritual and earthly authority.

Santo Stefano Rotondo

*Via di Santo Stefano Rotondo 7
(06 421 191).* **Open** *Oct-Mar* 9.30am-12.30pm, 3.30-5.30pm Tue-Sun. *Apr-Sept* 9am-noon, 4-6pm Tue-Sun.
Map p102 B5 ㉙

One of the very few round churches in Rome, Santo Stefano dates from the fifth century. In its first millennia, the church must have been exceptionally beautiful, with its Byzantine-inspired simplicity. The atmosphere changed pretty definitively in the 16th century when 34 horrifically graphic frescoes of martyrs being boiled, stretched and slashed were added.

Scala Santa & Sancta Sanctorum

*Piazza di San Giovanni in Laterano
(06 772 6641).* **Open** *Scala Santa* Oct-Mar 6.15am-noon, 3-6pm daily; Apr-Sept 6.15am-noon, 3.30-6.30pm daily. *Sancta Sanctorum* (booking obligatory) Oct-Mar 10.30-11.30am, 3-6pm daily; Apr-Sept 10.30-11.30am, 3.30-4.30pm daily. **Admission** *Scala Santa* free. *Sancta Sanctorum* €3.50. No credit cards. **Map** p103 D4 ㉚

Tradition says that these are the stairs that Jesus climbed in Pontius Pilate's house before being sent to his crucifixion. They were brought to Rome in the fourth century by St Helena, mother of Emperor Constantine. A crawl up the Scala Santa has been a fixture on every serious pilgrim's list ever since. At the top of the Holy Stairs (but also accessible by non-holy stairs to the left) is the pope's private chapel, the Sancta Sanctorum. In a glass case on the left wall is a fragment of the table on which the Last Supper was supposedly served. The exquisite 13th-century frescoes in the lunettes and on the ceiling are attributed to Cimabue.

Eating & drinking

Café Café

Via dei Santi Quattro 44 (06 700 8743). **Open** 11am-1am Mon, Tue, Thur-Sun. **Map** p102 B4 ㉛

A café, yes, but also a perfect lunch spot – with soups, salads and pasta dishes – after a romp around the Colosseum. There's a brunch buffet from 11.30am to 4pm on Sundays. Opens daily in summer.

Il Bocconcino

NEW *Via Ostilia 23 (06 7707 9175).* **Meals served** 12.30-3.30pm, 7.30-11.30pm Mon, Tue, Thur-Sun. Closed 3wks Aug. €€. **Map** p102 B4 ㉜

This trat near the Colosseum looks like it's been around for generations but it's a recent addition. Expect a friendly welcome, good renditions of Roman favourites – plus some more adventurous dishes like pasta with fresh tuna, tropea onions and capers stewed in wine – and a small, well-priced wine list. Be warned: service can be very slow.

Luzzi

Via Celimontana 1 (06 709 6332). **Meals served** noon-3pm, 7pm-midnight Mon, Tue, Thur-Sun. Closed 2wks Aug. €€. **Map** p102 B4 ㉝

On busy nights (and most of them are) this neighbourhood trat is the loudest and most crowded 40 square metres in the whole of Rome. It serves perfectly decent pizzas, pasta dishes and *secondi*, which, on our last visit, included an excellent baked *orata* (bream) with potatoes. The outside tables operate all year round.

Shopping

Immediately outside the city walls by the basilica of San Giovanni, via Sannio is home each morning Monday to Friday and all day Saturday to three long corridors of stalls piled high with new and second-hand low-priced clothes.

Soul Food

*Via San Giovanni in Laterano 192-194
(06 7045 2025).* **Open** 10.30am-1.30pm, 3.30-8pm Tue-Sat. Closed 2wks Aug. **Map** p102 C4 ㉞

This vintage record shop is a record collector's heaven: indie, punk, '60s beat, exotica, lounge, rockabilly and more. Most musical tastes are catered for.

ROME BY AREA

Nightlife

Coming Out

Via San Giovanni in Laterano 8 (06 700 9871/www.comingout.it). **Open** 10am-2am daily. **Map** p102 B4 ❸

This unassuming pub offers beers, cocktails and a fair range of snacks to a predominantly youthful crowd of gay men and women. A good place to meet before heading off in search of something a bit more frantic.

Micca Club

Via Pietro Micca 7A (06 8744 0079/www.miccaclub.com). **Open** 10pm-2am Wed; 10pm-4am Thur-Sat; 6pm-2am Sun. Closed June-Aug. **Admission** free Wed, Thur, Sun; €5 Fri, Sat; €10 special events. **Map** p103 E3 ❸

A huge spiral staircase leads down to this cavernous underground venue with one of Rome's most eclectic nightlife programmes, ranging from themed and fancy dress nights (toga parties, Hammond organ nights) to live acts (on Sundays) and international DJ sets. There's a music-fuelled Sunday vintage market from 6pm.

Skyline

NEW *Via Pontremoli 36 (06 700 9431/www.skylineclub.it).* **Open** 10.30pm-4am daily. **Map** p103 E5 ❸

Skyline keeps getting better, even more so now that it has new, two-floor premises. The crowd is relaxed and a mix of gay and straight, with constant movement between the bar areas, the video parlour and the cruisy cubicle and dark areas. The club hosts naked parties on Mondays.

San Lorenzo

Colourful, hopping San Lorenzo retains some of its threadbare, slightly down-at-heel, working-class character. A constant influx of students and aspiring artists mingles with a (sadly diminishing) local population that remains proud of its impeccably unswerving anti-Fascist history.

The area has a history of rebellion. It was designed in the 1880s as a working-class ghetto, with few public services or basic amenities, and soon developed into Rome's most radical district. Along the north-east side is the vast Verano Cemetery, with the basilica of **San Lorenzo fuori le Mura** by its entrance.

To the north-west, the Città universitaria (the main campus of Europe's biggest university, La Sapienza), with buildings designed in the 1930s by Marcello Piacentini and Arnaldo Foschini, shows the Fascist take on the architecture of higher education.

Sights & museums

San Lorenzo fuori le Mura

Piazzale del Verano 3 (06 491 511). **Open** *Oct-Mar* 7.30am-12.30pm, 3-7pm daily. *Apr-Sept* 7.30am-12.30pm, 3-8pm daily. **Map** p103 F1 ❸

This basilica was donated by Constantine to house the remains of St Lawrence after the saint met his fiery end on a griddle. Rebuilt in the sixth century, it was later united with a neighbouring church. Bombs plunged through the roof in 1943, making San Lorenzo the only Roman church to suffer war damage, but it was painstakingly reconstructed by 1949. On the right side of the 13th-century portico are frescoes from the same period, showing scenes from the life of St Lawrence. Inside the triumphal arch are sixth-century mosaics.

Eating & drinking

Arancia Blu

Via dei Latini 55-65 (06 445 4105). **Meals served** 8.30-midnight daily. €€. No credit cards. **Map** p103 E2 ❸

This vegetarian restaurant has shaken off its rather earnest macrobiotic origins to become a stylish urban bistro with a great wine list; good-value meat-free fare in a space with a jazzy,

Piazza Immacolata

alternative atmosphere. The potato-filled ravioli topped with pecorino cheese and mint is excellent; the large cheese selection is a plus.

Bar à Book

NEW *Via dei Piceni 23 (06 4544 5438/ www.barabook.it).* **Open** 4pm-midnight Tue-Thur; 4pm-2am Fri, Sat; 11am-8pm Sun. Closed Aug. **Map** p103 F2 ④

With its long wooden central table and shelves piled high with books, this café in artsy San Lorenzo looks like the design-conscious study of an eccentric '60s-loving academic. In fact, it's the latest creation of the people who own Tram Tram, a restaurant just around the corner (via dei Reti 44, closed Mon, €€), which serves excellent creative Roman and Puglian specialities. In the bar, *aperitivi* come with a DJ on Saturdays from 7.30pm.

B-Said

NEW *Via Tiburtina 135 (06 446 9204/ www.said.it).* **Open** 10am-10pm Mon-Sat. **Map** p103 E2 ④

Said has been producing exquisite chocolate in this factory since 1923. But its industrial-chic tea room-restaurant, with a fireplace, comfy armchairs and glassed-over courtyard, is a recent addition. Chocolate pops up in unexpected places on the full lunch menu (€€); from 7.30pm, €10 gets you a glass of wine plus anything you like from a buffet of delicious quiches and salads.

Marcello

Via dei Campani 12 (06 446 3311). **Meals served** 7.30-11.30pm Mon-Fri. Closed 3wks Aug. **€**. No credit cards. **Map** p103 E3 ④

Inside this anonymous-looking trat, hordes of hungry students wolf food down at old wooden tables. Alongside specialities like tripe and intestines are more creative dishes such as *straccetti ai carciofi* (veal with artichokes).

Uno e Bino

Via degli Equi 58 (06 446 0702). **Meals served** 8.30-11.30pm Tue-Sun. Closed 2wks Aug. **€€€**. **Map** p103 E3 ④

An elegantly minimalist, creative Italian restaurant with one of the best quality-price ratios in Rome. With such pared-back decor the place needs to be full to really work. New chef Giovanni Passerini has brought in new dishes of his own, which, however, maintain the restaurant's reputation for audacious combinations of vegetables and herbs with fish, meat and game. Book well in advance.

Nightlife

Circolo degli Artisti

Via Casilina Vecchia 42 (06 7030 5684/www.circoloartisti.it). **Open** 9.30pm-3.30am Tue-Thur; 9pm-4.30 am Fri-Sun. Closed Aug. **Admission** varies, €6 and up. No credit cards. **Map** off p103 F4 ④

This is Rome's most popular venue for small- to medium-sized alternative bands. There's a popular gay night on Fridays. On Saturdays, 'Screamadelica' offers top-quality concerts by some of Europe's best alternative artists and emerging Italian bands.

La Palma

Via G Mirri 35 (06 4359 9029/ www.lapalmaclub.it). **Open** 8.30pm-1.30am Tue-Thur; 8.30pm-5am Fri, Sat. Closed Aug. **Admission** (with annual €2 membership) varies, up to €15. **Map** off p103 F1 ④

Beyond San Lorenzo, La Palma is an oasis in a post-industrial landscape, offering good concerts and quality DJ sets. The schedule is eclectic, though very jazz-focused. In the summer, it hosts a jazz festival in a spacious courtyard with restaurant.

Locanda Atlantide

Via dei Lucani 22B (06 4470 4540/ www.locandatlantide.it). **Open** 9.30pm-3am Tue-Sun. Closed mid June-Sept. **Admission** €3-€10. No credit cards. **Map** p103 E3 ④

An unpretentious venue hosting an array of events ranging from concerts and DJ sets to theatrical performances. It pulls an alternative crowd. Extra charge for concerts.

San Paolo fuori le Mura p122

The Aventine
& Testaccio

Aventine & Caracalla

King Ancius Marcius first colonised the Aventine hill in the seventh century BC; later, foreigners, sailors, merchants and other undesirables crept up the hill from the rough-and-tumble river port below.

In 456 BC, the Aventine hill was earmarked for plebeians, and there they remained, organising their guilds and building their temples. As they became more successful, so their villas became gentrified. By the time the Republic gave way to the Empire, this was a very exclusive neighbourhood. It still is.

The Aventine is lovely place for a walk. The delightful, recently revamped Parco Savello – still surrounded by the crenellated walls of a 12th-century fortress of the Savello family – has dozens of orange trees and a spectacular view over the city, especially at sunset. In nearby piazza Cavalieri di Malta, peek through the keyhole of the priory of the Knights of Malta to enjoy the surrealistic surprise designed by Gian Battista Piranesi – a telescopic view of St Peter's dome.

Across busy viale Aventino is the similarly well-heeled San Saba district and, beyond the white cuboids of the UN's Food and Agricultural Organisation, the giant **Baths of Caracalla**.

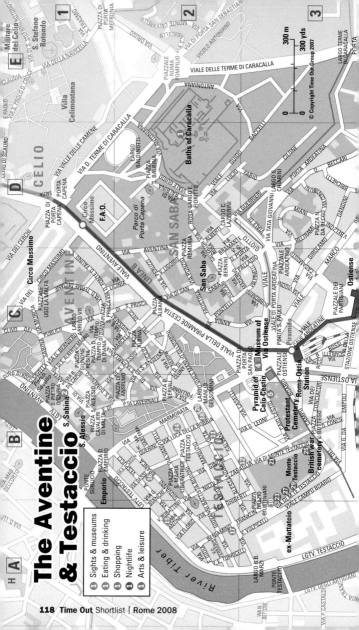

The Aventine & Testaccio

- Sights & museums
- Eating & drinking
- Shopping
- Nightlife
- Arts & leisure

© Copyright Time Out Group 2007

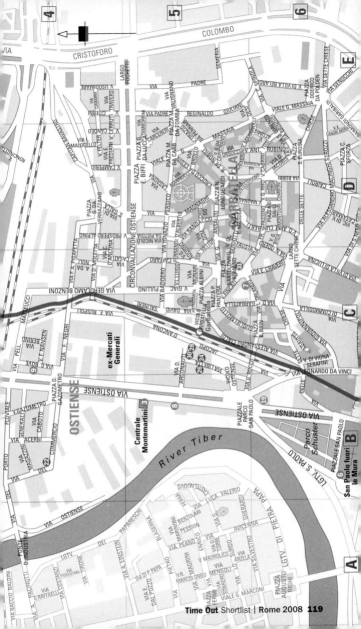

Sights & museums

Baths of Caracalla

Viale delle Terme di Caracalla 52 (06 3996 7700). **Open** 9am-2pm Mon; 9am-sunset Tue-Sun. **Admission** €6; €3.50 reductions. No credit cards. **Map** p118 D2 ❶

The high-vaulted ruins of the Terme di Caracalla are peaceful today, but were anything but tranquil in their heyday, when up to 1,600 Romans could sweat it out in the baths and gyms. You can get some idea of the original splendour of the baths from the fragments of mosaic and statuary littering the site, although the more impressive finds are in the Vatican Museums (p145).

The baths were built between AD 213 and 216. The two cavernous rooms down the sides were the gymnasia, where Romans engaged in such strenuous sports as toss-the-beanbag. There was also a large open-air *natatio* (pool), saunas and baths of varying temperatures, as well as a library, a garden, shops and stalls. Underneath it all was a network of tunnels where slaves treaded the giant wheels that pumped clean water up to bathers. Caracalla's baths were in use until 537, when the Visigoths sacked Rome and severed the city's aqueducts.

Santa Sabina

Piazza Pietro d'Illiria 1 (06 574 3575). **Open** 6.30am-12.45pm, 3-7pm daily. **Map** p118 B1 ❷

Santa Sabina was built in the fifth century over an early Christian place of worship; the bit of mosaic floor visible through a grate at the entrance is all that remains. Restored mercilessly in the 1930s, the church is now arguably the closest thing to an unadulterated ancient basilica in Rome. The fifth-century cypress doors are carved with biblical scenes. The nave's Corinthian columns support an arcade decorated with ninth-century marble inlay work; the choir dates from the same period. Selenite has been placed in the windows as it would have been in the ninth century. A window in the entrance porch looks on to the place where St Dominic is said to have planted an orange tree brought from Spain in 1220. The beautiful 13th-century cloister has just been restored.

Testaccio & Ostiense

Tucked below the quiet heights of the Aventine is bustling, workaday Testaccio. The stridently – even brusquely – salt-of-the-earth long-term residents have taken an influx of young(ish) professionals in their stride. Locals of all stripes mix happily in the gardens of piazza Santa Maria in Liberatrice on warm evenings, linked by an almost universal devotion to the AS Roma football team and an indulgent fondness for the elderly ladies who still traipse to the market in their slippers of a morning.

No wondrous monuments beckon here, just sites that tell of Testaccio's industrious past: an ancient river port and *emporio* (warehouse; closed but visible from lungotevere Testaccio), a rubbish tip composed of discarded potsherds (Monte Testaccio) and an abandoned slaughterhouse (il Mattatoio), now destined to become a cultural centre. And, incongruously, Rome's most happening nightlife hub.

Further south, via Ostiense slices through once run-down suburbs earmarked for some interesting development: Dutch architectural superstar Rem Koolhas is turning the former wholesale fruit and vegetable market into a complex of youth-oriented exhibition spaces, sports centres and shopping centres… what authorities like to describe as 'Rome's Covent Garden'.

Signs of a transformation have been around for a while, though, since the **Centrale Montemartini** power station was converted into one of the capital's most striking

View from Parco Savello

museums, the **Teatro Palladium** reopened, revamped and with a fascinating programme, and Testaccio's vibrant after-hours activity began seeping south.

Sights & museums

Centrale Montemartini

Via Ostiense 106 (06 574 8030/ www.museicapitolini.org). **Open** 9am-7pm Tue-Sun. **Admission** €4.50; €2.50 reductions. *Special exhibitions* extra charge (varies). No credit cards. **Map** p119 B5 ❸

The Centrale Montemartini contains the leftover ancient statuary from the Capitoline Museums – but the dregs are pretty impressive; moreover, the setting itself is worth a visit. Fauns and Minervas, bacchic revellers and Apollos are all starkly white but oddly at home against the gleaming machinery of this former generating station.

Museum of Via Ostiense

Via R Persichetti 3 (06 574 3193). **Open** 9.30am-1.30pm, 2.30-4.30pm Tue, Thur; 9.30am-1.30pm Wed, Fri, Sat, 1st & 3rd Sun of mth. **Admission** free. **Map** p118 C3 ❹

This third-century AD gatehouse, called Porta Ostiensis in antiquity and Porta San Paolo today, contains a quaint collection of artefacts and prints describing the history of via Ostiense – the Ostian Way, built in the third century BC to join Rome to its port at Ostia. There's also a large-scale model of the ancient port. Best of all, you can cross the crenellated walkway for a bird's-eye view of the true finesse of the modern Roman motorist.

Protestant Cemetery

Via Caio Cestio 6 (06 574 1900/www. protestantcemetery.it). **Open** 9am-5pm Mon-Sat. **Admission** free (donation expected). **Map** p118 B3 ❺

This heavenly oasis of calm in the midst of a ruckus of traffic has been the resting place for foreigners who have passed on to a better world since 1784. Officially the 'non-Catholic' cemetery, this charmingly old-world corner of the city accommodates Buddhists, Russian Orthodox Christians and atheists. In the older sector you'll find the grave of John Keats, who coughed his last at the age of 26. Close by is the tomb of Shelley, who died a year after Keats in a boating accident.

Centrale Montemartini p121

San Paolo fuori le Mura

Via Ostiense 184 (06 541 0341). **Open** *Basilica* 7am-7pm daily. *Cloister* 9am-1pm, 3-6pm daily. **Map** p119 B6 ⑥

Constantine founded this basilica to commemorate the martyrdom of St Paul nearby. The church has been destroyed and rebuilt several times; most of the present church is only 150 years old. Features to have survived include 11th-century doors; a strange 12th-century Easter candlestick featuring human-, lion- and goat-headed beasts spewing the vine of life from their mouths; and a 13th-century ciborium (canopy) above the altar, by Arnolfo di Cambio. In the nave are mosaic portraits of all the popes from Peter to the present incumbent. There are only seven spaces left; once they are filled, the world, apparently, will end. In the confessio beneath the altar is the tomb of St Paul, topped by a stone slab pierced with holes through which devotees stuff bits of cloth to imbue them with the apostle's holiness.

Eating & drinking

See also Volpetti (p126).

Al Ristoro degli Angeli

Via Luigi Orlando 2 (06 5143 6020/ www.ristorodegliangeli.it). **Meals served** 8-11.30pm Mon-Sat. €€€. **Map** p119 C5 ❼

Rather off the beaten track in the charming 1920s workers' suburb of Garbatella, the Ristoro's vibe is old-style French bistro but the excellent food is all Italian. Many organic products go into dishes such as a soup of chickpeas and fried baby squid, or beef millefeuille with radicchio and smoked provola cheese. There are always fish and vegetarian options. The wine list is small but interesting, the home-made desserts are luscious and there are tables in the arcade outside.

Bishoku Kobo

Via Ostiense 110B (06 574 4190). **Meals served** 7.30-midnight Mon, Sat; 12.30-3pm, 7.30-midnight Tue-Fri. Closed 1wk Aug. €€. No credit cards. **Map** p119 B5 ❽

This Japanese restaurant is well placed for visitors to the collection of antique statues in the Centrale Montemartini. The food is classic Japanese, the ambience is pure neighbourhood trattoria.

Caffè Letterario

NEW *Via Ostiense 83 (392 069 3460/ www.caffeletterarioroma.it).* **Open** 10am-2am Mon-Fri; 3pm-2am Sat, Sun. Closed 1wk Aug. No credit cards. **Map** p119 C4 ❾

In super-hip Ostiense, at the centre of a complex that comprises a bookshop, gallery and a TV studio, this design-conscious book-lined bar hosts book launches, political debates, concerts and other events, as well as serving good coffee and cocktails.

Checchino dal 1887

Via di Monte Testaccio 30 (06 574 6318/www.checchino-dal-1887.com).

Meals served 12.30-3pm, 8pm-midnight Tue-Sat. Closed Aug; 1wk Dec. €€€€. **Map** p118 A3 ❿

Imagine a pie shop becoming a top-class restaurant, and the odd mix of humble decor, elegant service, hearty food and huge cellar falls into place. Vegetarians should give the Mariani family's restaurant a wide berth: offal is the speciality. Pasta dishes like the *bucatini all'amatriciana* are delicious.

Da Felice

Via Mastro Giorgio 29 (06 574 6800). **Meals served** 12.30-3pm, 8-11.30pm Mon-Sat; 12.30-3pm Sun. Closed 3wks Aug. €€€. **Map** p118 B2 ⓫

This former spit-and-sawdust trat has had a stylish makeover but its high-quality traditional fare – including classics such as *tonarelli cacio e pepe* (p189) and *abbacchio al forno con patate* (baked lamb with potatoes) – remains as good as ever. In fact, some lighter, more creative additions – plus a good wine list – are improvements.

Il Seme e la Foglia

Via Galvani 18 (06 574 3008). **Open** 7.30am-2am Mon-Sat; 6pm-2am Sun. Closed 3wks Aug. No credit cards. **Map** p118 B3 ⓬

This lively daytime snack bar and evening pre-club stop is always packed with students from the music school opposite. At midday there's generally a pasta dish, plus large salads (€5-€7) and creative filled rolls.

L'Acino Brillo

NEW *Piazza Santa Eurosia 2 (06 513 7145/www.acinobrillo.it).* **Meals served** 8-11.30pm Tue-Sun. Closed Aug. €€€. **Map** p119 D6 ⓭

It's a long trek into unlikely territory – the glorious Fascist ideal workers' suburb of Garbatella – to this brightly coloured, creative wine bar and restaurant, but the journey's worth it. Try the smoked cod-stuffed pasta packets and squid ink sauce on a bed of roast peppers; follow up with lamb in a pistachio crust with a sauce of cheese, artichoke and wild mint. There are some unusual wines on the fairly priced list.

ROME BY AREA

L'Oasi della Birra

Piazza Testaccio 38 (06 574 6122).
Open 7pm-12.30am daily. Closed 2wks
Aug. **Map** p118 B2 ⑭

The 'Oasis of Beer' has more than 500
brews on offer, including beers from
award-winning Italian micro-breweries.
The selection of wines by the bottle is
almost as impressive. Food ranges from
snacks (*crostini, bruschette*, a well-
stocked cheese board) to full-scale meals
with a Teutonic slant. Outside tables.

Piccolo Alpino

Via Orazio Antinori 5 (06 574 1368).
Meals served 12.30-2.30pm, 6-11pm
Tue-Sun. **€.** No credit cards.
Map p118 A2 ⑮

There are no frills in this very cheap,
very cheerful eaterie where the pizzas
are good and some of the pasta dishes
– the *spaghetti con le vongole* stands out
– are perfectly acceptable too (though
these will push the bill into the €€
bracket). Neighbours often shout down
to friends dining at the outside tables.

Remo

*Piazza Santa Maria Liberatrice 44
(06 574 6270).* **Meals served** 7pm-
1am Mon-Sat. Closed 3wks Aug. **€.**
No credit cards. **Map** p118 B2 ⑯

This pizzeria is a Testaccio institution.
You can choose to sit at wonky tables
balanced on the pavement, or in the
deafening interior. The thin-crust
Roman pizzas are excellent, as are the
bruschette al pomodoro.

Tallusa

NEW *Via Beniamino Franklin 11
(333 752 3506).* **Open** 11am-1.30am
daily. **€. Map** p118 A2 ⑰

Always packed, this tiny eat-in or
takeaway joint specialises in southern
and eastern Mediterranean cuisine –
ranging from Sicilian specialities to
falafel and a full range of Lebanese-style
mezedes. Very friendly, very cheap but
rather erratic in its opening times.

Tuttifrutti

*Via Luca della Robbia 3A (06 575
7902).* **Meals served** 8-11.30pm
Mon-Sat. Closed 3wks Aug. **€€€.**
Map p118 B2 ⑱

Behind an anonymous frosted-glass
door, this trattoria is Testaccio's best-
value dining experience, at the lower
end of this price bracket. Michele
guides you through a changing menu
of creative pan-Italian fare, which
might include fusilli with sun-dried
tomatoes, pecorino, bacon and pine
nuts and then baked lamb with potatoes and rosemary. There are always
a few veggie options and the wine is
excellently priced.

Zampagna

Via Ostiense 179 (06 574 2306).
Meals served 12.30-2.30pm Mon-
Sat. Closed Aug. **€€.** No credit cards.
Map p119 B6 ⑲

This is basic Roman cooking as it once
was, with filling dishes for the refined
carnivore. Primi include *spaghetti alla
carbonara* or *tagliatelle alla gricia* (with
bacon and pecorino cheese), while most
of the second courses are served swimming in the thick house *sugo* (tomato
sauce). Service is brisk.

Remo

Eating foreign

Doozo

Mangiare straniero (eating foreign) was well nigh impossible in Rome until not so long ago. There *were* ethnic places – most notably innumerable empty Chinese restaurants – but they weren't considered serious dining options. These days, however, stick-in-the-mud Romans are branching out.

The transition came, perhaps, with the advent of fusion at the city's more sophisticated eateries around the turn of the millennium. Though this trend, on the whole, passed as locals rediscovered their traditional (though often now with superchef twists) fare, previously unheard-of ingredients made their way into the Roman consciousness, and a new age of gastronomic openness dawned.

The quick snack kebab option is a rather *recherché* experience here. **Le Piramidi** (p69) near campo de' Fiori has been doing it for years but **Tallusa** (p124) in Testaccio is a relative newcomer.

Offered a sag aloo or a rogan josh, your average Roman will look blank. Yet more and more locals pile into the city's handful of Indian eateries, jostling with the South Asians tucking in.

Jaipur (p135) in Trastevere turns out perfectly acceptable versions of tandoori and other favourites. Also in Trastevere is the slightly more expensive **Suriya Mahal** (piazza Trilussa 50, 06 589 4554), with dishes that sometimes make too many concessions to Italians' lack of adventurousness; its lovely terrace is marred by the squalor in the piazza outside.

In trendy Monti, **Maharajah** (via dei Serpenti 124, 06 474 7144) and **Guru** (via Cimarra 4-6, 06 474 4110) serve up all the usual Indian staples; the former is slightly more upmarket. For great food to go, try **Indian Fast Food** (p107) near piazza Vittorio.

Colourful, bustling **Hang Zhou** (p107) has long been the Chinese option of choice for Romans. But **Green T** (p78), just round the corner from the Pantheon, is more stylish and laid back – good for a light lunch or an evening meal.

The past couple of years have seen an explosion of Japanese cuisine, with sushi joints – many of dubious merit – springing up in their dozens. The long-running **Bishoku Kobo** (p123) draws lovers of Japanese food to the southern suburbs, while **Zen** (via degli Scipioni 243, 06 321 3420) serves upmarket fare in Prati, north of the Vatican. But lunch in the peaceful garden of the new **Doozo** (p107) is a more central spot for experiencing good Japanese dining in Rome.

ROME BY AREA

Shopping

The produce market in piazza Testaccio, arguably Rome's best, is an excellent place to pick up the wherewithal for a picnic. Nearby streets, and the north-western aisle of the market itself, have been colonised by vendors of shoes of every description, including some bargains on last season's models.

Volpetti

Via Marmorata 47 (06 574 2352/ www.fooditaly.com). **Open** 8am-2pm, 5-8.15pm Mon-Sat. **Map** p118 B2 ⑳

This is one of the best delis in Rome. It's hard to get away without one of the jolly assistants loading you up with samples – pleasant, but painful on the wallet. Around the corner is Volpetti Più (via A Volta 8-10, 06 574 4306, open 10am-3.30pm, 5.30-9.30pm), a self-service restaurant where you can taste the deli's delicious cured meats and cheeses, along with pizza, salads and more.

Nightlife

Akab

Via di Monte Testaccio 68-69 (06 5725 0585/www.akabcave.it). **Open** midnight-5am Tue-Sat. Closed Aug. **Admission** (incl 1 drink) €10-€20. **Map** p118 B3 ㉑

This long-term fixture of the Testaccio scene has an underground cellar and a street-level room, plus a garden for warmer months. Tuesday L-Ektrica sessions feature international DJs. There's retro on Wednesday, R&B on Thursday and house on Friday and Saturday.

Alpheus

Via del Commercio 36 (06 574 7826/ www.alpheus.it). **Open** 10.30pm-4am Fri-Sun; other days vary. Closed July & Aug. **Admission** €5-€20. **Map** p119 B4 ㉒

An eclectic club with a varied crowd, the Alpheus has four halls for live gigs, music festivals, theatre and cabaret, all followed by a disco. The music changes nightly and from room to room: rock, chart R&B, Latin, world

music, retro and happy trash. It's also the venue for Tocodance (www.tocodance.it), a word-of-mouth dance event frequented by a creative, international crowd of thirty- and forty-somethings.

Caruso-Café de Oriente

Via di Monte Testaccio 36 (06 574 5019/www.carusocafedeoriente.com). **Open** 10.30pm-3.30am Tue-Thur, Sun; 11pm-4.30am Fri, Sat. Closed July-mid Sept. **Admission** (incl 1 drink) €8-€15; free Sun. No credit cards. **Map** p118 B3 ㉓

A must for lovers of salsa, this club offers Latin American tunes every night apart from Saturday (anything from reggae to hip hop), and live acts almost daily. There's a roof terrace.

Classico Village

Via Libetta 3 (06 574 3364/www. classico.it). **Open** 9pm-1.30am Mon-Thur; 9pm-4am Fri, Sat. **Admission** €5-€15. **Map** p119 C5 ㉔

This former factory in trendy Ostiense can offer up to three (mainly rock-based) events simultaneously in its large spaces, all of which face on to a courtyard – a heavenly spot to chill on warm evenings. DJ sets follow shows.

Fake

Via di Monte Testaccio 64 (347 794 8859). **Open** 11.30pm-4am Wed, Thur; midnight-4am Fri, Sat; 7pm-2am Sun. Closed June-Sept. **Admission** free; €10 Fri, Sat. **Map** p118 B3 ㉕

This recent arrival certainly looks the part with its stunning mix of white, '60s space-age design, pop-art motifs and ancient brick. But the vibe still isn't quite right, and the music on offer from global DJs can disappoint: mainly electronica, it stretches to hip hop, R&B and '60s beat. There's a garden.

Goa

Via Libetta 13 (06 574 8277). **Open** midnight-4am Wed-Sat. Closed mid May-mid Sept. **Admission** (incl 1 drink) €10-€25. **Map** p119 C5 ㉖

One of the best of Rome's fashionable clubs, Goa is a techno-ethno fantasy of iron and steel with oriental-style statues and colours. Thursday's Ultrabeat

Goa

brings Europe's top electronic music DJs. Goa also opens some Sundays (5pm-4am); there's a women-only event on the last Sunday of the month.

L'Alibi

Via di Monte Testaccio 40-44 (06 574 3448). **Open** 11.30pm-5am Thur-Sun. **Admission** (incl 1 drink) €15. **Map** p118 B3 ㉗
Rome's original gay club, the Alibi is still, in theory, a great place to dance away, with a well-oiled sound system. But it's showing its age. A new straight-friendly approach and Friday hetero night has proved a turn-off all round.

La Saponeria

Via degli Argonauti 20 (393 966 1321/www.lasaponeria.com). **Open** 11.30pm-5am Thur-Sat. Closed mid May-mid Sept. **Admission** €5-€15. **Map** p119 C5 ㉘
One of the liveliest clubs in Ostiense, this stylish, curvy, white space gets hopelessly packed on weekends. Friday is hip hop and R&B, Saturday is house.

Metaverso

Via di Monte Testaccio 38A (06 574 4712/www.metaverso.com). **Open** 10.30pm-5am Fri, Sat. Closed July

& Aug. **Admission** €5-€7. No credit cards. **Map** p118 B3 ㉙
This inexpensive, friendly little club hosts international and Roman DJs, pulling in an alternative crowd. Electronica and hip hop dominate except the one Saturday a month given over to the cool '60s 'Twiggy' party and another to gay extravaganza 'Phag Off'.

Rashomon

NEW *Via degli Argonauti 16 (347 340 5710).* **Open** 11pm-4am Thur-Sat. Closed July & Aug. **Admission** free-€10. No credit cards. **Map** p119 C5 ㉚
Run by afficionados of alternative clubs in London and Berlin, Rashomon offers electro-rock, indie, electronica and new wave. There are live acts, including emerging locals.

Arts & leisure

Teatro Palladium

Piazza Bartolomeo Romano 8 (06 5706 7768/www.teatro-palladium.it). **Map** p119 C5 ㉛
This beautiful 1920s theatre in Garbatella offers a mix of top-quality electronic music acts, cutting-edge theatre, art performances and, oddly, university seminars on diverse topics.

ROME BY AREA

Piazza Sant'Egidio

Trastevere & the Gianicolo

Trastevere

If you've done your duty around the mighty ruins and splendid galleries of Rome, and are seeking relief in the kind of picturesque, ivy-draped warren that makes fewer cultural demands, then Trastevere is the place for you.

Here – across the Tiber (*trans Tiberim*) – your main tasks will include rambling in leisurely fashion through narrow cobbled streets, and selecting the likeliest-looking bar for *aperitivi*. And if your fellow ramblers are more likely to be tourists than the salt-of-the-earth Romans that the remaining *trasteverini* (those who haven't been priced out of this exclusive enclave) like to consider themselves, well… that's not so bad. After all, you can eat well, soak up the rustic charm and generally bask in the sense that there's little here in the way of pressing must-do sights.

Trasteverini claim descent from slave stock. Through the Imperial period, much of the *trans Tiberim* area was agricultural, with farms, vineyards, country villas and gardens laid out for the pleasure of the Caesars. Trastevere was a working-class district in papal Rome and remained so until well after Unification.

Viale Trastevere slices the district in two. At the hub of the much-visited western part is piazza **Santa Maria in Trastevere** with its eponymous church. Fewer tourists make it to the warren of cobbled alleys in the eastern half, where craftsmen still ply their trades around the lovely church of **Santa Cecilia in Trastevere**.

Further upriver, Ponte Sisto provides handy pedestrian access back across to the *centro storico*.

Sights & museums

Museo di Roma in Trastevere

Piazza Sant'Egidio 1B (06 581 6563/ www.museodiromaintrastevere.it). **Open** 10am-8pm Tue-Sun. **Admission** €3; €1.50 reductions. No credit cards. **Map** p130 C3 ❶

Rome's folklore museum, housed in a 17th-century convent, has a series of watercolours by Ettore Roesler Franz of 19th-century Rome and some whiskery waxwork tableaux evoking the life, work, pastimes and superstitions of the 18th- and 19th-century *trasteverini*. There are occasional good photo exhibits in the pretty courtyard.

Orto botanico (Botanical Gardens)

Largo Cristina di Svezia 24 (06 4991 7135). **Open** *Nov-Mar* 9.30am-5.30pm Mon-Sat. *Apr-Oct* 9.30am-6pm Mon-Sat. **Admission** €4; €2 reductions. No credit cards. **Map** p130 B2 ❷

Established in 1883, Rome's Botanical Gardens are a welcome haven from the rigours of a dusty, hot city: plants tumble over steps and into fountains and fish ponds, creating luxuriant hidden corners that are now disturbed only by frolicking children. There's a touch and smell garden for the vision-impaired.

Palazzo Corsini – Galleria Nazionale d'Arte Antica

Via della Lungara 10 (06 6880 2323/ www.galleriaborghese.it). **Open** 9.30am-1.50pm Tue-Sun. **Admission** €4; €2 reductions. No credit cards. **Map** p130 C2 ❸

Note: Due to staff shortages, it's only possible to enter the gallery at 9.30am, 11am and 12.30pm.

A 17th-century convert to Catholicism, Sweden's Queen Christina established her glittering court here in 1662. The stout monarch smoked a pipe, wore trousers and entertained female and (ordained) male lovers here. Today her home houses part of the national art collection, with scores of Madonnas and Children (the most memorable is a Madonna by Van Dyck). Other works include a pair of Annunciations by Guercino; two St Sebastians (one by Rubens, one by Annibale Carracci); Caravaggio's unadorned *Narcissus*; and a triptych by Fra Angelico. There's also a melancholy *Salome* by Guido Reni.

San Francesco a Ripa

Piazza San Francesco d'Assisi 88 (06 581 9020). **Open** 7am-noon, 4-7pm Mon-Sat; 7am-1pm, 4-7.30pm Sun. **Map** p131 E5 ❹

This church stands on the site of the hospice where St Francis of Assisi stayed when he visited Rome in 1219; a near-contemporary portrait hangs in the cell where the saint stayed. The original 13th-century church was rebuilt in the 1680s. It contains Bernini's sculpture of the Beata Ludovica Albertoni (1674), showing the aristocratic Franciscan nun dying in an agonised, sexually ambiguous Baroque ecstasy.

Santa Cecilia in Trastevere

Piazza Santa Cecilia (06 581 2140). **Open** *Church* 9.30am-1.15pm, 4-8pm daily. *Cavallini frescoes* 10.15am-12.30pm Mon-Sat; 11.30am-12.30pm Sun. *Excavations* 7am-12.30pm, 4-6.30pm daily. **Admission** *Frescoes* €2.50. *Excavations* €2.50. No credit cards. **Map** p131 E4 ❺

This church stands on the site of a fifth-century building that was itself built over an older Roman house, part of which can be visited. According to legend it was the home of the martyr Cecilia: after an attempt to suffocate her in her bath, her persecutors tried to behead her with three strokes of an axe (the maximum permitted). She sang for the several days it took her to die, and so became the patron saint of music. Her

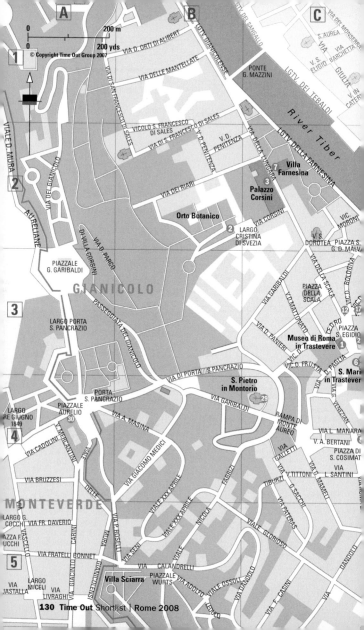

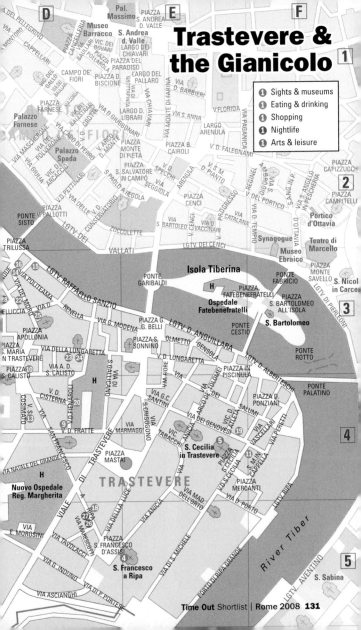

Trastevere & the Gianicolo

❶ Sights & museums
❶ Eating & drinking
❶ Shopping
❶ Nightlife
❶ Arts & leisure

tomb was opened in 1599, revealing her undecayed body. It disintegrated, but not before a sketch was made, on which Stefano Maderno based the sculpture below the high altar. Her sarcophagus is in the crypt. In the upstairs gallery is a small fragment of what must have been one of the world's greatest frescoes. In this 13th-century *Last Judgment*, Pietro Cavallini flooded the apostles with a totally new kind of light – the same that was to reappear in Giotto's work.

Santa Maria in Trastevere

Piazza Santa Maria in Trastevere (06 581 4802). **Open** 7.30am-9pm daily. **Map** p130 C3 ⑥
Legend has it that a miraculous well of oil sprang from the ground where Santa Maria now stands the moment that Christ was born, and flowed to the Tiber all day. The first church on this site was begun in 337; the present building was erected in the 12th century, and has wonderful mosaics.

Those on the façade – from the 12th and 13th centuries – show Mary breast-feeding Christ, and ten women with crowns and lanterns (they may represent the parable of the wise and foolish virgins). Inside, the apse has a 12th-century mosaic of Jesus and his mother. Lower down, between the windows, there are beautiful 13th-century mosaics showing scenes from the life of the Virgin by Pietro Cavallini. The Madonna and Child with rainbow overhead is also by Cavallini. In the chapel immediately to the left of the high altar is a very rare sixth-century painting on wood of the Madonna.

Villa Farnesina

Via della Lungara 230 (06 6802 7268/ www.lincei.it). **Open** 9am-1pm Mon-Sat. **Admission** €5; €4 reductions. No credit cards. **Map** p130 C2 ⑦
Built in 1508-11 for rich papal banker Agostino Chigi, this palazzo became the property of the powerful Farnese family in 1577. Chigi was one of Raphael's

Freni e Frizioni p135

principal patrons. The stunning frescoes in the ground-floor Loggia of Psyche were designed by Raphael but executed by his followers while the master dallied with his mistress. The Grace with her back turned, to the right of the door, is attributed to him. Around the corner, in the Loggia of Galatea, Raphael himself created the victorious goddess in her seashell chariot.

Eating & drinking

See also Lettere Caffè (p137).

Alberto Ciarla

NEW *Piazza San Cosimato 40 (06 581 8668/www.albertociarla.com).* **Open** *Bottiglieria* noon-midnight Mon-Sat. **Meals served** *Restaurant* 8.30pm-midnight Mon-Sat. Closed 1wk Aug. **€€-€€€€**. **Map** p130 C4 ❽

This mirrors-and-glitz time-warp of a restaurant serves some of Rome's best fish, with the emphasis on raw seafood. The Ciarla experience is unfailingly wonderful, but if the (justifiably hefty) bill worries you, go for one of the taster menus (from €50) or check out Alberto's stylish new wine bar, La Bottiglieria di Alberto Ciarla, where traditional Roman dishes are given a creative twist and offered along with a daunting selection of excellent wines. Here you can perch and nibble or go for a full meal; either way, the price tag will be considerably lower than at the restaurant next door.

Alle Fratte di Trastevere

Via delle Fratte di Trastevere 49-50 (06 583 5775/www.allefrattedi trastevere.com). **Meals served** 12.30-3pm, 6.30-11.30pm Mon, Tue, Thur-Sat; 6.30-11.30pm Sun. Closed 2wks Aug. **€€**. **Map** p131 D4 ❾

The cheerful Alle Fratte does honest Roman trattoria fare with Neapolitan influences. Service is friendly, attentive and bilingual. First courses, such as *pennette alla sorrentina* (pasta with tomatoes and mozzarella), come in generous portions. *Secondi* include roast sea bream and veal escalopes in marsala. Post-prandial *digestivi* flow freely.

Bar San Calisto

Piazza San Calisto (no phone). **Open** 5.30am-2am Mon-Sat. No credit cards. **Map** p131 D3 ❿

Harsh lighting in a dingy space means this bar is no picture postcard. But arty and fringe types flock here, to down a beer or an *affogato* (ice-cream swamped with liqueur), or savour some of the best chocolate in Rome: hot and thick with whipped cream in winter, and as creamy *gelato* in warmer months.

b-Gallery

NEW *Piazza Santa Cecilia 16 (06 5833 4365).* **Open** 10am-10pm Mon-Wed; 10am-midnight Thur-Sat. **Map** p131 F4 ⓫

Recently taken over by a design and marketing concern (www.b-egg.com), this pared-back space is primarily a gallery, showcasing photography and a range of contemporary artworks. But its welcoming bar (with *aperitivo* snacks available from 6pm), its shelves displaying the sleekest of design-related publications and its comfy armchairs make it a great place for a fashion-conscious drink.

Dar Poeta

Vicolo del Bologna 45 (06 588 0516). **Meals served** 7.30pm-midnight daily. **€€**. **Map** p130 C3 ⓬

Dar Poeta does high-quality pizza with creative toppings, such as the house pizza (with courgettes, sausage and spicy pepper) and the *bodrilla* (with apples and Grand Marnier). The varied *bruschette* are first-rate, and healthy salads offer a break from all those carbs. Be prepared to queue, as they don't take bookings.

Da Vittorio

Via di San Cosimato 14A (06 580 0353). **Meals served** 7.30pm-midnight Mon-Sat. Closed 1wk Aug. **€€**. **Map** p131 D4 ⓭

Vittorio is as expansively *napoletano* as they come, and so are his succulent pizzas, which include the self-celebratory Vittorio (mozzarella, parmesan, fresh tomato and basil). Kids will delight in his heart-shaped junior specials.

Bars with a mission

Cinecaffè

Romans have never needed a reason to step into a bar: their function as a pitstop for a speedy caffeine injection more than suffices. If they also supply a splendid pavement spot for catching lunchtime rays, or a cosy corner for some post-work *aperitivi*, so much the better.

But a recent spate of themed bar openings has provided a number of new motives for sipping a cappuccino or nursing a cocktail. And Romans have taken to the idea with gusto.

Book bars are the most numerous. From bookshops with a café attached – such as **Bibli** in Trastevere (via dei Fienaroli 20, 06 581 4534, www.bibli.it) – these have expanded into fully-fledged day-and-night drinking and gathering spots where the books that line the walls and

clutter the surfaces are… well, if not the whole point, at least an added incentive.

At sleek **Salotto 42** (p78), the tasteful tomes on art and design act as foils for the sleek, tasteful crowd that flocks here. **Lettere Caffè** (p137), on the other hand, has poetry slams and a host of readings (before, that is, its good live concerts begin later in the evening). As the name implies, **b-Gallery** (p133) is an art gallery – but the mix of this with welcoming bar and the coolest of design publications is a winning one.

In trendy Ostiense, the **Caffè Letterario** (p123) is at the heart of a media-and-design complex, which includes gallery space and a TV studio. It has become *the* place for major book launches. In San Lorenzo, on the other hand, the **Bar à Book** (p116) looks like the comfortably messy study of some erudite character with an eye for design: there are readings and theatrical happenings, as well as a Saturday evening *aperitivi* with-DJ fixture from 7.30pm.

If books aren't your thing, how about the movies?

Earnest cineastes gather in the little bar in the foyer of the **Nuovo Sacher** (largo Ascianghi 1, 06 581 8116), the Trastevere cinema of cult director Nanni Moretti. Note also that non-Italian films are shown here in their original language on Mondays and Tuesdays. The **Cinecaffè** (p94), inside the Villa Borghese park, also buzzes with celluloid fans. Lined with film memorabilia, the **Caffè Fandango** (p76) hosts film-related events and talks, and some screenings.

Enoteca Ferrara

Piazza Trilussa 41A (06 5833 3920).
Open *Wine bar & shop* 11am-2am
daily. **Map** p131 D3 ⓮
This warren of a place may also be a
restaurant (8-11.30pm daily, €€€€) but
we recommend sticking to the comfortable, dimly-lit wine bar with its good
choice of wines by the glass, and an
encyclopedic (though rather expensive)
bottle menu. From 6pm to 2am you can
graze through an appetising selection
of tapas-style bar snacks for €7-€9.

Freni e Frizioni

*Via del Politeama 4-6 (06 5833 4210/
www.freniefrizioni.com).* **Open** 10am-
2am daily. **Map** p131 D3 ⓯
Bar of the moment, 'Brakes and Clutch'
is a shabby-chic temple to the Turinese
aperitivo cult. It occupies a former car
mechanic's workshop in a small square
just downriver from piazza Trilussa,
but uncontainable crowds spill across
the square outside.

Friends Art Café

Piazza Trilussa 34 (06 581 6111).
Open 7.30am-2am Mon-Sat; 6.30pm-
2am Sun. Closed 1wk Aug. **Map**
p131 D3 ⓰
Habitués meet in this lively bar for
everything from breakfast to after-
dinner cocktails. The chrome detailing
and brightly coloured plastic chairs,
plus the constant din of fashion TV,
lend the place a retro-'80s funhouse
feel. Lunch and dinner menus offer
bruschette, salads and pastas at quite
reasonable prices.

Glass Hostaria

Vicolo del Cinque 58 (06 5833 5903).
Meals served 8pm-midnight Tue-
Sat. Closed 2wks Jan-Feb. €€€.
Map p130 C3 ⓱
Don't be misled by the ultra-modern
design: though Glass Hostaria kicks
against the trad Trastevere dining
scene, the service is surprisingly warm,
the wine list interesting, and the pan-
Italian food a lot less pretentious than
you might expect (outside of a couple of
kooky numbers). It's also unexpectedly
good value, given the setting.

Jaipur

*Via di San Francesco a Ripa 56
(06 580 3992/www.ristorantejaipur.it).*
Meals served 7pm-midnight Mon;
noon-3pm, 7pm-midnight Tue-Sun.
€€. **Map** p131 D5 ⓲
Jaipur does some of Rome's best
Indian food (not that there's much
competition), and it's good value too –
which all helps make up for the rather
garish lighting and colour scheme.
The menu ranges from basic starters
to an extensive selection of tandoori
specials, curries and murghs, plus a
range of vegetarian dishes.

Le Mani in Pasta

NEW *Via de' Genovesi 37 (06 581
6017/www.lemaniinpasta.com).* **Meals
served** 12.30-3pm, 7.30-11.30pm Tue-
Sat. Closed 3wks Aug; 1wk Dec. €€€.
Map p131 E4 ⓳
This newcomer offers decent, creative
home cooking, huge portions, friendly
informal service and great value for
money, all of which make it popular,

Via dei Fienaroli

Piazza San Cosimato

so book ahead. Antipasti such as the chargrilled vegetables or sautéed clams and mussels, and huge mountains of pasta, such as the spaghetti with cuttlefish and artichokes, may mean you never get as far as good main courses like fillet steak with green peppercorns.

Libreria del Cinema

Via dei Fienaroli 31 (06 581 7724/ www.libreriadelcinema.roma.it). **Open** 4-9pm Mon; 10am-2pm, 3-9pm Tue-Fri; 11am-11pm Sat; 11am-9pm Sun. Closed 1wk Aug. **Map** p131 D4 ⓴
This is a heaven for movie buffs, with its vast stock of cinema-related books, its busy events programme and its intimate little bar where aficionados swap cinema tales.

Ombre Rosse

Piazza Sant'Egidio 12 (06 588 4155). **Open** 7.30am-2am Mon-Sat; 6.30pm-2am Sun. Closed 1wk Aug.
Map p130 C3 ㉑
In the heart of Trastevere, this café is a meeting spot day and night: perfect for morning coffee, a late lunch or a light dinner (try the chicken salad or fresh soups). It fills to bursting after

dark, when snagging an outside table is a coup. Service is slow but friendly: as the bartender hand-crushes the ice for your next caipiroska, you have plenty of time to watch the world go by.

Shopping

Piazza San Cosimato is home to a produce market (early to about 2pm Mon-Sat) which manages to retain a local feel in this heavily touristed area. On Sunday mornings, the Porta Portese flea market engulfs via Portuense and surrounding streets: watch out for pickpockets as you root through bootleg CDs, clothes, bags and fake designer gear.

The Almost Corner Bookshop

Via del Moro 45 (06 583 6942). **Open** 10am-1.30pm, 3.30-8pm Mon-Sat; 11am-1.30pm, 3.30-8pm Sun.
Map p131 D3 ㉒
This English language bookshop has a good selection of fiction, as well as history, art, archaeology and more. Check the noticeboard if you're seeking work, lodgings or Italian lessons.

Antico Arco p138

Giokeb

*Via della Lungaretta 79 (06 589
6891).* **Open** 10am-8pm Mon-Sat.
Map p131 D3 ㉓
Giokeb has a sparkling array of silver
settings adorned with natural stones,
including a stylish amber collection.
Original, but at prices that won't make
your eyes water.

Roma – Store

*Via della Lungaretta 63 (06 581
8789).* **Open** 10am-8pm daily.
Map p131 D3 ㉔
This blissful sanctuary of lotions and
potions stocks an array of gorgeous
scents: old-school Floris, Creed and
Penhaligon's rub shoulders with mod-
ern classics such as home-grown
Acqua di Parma and Lorenzo Villoresi.
Staff can be very abrupt, though.

Valzani

Via del Moro 37B (06 580 3794).
Open 2-8pm Mon, Tue; 9.30am-8pm
Wed-Sun. **Map** p131 D3 ㉕
Sachertorte and spicy, nutty *pangiallo*
are the specialities in this Trastevere
institution, but they are the tip of a
sweet-toothed iceberg.

Nightlife

See also Freni e Frizioni, Friends
Art Café (both p135) and Ombre
Rosse (p136).

Big Mama

*Vicolo San Francesco a Ripa 18
(06 581 2551/www.bigmama.it).*
Open 9pm-1.30am Tue-Sat. Closed
June-mid Sept. **Admission** free with
membership (annual €13, monthly €8);
extra charge (€8-€22) for big acts.
Map p131 D5 ㉖
Rome's temple to blues, where an array
of respected Italian and international
artists play regularly, guaranteeing
a quality night out for live-music
aficionados. There's jazz too. Food is
served: book to ensure you get a table.

Lettere Caffè

*Via San Francesco a Ripa 100-101
(06 6456 1919/www.lettercaffe.org).*
Open 5pm-2am daily. Closed Aug.
Map p131 D5 ㉗
Poetry slams and readings compete
with live concerts – from rockabilly to
jazz via '60s beat, beginning at 10.30pm
– and DJ sets in this bookish bar
where a quality selection of well-priced

ROME BY AREA

wines and spirits and yummy home-made cakes complete the picture. Enthusiastic new management has given the café a shot in the arm.

Arts & leisure

L'Albero e la Mano
Via della Pelliccia 3 (06 581 2871/ www.lalberoelamano.it). Closed Sun & mid July-mid Sept. **Rates** €12-€13 per class. No credit cards. **Map** p131 D3 ㉗
This incense-scented studio offers Shiatsu, Ayurvedic and Thai massages. There are also daily classes in Ashtanga and Hatha yoga, as well as several classes per week in stretching, t'ai chi and belly-dancing.

The Gianicolo & Monteverde

Every day at noon a cannon is fired from beneath the terrace on the Gianicolo where an equestrian statue of Unification hero Giuseppe Garibaldi stands. The view over the city from this terrace is superb.

To the south, tortuous via Garibaldi passes by the Baroque Fontana Paola, an extravagant fountain made in 1612 to celebrate the reopening of an ancient Roman aqueduct; the columns come from the original St Peter's. Between the fountain and the church of **San Pietro in Montorio** – with the exquisite **Tempietto** in its courtyard – stands the unlikely Fascist-era Ossario Garibaldo (open 9am-1pm Tue-Sun) containing the remains of heroes of the Risorgimento, Italy's struggle for Unification.

West of here stretches the leafy well-heeled suburb of Monteverde, home to vast, green expanses of the Villa Pamphili park. Rome's largest public green space, it's a wonderful place to stroll of a summer evening. Nearby, to the south-east, is the smaller but equally lovely Villa

Sciarra garden, with multi-hued rose arbours, a children's play area and a miniature big dipper.

Sights & museums

Tempietto di Bramante & San Pietro in Montorio
Piazza San Pietro in Montorio 2 (06 581 3940). **Open** *Tempietto* Oct-Mar 9.30am-12.30pm, 2-4pm Tue-Sun; Apr-Sept 9.30am-12.30pm, 4-6pm Tue-Sun. *Church* 8am-noon, 4-6pm daily. **Map** p130 C4 ㉙
High up on the Gianicolo, on one of the spots where St Peter was said to have been crucified (St Peter's is another), San Pietro in Montorio conceals an architectural gem in its courtyard: the Tempietto, designed by Bramante in 1508. This round construction, with its Doric columns, was the first modern building to follow exactly the proportions of one of the classical orders. In 1628, Bernini added the staircase down to the crypt. The 15th-century church has a chapel by Bernini (the second on the left). Paintings include Sebastiano del Piombo's *Flagellation* and a *Crucifixion of St Peter* by Guido Reni.

Eating & drinking

Antico Arco
Piazzale Aurelio 7 (06 581 5274). **Meals served** 7.30-11.30pm Mon-Sat. Closed 2wks Aug. €€€€. **Map** p130 A4 ㉚
A January 2007 refit has given the Antico Arco a minimalist-but-warm new interior, served up with some interesting innovations – including a delicious *tonnarelli* pasta with mullet roe, artichokes and coriander – in the kitchen. But the old favourites are still there too, from the outstanding onion flan with grana cheese sauce, to *primi* like risotto with castelmagno cheese. The *secondi* cover the board from meat to fish to game, and the desserts are fantastic. Sommelier Maurizio will steer you a course through an extensive, well-priced wine list. Book at least a couple of days in advance.

Alexanderplatz p151

The Vatican & Prati

The Vatican & Borgo

In AD 54, Emperor Nero built a circus in the *campus vaticanus*, a marshy area across the river from the city centre known mainly for its poor-quality wine.

Ten years later, a fire destroyed two-thirds of Rome. Most Romans blamed Nero; he in turn blamed the Christians, and the persecution of this troublesome new cult began in earnest. Nero's circus was the main venue for Christian-baiting. Top apostle Peter is believed to have been crucified here and buried close by on the spot where, in AD 326, Emperor Constantine built the first church of St Peter.

Not all of the following popes resided here but throughout the Christian era, pilgrims have flocked to the tomb of the founder of the Roman Church. Around it, Borgo grew up to service the burgeoning Dark Age tourist industry. Pope Leo IV (847-55) enclosed Borgo with the 12-metre-high (40 feet) Leonine Wall. Pope Nicholas III (1277-80) extended the walls and provided a papal escape route, linking the Vatican to the huge, impregnable Castel Sant'Angelo by way of a long *passetto* or covered walkway.

After the Sack of Rome in 1527, Pope Paul III got Michelangelo to build bigger, better walls but the popes moved to the Lateran, then the Quirinal, palaces. Only in 1870, with the Unification of Italy, were they forced back across the Tiber once more. Until 1929 the pope pronounced the Italian state to

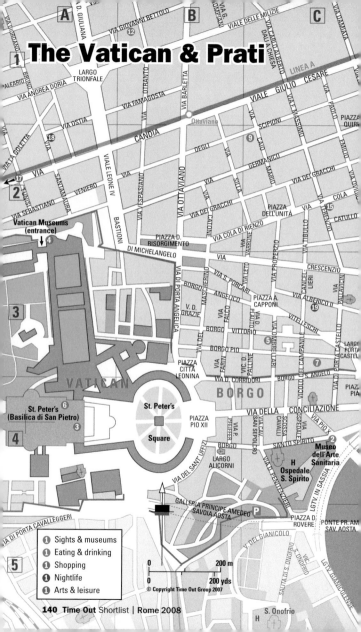

The Vatican & Prati

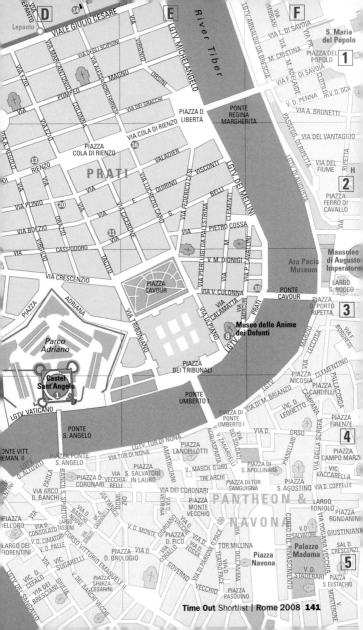

be sacrilegious. But on 11 February 1929 Pius XII and Mussolini signed the Lateran Pacts, awarding the Church a huge cash payment, tax-free status and a constitutional role that led to an important and continuing moral influence over legislation on social issues.

The Vatican City occupies an area of less than half a square kilometre, making it the world's smallest state. Despite having fewer than 800 residents, it has its own diplomatic service, postal service, army (the Swiss Guard), heliport, station, supermarket, and radio and TV stations. It has observer status at the UN, and issues its own stamps and currency. Outside in Borgo, locals mingle with off-duty Swiss Guards and priests from the Vatican Curia (administration).

Vatican tips

■ **Dress code**: the Vatican enforces its dress code strictly, both in St Peter's and in the Vatican Museums. Anyone wearing shorts or a short skirt, or with bare shoulders or midriff, will be turned away.

■ **Timing**: the queues to visit both St Peter's and the Vatican Museums (ten minutes' brisk walk between the two) are usually huge. Factor in an hour or more of waiting time for each.

■ **Papal audiences**: when in Rome, the pope addresses crowds in St Peter's Square at noon on Sunday. On Wednesday mornings he holds a general audience in St Peter's Square, if the weather is fine, otherwise in the modern Sala Nervi audience hall. If you wish to attend, make your request well in advance to the Prefettura della Casa Pontificia (06 6988 4857, fax 06 6988 5863, open 9am-1.30pm Mon-Sat). See also box p37.

■ **Vatican Gardens**: the Vatican walls surround splendid formal gardens, which can be visited daily – weather permitting – on guided tours (€12, €8 reductions). Phone 06 6988 4676 at least one week in advance to book.

Sights & museums

Castel Sant'Angelo
Lungotevere Castello 50 (06 681 9111). **Open** 9am-7pm Tue-Sun. **Admission** €5; €2.50 reductions. *Special exhibitions* €3 extra. No credit cards. **Map** p141 D4 ❶
Begun by Emperor Hadrian in AD 135 as his own mausoleum, Castel Sant'Angelo has been a fortress, prison and papal residence. It now plays host to temporary art shows, although the real pleasure of a visit lies in wandering from Hadrian's original spiralling ramp entrance to the upper terraces, with their superb views over the city. Between, there is much to see: lavish Renaissance salons, decorated with spectacular frescoes and trompe l'oeils; the glorious chapel in the *Cortile d'Onore* designed by Michelangelo; and, halfway up an easily missed staircase, Clement VII's tiny bathroom, painted by Giulio Romano.

Museo Storico Nazionale dell'Arte Sanitaria
Lungotevere in Sassia 3 (06 689 3051). **Open** 10am-noon Mon, Wed, Fri. Closed Aug. **Admission** €3. No credit cards. **Map** p140 C4 ❷
A hostel and church was established here in around 726 by King Ine of Wessex to cater for weary pilgrims from the north. Known as the *burgus saxonum* or 'in Sassia', this became the nucleus of the world's first purpose-built hospital. British funds for the hostel were cut off with the Norman invasion of England in 1066, after which it passed into papal hands and thence to the Templar knight Guy de Montpellier, who founded the Order of the Holy Spirit. A few rooms of the modern hospital here house a gruesome collection of medical artefacts. Two massive 15th-century frescoed

Museo Storico Nazionale dell'Arte Sanitaria

wards were emptied not all that long ago of their beds to provide space for itinerant exhibitions.

St Peter's (Basilica di San Pietro)

Piazza San Pietro (06 6988 1662). No credit cards. **Map** p140 A4 ❸
Basilica Open *Oct-Mar* 7am-6pm daily. *Apr-Sept* 7am-7pm daily. **Admission** free. *Audio guide* €5.
Dome Open *Oct-Mar* 8am-5pm daily. *Apr-Sept* 8am-6pm daily. **Admission** €4; €7 with lift.
Grottoes Open *Oct-Mar* 7am-5pm daily. *Apr-Sept* 7am-6pm daily. **Admission** free.
Necropolis Apply at the Uffizio degli Scavi (06 6988 5318/fax 06 6988 5518/scavi@fsp.va). **Open** *Guided tours* 9am-5pm Mon-Sat. **Admission** €10.
Treasury Museum Open *Oct-Mar* 9am-5.15pm daily. *Apr-Sept* 9am-6.15pm daily. **Admission** €6; €4 reductions.

The current St Peter's was consecrated on 18 November 1626 by Urban VIII, exactly 1,300 years after the consecration of the first basilica on the site. By the mid 15th century, the south wall of the original basilica was collapsing.

Pope Nicholas V had 2,500 wagonloads of masonry from the Colosseum carted here, just for running repairs. It took the arrogance of Pope Julius II and his pet architect Donato Bramante to knock the millennia-old basilica down, in 1506.

Following Bramante's death in 1514, Raphael took over the work. In 1547 he was replaced by Michelangelo; he died in 1564, aged 87, after coming up with a plan for a massive dome. Completed in 1590, this was the largest brick dome ever constructed, and still the tallest building in Rome. In 1607 Carlo Maderno designed a new façade, crowned by enormous statues of Christ and the apostles.

After Maderno's death Bernini took over and became the hero of the hour with his sumptuous baldachin and elliptical piazza. This latter was built between 1656 and 1667; the oval measures 340 by 240 metres (1,115 by 787 feet), and is punctuated by the central Egyptian obelisk and two symmetrical fountains by Maderno and Bernini. The 284-column, 88-pillar colonnade is topped by 140 statues of saints.

In the portico (1612), opposite the main portal, is a mosaic by Giotto

ROME BY AREA

St Peter's Square

(c1298), from the original basilica. Five doors lead into the basilica: the central ones come from the earlier church, while the others are all 20th century. The last door on the right is opened only in Holy Years by the pope himself. Inside, a series of brass lines in the floor show the lengths of other churches around the world that are not as big. Bernini's vast *baldacchino* (1633), cast from bronze purloined from the Pantheon, hovering over the high altar, is the real focal point. Below the altar, two flights of stairs lead to the *confessio*, where a niche contains a ninth-century mosaic of Christ, the only thing from old St Peter's that stayed in the same place. Far below lies the site of what is believed to be St Peter's tomb, discovered during excavations in 1951.

Pilgrims head straight for the last pilaster on the right before the main altar, to kiss the big toe of Arnolfo da Cambio's brass statue of St Peter (c1296), or to say a prayer before the crystal casket containing the mummified remains of Pope John XXIII, who was beatified in 2002. Tourists make a beeline for the first chapel on the right,

where Michelangelo's *Pietà* (1499) is found. Proceeding around the basilica in an anti-clockwise direction, the third chapel has a tabernacle and two angels by Bernini, plus St Peter's only remaining painting: a *Trinity* by Pietro da Cortona (the others have been replaced by mosaic copies).

Bernini's Throne of St Peter (1665) stands at the far end of the nave. Encased within Bernini's creation is a wood and ivory chair, probably dating from the ninth century but for many years believed to have belonged to Peter himself. To the right of the throne is Bernini's 1644 monument to his patron Urban VIII.

On the pillars supporting the main dome are much-venerated relics, including a chip off the True Cross. In the left aisle, beyond the pilaster with St Veronica holding the cloth with which she wiped Christ's face, Bernini's tomb for Pope Alexander VII shows the pope seated above a doorway shrouded with a cloth of reddish marble, from beneath which struggles a skeleton clutching an hour-glass. Near the portico end of the left aisle is a group of monuments

to the Sistine Chapel to a five-hour plod around the lot. There are also itineraries for wheelchair users. Wheelchairs can be borrowed at the museum: you can't book them, but you can call ahead (06 6988 3860) to check there's one free.

Borgia Rooms

This six-room suite was adapted for the Borgia Pope Alexander VI (1492-1503) and decorated by Pinturicchio with a series of frescoes on biblical and classical themes.

Galleria Chiaramonte

Founded by Pius VII in the early 19th century, this is an eclectic collection of Roman statues, reliefs and busts.

Gallerie dei Candelabri & degli Arazzi

The long gallery, which is studded with candelabra, contains Roman statues, while the next gallery has ten huge tapestries (*arazzi*), woven by Flemish master Pieter van Aelst from cartoons by Raphael.

Galleria delle Carte Geografiche

A 120m-long (394ft) gallery, with the Tower of the Winds observation point at the north end. Ignazio Danti drew the extraordinarily precise maps of Italian regions and cities.

Egyptian Museum

Founded in 1839, this selection of ancient Egyptian art from 3000 BC to 600 BC includes statues of a baboon god, painted mummy cases, real mummies and a marble statue of Antinous, Emperor Hadrian's lover.

Etruscan Museum

This collection contains Greek and Roman art as well as Etruscan masterpieces, including the contents of the Regolini-Galassi Tomb (c650 BC).

Museo Paolino

Highlights of this collection of Roman and neo-Attic sculpture include a beautifully draped statue of Greek tragedian Sophocles and a trompe l'oeil mosaic of an unswept floor.

Museo Pio-Clementino

The world's largest collection of classical statues fills 16 rooms. Don't miss the first-century BC *Belvedere Torso*

to the Old Pretender James Edward Stuart and family.

Beneath the basilica are the Vatican Grottoes – Renaissance crypts containing papal tombs. The Necropolis, where St Peter is said to be buried, lies under the grottoes. The small treasury museum off the left nave of the basilica contains stunning liturgical relics. The dome, reached via hundreds of stairs (there's a cramped lift as far as the basilica roof, then 320 steps to climb to get to the very top), offers fabulous views.

Vatican Museums

Viale del Vaticano (06 6988 3333).
Open *Nov-Feb* 10am-1.45pm Mon-Sat. *Mar-Oct* 10am-4.45pm Mon-Fri; 10am-2.45pm Sat. *Year-round* last Sun of month 9am-1.45pm. Closed Catholic holidays. **Admission** €13; €8 reductions; free last Sun of month. No credit cards. **Map** p140 A3 ❹

Begun by Pope Julius II in 1503, this immense collection represents the accumulated fancies and obsessions of a long line of strong, often contradictory personalities. The sign-posted routes cater for anything from a dash

by Apollonius of Athens, the Roman copy of the bronze *Lizard Killer* by Praxiteles and, in the octagonal Belvedere Courtyard, the exquisite *Belvedere Apollo* and *Laocoön*.

Pinacoteca

The Pinacoteca (picture gallery) holds many of the pictures that the Vatican managed to recover from France after Napoleon whipped them in the early 19th century. The collection ranges from Byzantine school works and Italian primitives to 18th-century Dutch and French old masters, and includes Giotto's *Stefaneschi Triptych*; a *Pietà* by Lucas Cranach the Elder; several delicate Madonnas by Fra Filippo Lippi, Fra Angelico, Raphael and Titian; Raphael's last work, *The Transfiguration*; Caravaggio's *Entombment*; and a chiaroscuro *St Jerome* by Leonardo da Vinci.

Sistine Chapel

The world's most famous frescoes cover the ceiling and one immense wall of the Cappella Sistina, built by Sixtus IV in 1473-84. For centuries it has been used for popes' private prayers and papal elections. In the 1980s and '90s, the 930 sq m (10,000 sq ft) of *Creation* (on the ceiling) and the *Last Judgment* (on the wall behind the altar) were subjected to a controversial restoration.

In 1508 Michelangelo was commissioned to paint some undemanding decoration on the ceiling of the chapel. He offered to do far more than that, and embarked upon his massive venture alone, spending the next four and a half years standing (only Charlton Heston lay down) on 18m-high (60ft) scaffolding. A sequence of biblical scenes, from the Creation to the Flood, begins at the *Last Judgment* end; they are framed by monumental figures of Old Testament prophets and classical sibyls.

In 1535, aged 60, Michelangelo returned. Between the completion of the ceiling and the beginning of the wall, Rome had suffered. From 1517, the Protestant Reformation threatened the power of the popes, and the sack of the city in 1527 by Imperial troops was seen by Michelangelo as the wrath of God. The *Last Judgment* dramatically reflects this gloomy atmosphere. In among the larger-than-life figures, Michelangelo painted his own miserable face on the human skin held by St Bartholomew, below and to the right of the powerful figure of Christ.

Before Michelangelo set foot in the chapel, the stars of the 1480s – Perugino, Cosimo Roselli, Botticelli, Ghirlandaio – had created the paintings along the walls.

Raphael Rooms

Pope Julius II gave 26-year-old Raphael carte blanche to redesign four rooms of the Papal Suite. The Study (Stanza della Segnatura, 1508-11) covers philosophical and spiritual themes. The star-packed *School of Athens* fresco has contemporary artists as classical figures: Plato is Leonardo; the glum thinker on the steps at the front – Heraclitus – is Michelangelo; Euclid is Bramante; and Raphael himself is on the far right-hand side behind a man in white. Raphael next turned to the Stanza di Eliodoro (1512-14), where the portrayal of God saving the temple in Jerusalem from the thieving Heliodorus was intended to highlight the divine protection enjoyed by Pope Julius. The Dining Room (Stanza dell'Incendio; 1514-17) is dedicated to Pope Leo X (the most obese of the popes, he died from gout aged 38). The room is named for the *Fire in the Borgo*, which Leo IV apparently stopped with the sign of the cross. The Reception Room (Sala di Constantino, 1517-24) was completed by Giulio Romano after Raphael's death in 1520, and tells the legend of Emperor Constantine's miraculous conversion. The Loggia di Raffaello (usually closed) has a beautiful view over Rome; started by Bramante in 1513, and finished by Raphael, it has 52 small paintings on biblical themes, and leads into the Sala dei Chiaroscuri. The adjacent Chapel of Nicholas V has scenes from the lives of saints Lawrence and Stephen by Fra Angelico (1448-50).

Latin lovers

San Giovanni in
Laterano p110

In the 1960s, the Second Vatican Council controversially did away with the Latin mass, modernising the Catholic Church's language, if not its message. In 2007, Pope Benedict XVI was going to ignore the advice of many of his bishops and reverse the ban, issuing a *motu proprio* ('own initiative') allowing priests to preach once again in this 'dead' language.

How handy, then, that in the Vatican, Latin is far from dead. The Holy Father himself speaks it fluently. The Holy See translates all its formal documents into the language of St Augustine. And it supplies a helpful on-line glossary for 21st-century would-be Latin conversationalists.

You never know when you might need useful words like *ovata pelvis* (bidet), *brevíssimae bracae femíneae* (hot pants), *hassum* (hashish), *foetris delumentum* (deodorant), *fístula nicotina* (cigarette) or *víschium Scóticum* (whisky). And of course, you can't chat about doctrine all the time, so you'll be wanting modern concepts like *voluntárius sui interemptor* (kamikaze), *largítio quaestusa* (bribe), *pecúniae male partae collocatio* (money laundering), *ruttianorum praednum*

grex (the Mafia), and *siderlis navigation* (space travel). For more, visit www.vatican.va and click on 'Other services'.

Unless you have a personal account at the Vatican bank you will never be asked by the Vatican City cash dispenser to *inserite scidulam quaeso ut faciendam cognoscas rationem* (insert card now and PIN number).

But if you're dying to use the language of the ancients, don't bother trying your *amo, amas, amat* on the legions of plastic-breastplated centurions who pose for unwary tourists in front of the Colosseum (the going rate for a snap is about €5); instead, brush up your Latin translating the city's many inscriptions. The new multi-storey Vatican coach and car park to the south of St Peter's is a good place to start: a large plaque by the exit explains the noble aims of this facility.

American Carmelite priest Father Reginald Foster is known as the pope's Latinist. His entertaining *Latin Lover* programme on Vatican radio each Saturday (download at www.vaticanradio.org/english) is almost as popular as Finnish radio's weekly news, *Nuntii Latini* (www.yleradio1.fi/nuntii).

ROME BY AREA

Il Ristoro

Eating & drinking

Enoteca Nuvolari
Via degli Ombrellari 10 (06 6880 3018). **Open** 6.30pm-2am Mon-Sat. No credit cards. **Map** p140 C3 ⑤
The younger denizens of Borgo hang out in this welcoming *enoteca*. The lively *aperitivo* hour (6.30-8.30pm) is accompanied by a free buffet; more filling soups and patés are on offer next door (8pm-1am) in the candlelit dining room.

Il Ristoro
NEW *Basilica di San Pietro (06 6988 1662).* **Open** *Oct-Mar* 8.30am-5pm Mon-Sat. *Apr-Sept* 8.30am-6pm Mon-Sat. No credit cards. **Map** p140 A4 ⑥
Take the St Peter's dome lift for Rome's most unlikely 'cappuccino with a view' – on the roof of the basilica. There's nothing but water, coffee and soft drinks on the menu, but the wonder of being up here between those giant marble saints will make you feel light-headed anyway.

Paninoteca da Guido
Borgo Pio 13 (06 687 5491). **Open** 8am-6pm Mon-Sat. No credit cards. **Map** p140 C3 ⑦

This hole-in-the-wall joint in the pedestrianised Borgo Pio is one of the best places to grab a snack in the Vatican area. Guido does filled rolls, made up while you wait from the ingredients behind the counter: ham, mozzarella, rocket, olive paste, etc. There are also a couple of pasta dishes. You'll have to fight for one of the few outside tables, though.

Prati

After Rome became capital of the newly unified Italian state in 1871, the meadows (*prati*) around the ramparts north of Borgo were required for housing for the staff of the ministries and parliament across the Tiber. The largest of the *piazze* by the Vatican walls was provocatively named after the Risorgimento, the movement that had destroyed the papacy's hold on Italy. Broad avenues were named after historic freedom fighters.

A solidly bourgeois district, Prati has a main drag – via Cola di Rienzo – that provides ample opportunities for retail therapy.

Imposing military barracks line viale delle Milizie, and the bombastic Palazzo di Giustizia (popularly known as il *palazzaccio*, 'the big ugly building') sits between piazza Cavour and the Tiber. On the riverbank is one of Catholic Rome's truly weird experiences: the Museo delle Anime dei Defunti.

Sights & museums

Museo delle Anime dei Defunti
Lungotevere Prati 12 (06 6880 6517). **Open** *mid Sept-June* 7-11am, 4.30-7.30pm daily. *July-mid Sept* 7-10am, 5.30-7.30pm daily. **Map** p141 E3 **⑧**

This macabre collection, attached to the neo-Gothic church of Sacro Cuore di Gesù in Prati, contains hand- and fingerprints left on the prayer books and clothes of the living by dead loved ones, to request masses to release their souls from purgatory.

Eating & drinking

Del Frate
Via degli Scipioni 118 (06 323 6437). **Meals served** 1-3pm, 6.30pm-12.30am Mon-Fri; 6.30pm-1.30am Sat, Sun. Closed 2wks Aug. **€€€**. **Map** p140 C2 **⑨**

This venerable Prati bottle shop expanded into a wine bar annexe a few years back. Of an evening, tables spill over into the *enoteca* itself, amid tall shelves crammed with bottles. The oven-baked ravioli with salmon and courgette sauce is a good demonstration of the modern approach; seconds might include a scallop of sea bass with pan-fried cicoria. The only off-note is the steep mark-up on wines.

Gran Caffè Esperia
Lungotevere dei Mellini 1 (06 3211 0016). **Open** *Oct-Apr* 7am-9.30pm daily. *May-Sept* 7am-midnight daily. **Map** p141 F3 **⑩**

The pavement tables at this newly restored belle-époque café are hotly contested when the sun shines on them

in the morning. Work on your tan while munching toasted *cornetti* with ham and cheese, or smoked salmon sandwiches. The coffee's great… or go straight for a prosecco.

L'Arcangelo
Via GG Belli 59-61 (06 321 0992). **Meals served** 1-2.30pm, 8-11.30pm Mon-Fri; 8-11pm Sat. Closed Aug. **€€€**. **Map** p141 D2 **⑪**

The elegant L'Arcangelo has wood panelling below tobacco-sponged walls, linen tablecloths and a soft jazz soundtrack. But it's what's on the plate that really impresses. A tartlet of octopus and potato with olive oil is simple but delicious, and fresh pasta *chitarrini* with marinated anchovies and fried artichokes a worthy follow-up. *Secondi*, like steamed *baccalà* (cod) with puréed broccoli and warm ricotta with cocoa beans, are clever variations on the Roman tradition. The wine list includes some real discoveries from small-scale Italian producers.

Osteria dell'Angelo
Via G Bettolo 32 (06 372 9470). **Meals served** 8-11pm Mon, Sat; 12.30-2.30pm, 8-11pm Tue-Fri. Closed 2wks Aug. **€€**. No credit cards. **Map** p140 B1 **⑫**

Recently expanded and given a lick of paint, this trat's decor still consists of photos of boxers and rugby players – the two sporting passions of host Angelo Croce. The menu – which, in the evening, comes at a fixed price (€25, or €30 for the luxe grilled-meat option), rough-and-ready house wine included – celebrates the Roman tradition in dishes like *tonnarelli cacio e pepe* (pasta with cheese and pepper) and meatballs flavoured with nutmeg, pine nuts and sultanas.

Pellacchia
Via Cola di Rienzo 103 (06 321 0807/ www.pellacchia.it). **Open** 6am-1am Tue-Sun. Closed 1wk Aug. **Map** p141 D2 **⑬**

This bar, located on Prati's busiest street, produces some of the tastiest ice-cream north of the river.

Vatican tack

If the rosary sellers who assail you before you even reach St Peter's Square get you down, spare a thought for medieval visitors: for them, the hard sell began almost as soon as they set foot in the Eternal City, with via de' Coronari (from *corona*, rosary) – then the main approach to the only bridge across to the Vatican – a regular snipers' alley of tack-sellers.

Then, souvenir-extras came in the shape of fingers and toes of 'saints', splinters of the 'True' cross, tatters of the 'Holy' shroud plus indulgences of very dubious origin. Nowadays, there are fewer body parts but no less bad taste in the objects on offer to remind you of your Holy Roman visit.

Stuck for a gift for the kids? How about a giant papal lollipop with Joseph Ratzinger's shining face etched in sugar – well worth €6.

Nothing for granny? Surely she'd treasure a gruesome, plasticised image of the crucified Jesus, with crown of thorns and mesmerising eyes that follow you around?

Colleagues in your office will no doubt appreciate that thoughtful ashtray in the shape of Bernini's colonnade and your mother-in-law will just love drying the dishes with her Sistine Chapel tea towel. Why not treat your brother to a bottle of imported German 'papal' beer on sale in the bottle shops and drinking holes of the Borgo?

For those difficult gifts, don't forget the life-size, hand-painted plaster busts of Pope John Paul II, or – easier to pack, and just what you need on sleepless nights – a glow-in-the-dark rosary. And you can hardly go wrong with a yellow and white Vatican City plastic car flag, or an extra large T-shirt with Michelangelo's *Pietà* emblazoned across the bosom.

Some souvenirs have obtained cult status, notably the press-out-and-play *Dressing up the Pope* book featuring items from John Paul's extensive ceremonial wardrobe (as yet, there's no Benedict version), or the Weeping Madonna of Civitavecchia car freshener. Wallet-sized religious images of the pope emitting an all too audible blessing were a recent sell-out.

Regular visitors to Rome stock up on purple knee-length bishop's socks from one of the numerous ecclesiastical suppliers located around Borgo Pio, and bulk-buy rare liqueurs, miracle-working cosmetics and fine chocolate, made by monks according to traditional recipes, at **Ai Monasteri** (corso Rinascimento 72, 06 6880 2783, www.monasteri.it).

Settembrini

*Via Luigi Settembrini 25 (06 323
2617).* **Meals served** 12.30-4pm,
8-11.30pm Mon-Sat. **€€€**. Closed
2wks Aug. **Map** off p141 D1 🄑

One of the most interesting newish kids
on the block, Settembrini mixes design
and tradition both in its warmly minimalist decor and in its menu. In chef
Marco Poddi's Italo fusion approach,
the flavours of his native Sardinia are
prominent (as in spaghetti with Cabras
sea urchins) and ingredients are sourced
with an obsessive regard for quality.
The place is open all day, from 11am
on, with *aperitivi* served from 6 to 8pm.

Shopping

Franchi

*Via Cola di Rienzo 200 (06 687
4651).* **Open** 8am-9pm Mon-Sat.
Map p140 C2 🄒

This dream of a deli has just about
anything you could ever want to eat:
cheeses from everywhere, cured meat
and fresh, ready-to-eat seafood dishes.
Perfect for picnic preparation.

Iron G

Via Cola di Rienzo 50 (06 321 6798).
Open 10.30am-7.30pm Mon-Sat.
Closed 2wks Aug. **Map** p141 E2 🄖

This warehousey boutique supplies
clubwear to the fashion victims of
this well-heeled neighbourhood. The
hippest labels mix with ethnic and
local accessories and some jewellery.

Studio Massoni

Via della Meloria 90 (06 322 7207).
Open 9am-1pm, 3-7pm Mon-Fri.
Closed Aug. No credit cards.
Map off p140 A2 🄗

There's a selection of classical busts in
gesso (plaster), while copies of just
about any statue that has taken your
fancy can be made to order.

Nightlife

Alexanderplatz

*Via Ostia 9 (06 3974 2171/www.
alexanderplatz.it).* **Open** 8.30pm-
1.30am daily. Closed June-Sept.

**Museo delle
Anime dei Defunti p149**

Admission free with monthly (€10)
membership. **Map** p140 A2 🄘

Rome's pioneer jazz club offers nightly
concerts with famous names from the
Italian and foreign scene.

The Place

*Via Alberico II 27 (06 6830 7137/www.
theplace.it).* **Open** 8.30pm-2.30am daily.
Closed mid June-Sept. **Admission**
€5-€15. **Map** p140 C3 🄙

A swish, vibrant jazz club with a
stage for live acts, The Place draws a
thirty- to forty-something crowd for
mostly Italian jazz bands, plus DJs
after the weekend acts.

Arts & Leisure

El Spa

*Via Plinio 15C/D (06 6819 2869/www.
elspa.it).* **Open** 10am-9pm Mon-Thur;
10am-10pm Fri, Sat; noon-9pm Sun.
Map p141 D2 🄛

Decorated in warm, Middle-Eastern
style, the spa specialises in holistic
treatments. Try the *mandi lulur*, an
ancient Indonesian treatment that
leaves you with silky-soft skin.

Parco degli Acquedotti

Out of Town

The Appian Way

Built in the fourth century BC
by statesman and censor Appius
Claudius Caecus, via Appia Antica
was Rome's first great military
highway, stretching to link *caput
mundi* with the Adriatic.

By the time it reached Brindisi in
121 BC, the Appia was the Romans'
main route to their eastern Empire
and had become known as the
regina varium, 'the Queen of Roads'.
Well-to-do Roman families built
their mausoleums alongside, and
soon it was lined with tombs, vaults
and sarcophagi.

Today only a fraction of this
magnificent funerary decoration
remains, but it suffices to make this
the most fascinating, and the most
picturesque, of the ancient roads.

Christians, too, began burying
their dead here (burial was always
performed outside a sacred city
boundary known as the *pomerium*),
initially in necropoli and later
underground, creating the 300-
kilometre (200-mile) network of
tunnels known as the **catacombs**.
This system wasn't used for secret
worship, as was once thought:
authorities were perfectly aware of
their existence. A Jewish catacomb
still exists at via Appia Antica 119.

Via Appia Antica suffered at the
hands of marauding Goths and
Normans; successive popes did as
much damage, grabbing any good
pieces of statuary or marble that
remained and reducing the ancient
monuments to unrecognisable
stumps. But this is still a wonderful
place to spend a day, preferably a

Sunday or holiday when all but local traffic is banned.

Explore more extensively by renting a bike at the **Centro Visite Parco dell'Appia Antica** (via Appia Antica 42, 06 512 6314, www.parcoappiaantica.org, open 9.30am-5.30pm Sun & holidays; on weekdays, call for information).

Another ancient route lies nearby: the great Roman aqueduct that brought fresh water from the hills near Tivoli dominates the **Parco degli Acquedotti**, accessible from viale Appio Claudio.

Getting there

You can take the hop-on, hop-off **Archeobus** (tickets €8), which leaves from Termini railway station about every 40 minutes between 9am and 4pm, and stops by most major sights. Alternatively, the following regular bus services ply part of the way:
118 from viale Aventino (Circo Massimo metro) to the catacombs of San Callisto and San Sebastiano.
218 from piazza San Giovanni to porta San Sebastiano, down the Appia to the Domine Quo Vadis? church, then along via Ardeatina.
660 from Colli Albani metro to the Circus of Maxentius and Tomb of Cecilia Metella.

Sights & museums

Catacombs of San Callisto
Via Appia Antica 78, 110 & 126 (06 513 0151/www.catacombe.roma.it).
Open 9am-noon, 2-5pm Mon, Tue, Thur-Sun. Closed late Jan-late Feb.
Admission €5; €3 reductions.
This is Rome's largest underground burial site. Buried in the 29km (12.5 miles) of tunnels were nine popes, dozens of martyrs and thousands of Christians. They are stacked down, with the oldest on the top. Named after third-century Pope Callixtus, the area became the first official cemetery of the

Church of Rome. The crypt of St Cecilia is the spot where this patron saint of music is believed to have been buried, before she was transferred to her eponymous church in Trastevere.

Catacombs of San Sebastiano
Via Appia Antica 136 (06 785 0350).
Open 9am-noon, 2-5pm Mon, Tue, Thur-Sat. Closed late Jan-late Feb.
Admission €5; €3 reductions.
The name 'catacomb' originated here, where a complex of underground burial sites situated near a tufa quarry was

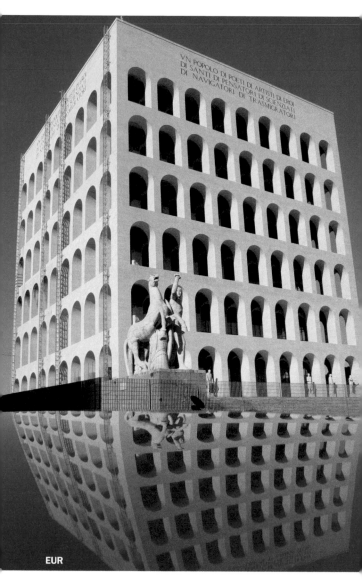

EUR

described as being *kata kymbas* – 'near the quarry'. The guided tour will take you into the crypt of St Sebastian, the martyr always depicted nastily pierced by a hail of arrows (though these were just one of several unpleasant tortures), who was buried here in the late third century. Above, the fourth-century basilica of San Sebastiano (open 8.30am-6pm daily) was originally called basilica Apostolorum, because the remains of Saints Peter and Paul were hidden here. On display is the marble slab in which Christ left his footprints during his miraculous apparition at the spot on the via Appia where the Domine Quo Vadis? church (open 7am-7pm daily) now stands.

Circus of Maxentius

Via Appia Antica 153 (06 780 1324).
Closed as this guide went to press; due to reopen late 2007.
This area of lovely green countryside contains one of the best-preserved Roman circuses. It was built by Emperor Maxentius for his private use, before his defeat and death at the hands of co-ruler Constantine in AD 312. Remains of the Imperial palace are perched above the track, at its northern end. Also found on this part of the site is the mausoleum Maxentius built for his beloved son Romulus.

Tomb of Cecilia Metella

Via Appia Antica 161 (06 780 0093).
Open *Nov-Mar* 9am-3.30pm daily. *Apr-Oct* 9am-6.30pm daily. **Admission** €6; €3 reductions. No credit cards.
Note: Opening hours are erratic.
This colossal cylinder of travertine is the final resting place of a woman who married into the wealthy Metella family in the first century BC. During the 14th century the powerful Caetani family incorporated the tomb into a fortress, adding the crenellations to the top of the structure. The spot where Cecilia was buried is a fine example of brick dome-making. Downstairs, pieces of the volcanic rock used in the construction of via Appia Antica can be seen.

EUR

Italian Fascism was at once monstrous and absurd, but out of it came some of 20th-century Europe's most fascinating architecture and urban planning.

In the early 1930s, Rome's governor Giuseppe Bottai – the leading arbiter of taste among the Fascists – had the idea of expanding landbound Rome along via Ostiense towards the sea, some 20km (12.5 miles) away. Using as an excuse the universal exhibition pencilled in for 1942, he intended to combine cultural and exhibition spaces with a monument to the regime.

Architect Marcello Piacentini was charged with co-ordinating the ambitious project, but the planning committee became so bogged down in argument that very little had been achieved by the outbreak of World War II. After the war, work resumed in an entirely different spirit. Still known as EUR (*Esposizione universale romana*), it's now a business district, where unrelieved planes of icy travertine and reinterpretations of classical monuments let you know you're not in Kansas any more.

A number of didactic museums – the Museo dell'Alto Medioevo, **Museo della Civiltà Romana** (now containing a new and very active astronomy museum and planetarium), Museo delle Arti e Tradizioni Popolari, the Museo Preistorico ed Etnografico – allow visitors a glimpse inside these grandiose monuments to the hubris of Italian Fascism.

Getting there

Take metro B to EUR Fermi or EUR Palasport, or buses 30Exp, 170, 714.

ROME BY AREA

Sights & museums

Abbazia delle Tre Fontane
Via Acque Salvie 1 (06 540 1655).
Open *Santi Vincenzo e Anastasio* 6am-12.30pm, 3-8pm daily. *Other churches* 8am-1pm, 3-6pm daily. *Shop* 9am-1pm, 3.30-7pm daily.

North-east of EUR centre (and reachable by buses 671, 707, 716, 761, 767) lies a haven of ancient, eucalyptus-scented green, with three churches commemorating the points where St Paul's head supposedly bounced after it was severed from his body in AD 67. (Being a Roman citizen, Paul was eligible for the relatively quick and painless head-chop, as opposed to the long, drawn-out crucifixion.) These are the grounds of the Trappist monastery of Tre Fontane, where water has gurgled and birds have sung since the fifth century. The church of San Paolo delle Tre Fontane is said to be built on the spot where the apostle was executed; apart from a column to which Paul is supposed to have been tied, all traces of the fifth-century church were done away with in 1599 by architect Giacomo della Porta, who was also responsible for the two other churches. Monks planted the eucalyptus trees in the 1860s, believing they would drive away the malarial mosquitoes; a liqueur is now brewed from the trees and sold in a little shop (no credit cards) along with chocolate and remedies for all ills.

Museo dell'Alto Medioevo
Viale Lincoln 3 (06 5422 8199). **Open** 9am-7.30pm Tue-Sun. **Admission** €2; €1 reductions. No credit cards.

Focusing on the decorative arts from the period between the fall of the Roman Empire and the Renaissance, this museum has intricate gold- and silver-decorated swords, buckles and horse tackle, as well as more mundane objects: ceramic bead jewellery and the metal frames of what may be Europe's earliest folding chairs.

Museo della Civiltà Romana
Piazza G Agnelli 10 (06 592 6135/06 592 6041). **Open** *Museum* 9am-2pm Tue-Sun. **Admission** *Museum* €6.50; €3 reductions. *Planetarium* (booking obligatory 06 8207 7304) €6.50; €4.50 reductions. No credit cards.

This museum dates from 1937, when Mussolini mounted a celebration to mark the second millennium of Augustus becoming the first emperor. The fact that the celebration came about 35 years too early was overlooked by *il Duce*, who was eager to draw parallels between Augustus' glory and his own.

With its blank white walls and lofty, echoing corridors, the building is Fascist-classical at its most grandiloquent. There's a fascinating cutaway model of the Colosseum's maze of tunnels and lifts, as well as casts of the intricate reliefs on Trajan's column. The centrepiece is a giant model of Rome in the fourth century AD, which puts the city's scattered fragments and artefacts into context. The palazzo also contains the brand new Museo dell'Astrologia and a planetarium (www2.comune.roma.it/planetario).

Museo delle Arti e Tradizioni Popolari
Piazza G Marconi 8 (06 592 6148/06 591 2669). **Open** 9am-4pm Tue-Fri; 9am-8pm Sat, Sun. **Admission** €4; €2 reductions. No credit cards.
Note: Staff shortages sometimes force this museum to close in the afternoon. It pays to call ahead.

This enormous collection is dedicated to Italian folk art and rural tradition. Exhibits include elaborately decorated carts and horse tackle, as well as craft-related implements and a bizarre collection of offerings left to local saints.

Museo Preistorico ed Etnografico L Pigorini
Piazza G Marconi 14 (06 549 521). **Open** 9am-2pm Tue-Sun. **Admission** €4; €2 reductions. No credit cards.

This museum displays prehistoric Italian artefacts together with material from a range of world cultures. The lobby contains a reconstruction of the prehistoric Guattari cave near Monte Circeo, south of Rome, with a genuine

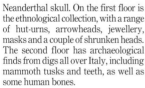

Ostia Antica

Neanderthal skull. On the first floor is the ethnological collection, with a range of hut-urns, arrowheads, jewellery, masks and a couple of shrunken heads. The second floor has archaeological finds from digs all over Italy, including mammoth tusks and teeth, as well as some human bones.

Ostia Antica

If you're contemplating the punishing day trip from Rome to Pompeii, do yourself a favour and come here instead. The excavated ruins (*scavi*) of Ostia Antica convey the everyday life of a working Roman town every bit as well as Pompeii does.

Five minutes' walk from the entrance to the excavations, the medieval village of Ostia Antica has a castle (built in 1483-86 for the bishop of Ostia, the future Pope Julius II) and picturesque cottages, which were inhabited by the people who worked in the nearby salt pans.

Getting there

Ostia Antica is a 20-minute train ride from Roma-Lido station, next to Piramide metro.

Sights & museums

Scavi di Ostia Antica

Viale dei Romagnoli 717, Ostia Antica (06 5635 8099/www.itnw.roma.it/ ostia/scavi). **Open** *Nov-Feb* 8.30am-4pm Tue-Sun. *Mar* 8.30am-5pm Tue-Sun. *Apr-Oct* 8.30am-6pm Tue-Sun. **Admission** €4; €2 reductions. No credit cards.
Legend says that Ostia was founded by Ancus Martius, the fourth king of Rome, in the seventh century BC, although the oldest remains date 'only' from c330 BC. Ostia was Rome's main port for more than 600 years.

Abandoned after sackings by barbarians in the fifth century, the town was gradually buried by river mud. Over the centuries, the coastline has receded, leaving Ostia landlocked and obsolete. Visit on a sunny weekday and bring a picnic (not actually allowed but keep a low profile and you probably won't be ejected).

The *decumanus maximus* (high street) runs from the Porta Romana for almost a kilometre (half a mile), past the theatre and forum, before forking left to what used to be the seashore. The right fork, via della Foce, leads to the Tiber. Either side of these main arteries lies a network of intersecting lanes where the best discoveries can be made.

Behind the theatre is one of Ostia's most interesting features: the Forum of the Corporations. Here the trade guilds had their offices, and mosaics on the floor of shops that ring the open square refer to the products each guild dealt in – shipowners had ships on the floor, ivory dealers had elephants. Further along on the right is the old mill, where the furrows ploughed by the blindfolded donkeys that turned them are still visible. In the tangle of streets between the decumanus and the museum, don't miss the *thermopolium* – an ancient Roman bar. Located off the forum to the south-east are the forum baths and nearby is the *forica*, or ancient public latrine. Off via della Foce, the House of Cupid and Psyche is an elegant fourth-century construction; the House of the Dioscuri has beautiful mosaics; the Insula of the Charioteers still has many of its frescoes.

ROME BY AREA

Tivoli

Just 20km (12.5 miles) from Rome, Tivoli (ancient Tibur) is home to two Unesco World Heritage Sites – **Villa d'Este**, in Tivoli itself, and **Hadrian's Villa**, five kilometres (three miles) down the hill – which make it an ideal destination for a day trip.

Getting there

Take the COTRAL bus from Ponte Mammolo metro station; note that the bus marked *autostrada* is a quicker service. If you're travelling by bus, visit Tivoli town first (the regular service is marked 'via Tiburtina' and takes about 45mins to Tivoli) and get off at the main square (piazza Garibaldi) for Villa d'Este. From the bus stop in front of the tourist office in piazza Garibaldi, frequent orange (local) buses serve Villa Adriana (10mins) down the hill. From Villa Adriana, both local and COTRAL buses travel to Rome.

Local trains go to Tivoli from Tiburtina station; bus 4 goes from Tivoli station to the centre of town for the Villa d'Este.

Sights & museums

Hadrian's Villa (Villa Adriana)

Via di Villa Adriana, Villa Adriana (0774 382 733). **Open** *Nov-Jan* 9am-5pm daily. *Feb* 9am-6pm daily. *Mar, Oct* 9am-6.30pm daily. *Apr, Sept* 9am-7pm daily. *May-Aug* 9am-7.30pm daily. **Admission** €6.50; €3.25 reductions. *Special exhibitions* €2.50 extra. No credit cards.

Villa Adriana, the retreat of Emperor Hadrian, is strewn across a gentle slope. Built from AD 118 to 134, it has some fascinating architectural spaces and water features.

Hadrian was an amateur architect and is believed to have designed many of the elements in his villa himself. In the centuries following the fall of the Empire it became a luxury quarry for treasure-hunters. At least 500 pieces of statuary in collections around the world have been identified as coming from this site.

The restored remains lie amid olive groves and cypresses and are still impressive. The model in the pavilion just up the hill from the entrance gives an idea of the villa's original size.

In the valley below is the lovely *Canopus*: a long, narrow pool, framed on three sides by columns and statues, including a marble crocodile. At the far (southern) end of the pool is a structure called the *Serapeum*, used for lavish entertaining. Summer guests enjoyed an innovative form of air-conditioning – a sheet of water poured from the roof over the open face of the building, enclosing diners.

Villa d'Este

Piazza Trento 1, Tivoli (0774 332 920/www.villadestetivoli.info). **Open** 8.30am-one hour before sunset Tue-Sun. **Admission** €6.50; €3.25 reductions. No credit cards.

Dominating the town of Tivoli is the Villa d'Este, a lavish pleasure palace built in 1550 for Cardinal Ippolito d'Este, son of Lucrezia Borgia, to a design by architect Pirro Ligorio. Inside the villa there are frescoes and paintings by Correggio, Da Volterra and Perin Del Vaga (including views of the villa shortly after its construction). But the gardens are the main attraction. Ligorio developed a complex 'hydraulic machine' that channelled water from the River Aniene (still the source today) through a series of canals under the garden. Using know-how borrowed from the Romans, he created 51 fountains spread around the terraced gardens. The sybils (pagan high-priestesses) are a recurring theme – it was at Tivoli that the Tiburtine sybil foretold the birth of Christ – and the grottoes of the sybils behind the vast fountain of Neptune echo with thundering artificial waterfalls.

Technological gimmickry was another big feature; the Owl Fountain (operates every two hours from 10am) imitated an owl's song using a hydraulic mechanism, while the *Fontana dell'organo idraulico* (restored and now in operation every two hours from 10.30am) used water pressure to compress air and play tunes.

Electric carts are provided free for disabled visitors to tour the gardens; booking is essential (0774 335 850).

Villa d'Este

Where the original entrance to the villa lay is uncertain; today, the first space you'll encounter after climbing the road from the ticket office is the *pecile* (or *poikile*), a large pool that was once surrounded by a portico with high walls, of which only one remains. Directly east of the *poikile*, the *Teatro marittimo* (Maritime Theatre) is one of the most delightful inventions in the whole villa. A circular brick wall, 45 metres (150 feet) in diameter, encloses a moat, at the centre of which is an island of columns and brickwork; today a cement bridge crosses the moat, but originally there would have been wooden bridges, which could be removed.

Beneath the building called the winter palace, visitors can walk along the perfectly preserved *cryptoporticus* (covered corridor).

FORTY 47 SEVEN
ALBERGO IN ROMA

Fortysevenhotel
Via Petroselli 47, 00186 – Rome
Tel +39.06.6787816; Fax +39.06.69190726
contact@fortysevenhotel.com
www.fortysevenhotel.com - www.circusbar.it

Essentials

Hotels

Until recently a city of polar opposite accommodation options – exorbitantly expensive, often soulless luxury hotels on the one hand; cheap *pensioni* of dubious cleanliness on the other – Rome has now started to generate the range of hotels you might expect for one of the most-visited destinations on the planet. The city's ever-increasing popularity has had an inevitable impact on hotel rates; Rome is a more expensive place to stay than many other European capitals. The days of the dirt-cheap hotel bed are well and truly over (though for anyone who doesn't mind a curfew or sleeping under a crucifix, there are still some bargain convents; see box p176) and you're as unlikely as ever to find a room with a view without making a sizeable dent in your holiday allowance.

It may not come cheap, but the general standard of accommodation in the Eternal City has improved dramatically in recent years. The luxury hotel market, in particular, has exploded, due partly to a council scheme to revamp old *palazzi* in down-at-heel areas like the Esquilino, and partly to upscale districts such as via Veneto experiencing a resurgence. The recent Italian trend for hotels created by fashion designers had seen haute couturiers sidelining Rome in favour of trendier Florence and Milan for their temples to style; a much-needed injection of glamour came in May 2006 with the opening

of fashion designer Ferragamo's swanky **Portrait Suites** (p172).

The mid-range market is also flourishing, and fierce competition from the boutique hotels popping up all over the *centro storico* means that older-style hotels and *pensioni* are being forced to upgrade both amenities and decor if they want to stay in business.

It's only at the lower end that Rome lags behind: in all but a few notable cases – for example, **The Beehive** (p175) – the gulf in standards between rock bottom and the lower edge of moderate is immense: in Rome, it's worth paying just a little bit more.

Location

There are now three five-star hotels within a stone's throw of Termini station, but the vast majority of hotels in this area – the **Esquilino** – are cheap *pensioni* swarming

ESSENTIALS

Buonanotte Garibaldi p179

with budget backpackers. It's not Rome's most picturesque corner, and almost certainly not what you dreamt of for your Roman holiday. It's definitely worth considering looking further afield, even if it costs you a bit more. Though Termini is only a few minutes' bus ride from the centre, you're likely to end up wishing you were more in the thick of things.

If you're staying for a few days, think about looking for a room in the *centro storico*. A shower between sightseeing and dinner, and a wander (rather than a bus) back to the hotel afterwards can make all the difference. The area around **campo de' Fiori** offers mid-priced hotels with lots of character, and a central piazza that is a lively market by day and a hip Roman hangout by night; the area around the **Pantheon** and **piazza Navona** is generally a bit pricier. Moving distinctly up the price range, Rome's top-end hotels have traditionally clustered around **via Veneto**; it's nothing like as lively as it was in its *dolce vita* heyday, and there's a strong whiff of expense accounts in the air. But brave efforts are underway to relaunch this famous street, and it definitely has a certain grandeur. The **Tridente** area near the Spanish Steps, hub of designer shopping, is full of elegant hotels at the upper end of the price scale.

If you're looking for some peace, the **Celio**, just beyond the Colosseum, offers a break from the frantic activity of the *centro storico*, as does another of Rome's seven hills: the **Aventine**, an exclusive residential outpost no distance at all from the *centro*.

Heading across the river, the characterful **Trastevere** district is a pleasant place to stay, with good bus and tram connections to the major sights; in recent years it has blossomed from hotel-desert to hotel-bonanza, offering an array of price options. Just north of Trastevere, the medieval alleys around the **Vatican** give on to the busy retail thoroughfares of **Prati**: it's lively during the day but hushed at night.

Booking a room

Always reserve a room well in advance, especially at peak times, which now means most of the year, with lulls during winter (January to March) and in the dog days of August. If you're coming at the same time as a major Christian holiday (Christmas or Easter) it's recommended to book weeks, or even months, ahead.

Increasingly, booking is via hotel websites, but you may also be asked to fax confirmation of a booking, with a credit card number as deposit. In high season, smaller hotels may ask for a money order to secure rooms. The www.venere.com booking service offers many hotels in all price ranges. If you arrive with nowhere to stay, try the **APT** tourist office (p187), which provides a list of hotels; you have to do the booking yourself. The **Enjoy Rome** tourist information agency (p187) offers a free booking service, as does the **Hotel Reservation** (www.hotelreservation.it) service, which has desks at Fiumicino airport (06 699 1000), Ciampino airport (06 7934 9427) and at Termini station (06 482 3952).

Avoid the touts that hang around Termini: you're likely to end up paying more than you should for a very grotty hotel.

Standards & prices

Italian hotels are classified on a star system, from one to five. One star usually indicates *pensioni*, which are cheap but have very few facilities; you may have to share a

ESSENTIALS

bathroom. The more stars, the more facilities a hotel will have, but bear in mind that a higher rating offers no guarantee of friendliness, cleanliness or decent service.

Prices generally rise by a relentless ten per cent a year in Rome, but it's worth keeping an eye out for low-season deals on hotel websites. If you're staying in a group or for a longish period, ask about discounts.

If you're visiting with children, most hotels will be happy to squeeze a cot or camp bed into a room, but they will probably charge 30 to 50 per cent extra for the privilege.

Our choice

The hotels listed in this guide have been chosen for their location, because they offer value for money, or simply because they have true Roman character. Unless stated, rates are for rooms with bathrooms, and include breakfast.

In the deluxe category (€€€€) the emphasis is on opulence and luxury; a standard double in high season is likely to set you back anywhere from €400 and up. Those in mid- to upper-price ranges (€€-€€€) are smaller, many in old *palazzi*, with pretty, though often small, bedrooms. Expect to pay between €100 and €250 for a moderately priced hotel, and anywhere from €250 to €400 for an expensive room. *Pensioni* (€-€€) are fairly basic, but those listed here are friendly and usually family-run; the cheapest cost less than €100 per night.

Few Roman hotels – with the exception of the grander ones – have access for the disabled. Though staff are generally very willing to help guests that have mobility difficulties, the real problem is that most places have so many stairs that there's not much they can do. As hotels renovate, they do tend to add a room for the disabled if they can.

A no-smoking law introduced in 2005 applies to hotels' public areas but most are still fairly laissez-faire when it comes to guests lighting up in the rooms so long as they open a window. Hotels which are strictly non-smoking, or which have designated non-smoking rooms, have been indicated in the text.

Il Centro

Abruzzi

Piazza della Rotonda 69 (06 9784 1369/www.hotelabruzzi.it). €€.
The splendid location is this hotel's selling point, although recent renovations have upgraded what used to be a dingy establishment. Many rooms have breathtaking views of the Pantheon; some are very small. Breakfast is taken in a nearby café.

Hotel Teatro di Pompeo p168

Campo de' Fiori

Piazza del Biscione 6 (06 6880 6865/ www.hotelcampodefiori.com). €€.
Just off busy campo de' Fiori, this hotel underwent a complete renovation in 2006, with impressive results: though not spacious, the rooms are finely fitted out in rich colours. The small but elegant bathrooms have bronze-effect tiles with antique mirrors. The pretty roof terrace has great views.

Due Torri

Vicolo del Leonetto 23-25 (06 6880 6956/www.hotelduetorriroma.com). €€.
In a labyrinth of cobbled streets, the Due Torri has a welcoming feel. The 26 rooms are cosy rather than spacious, and kitted out with dark wooden furniture. If you're persistent, you might get one of the rooms with a private terrace overlooking the rooftops.

Pensione Barrett

Largo Argentina 47 (06 686 8481 /www.pensionebarrett.com). €.
A bewildering number of antiques and curios decorate the hotel, giving it a vaguely eccentric feel. Rooms are a mishmash of faux-classical columns and mouldings, dark wood furniture, original wood-beamed ceilings and pastel walls; some have great views over largo Argentina. Breakfast (which costs extra) is served in the rooms; air-con is an extra €8 a night. Poet Elizabeth Barrett Browning stayed here in 1848.

Relais Palazzo Taverna & Locanda degli Antiquari

NEW *Via dei Gabrielli 92 (06 2039 8064/www.relaispalazzotaverna.com). €€.*
In a 15th-century building, these twin *residenze* have sleek, modern decor. Spacious bedrooms have white-painted wood ceilings, wallpaper with bold graphics and bedlinen in spicy tones. Breakfast is served in the rooms.

Residenza in Farnese

Via del Mascherone 59 (06 6889 1388/ www.residenzafarneseroma.it). €€€.

This converted convent in a narrow ivy-lined alley has been refurbished without losing its charm. A chandelier in the lobby lends a sense of opulence; details like home-made baked goods and jams for breakfast reflect the homely charm of the place. Rooms run the gamut from basic updated cells with small marble bathrooms to more comfortable pastel-hued rooms with hand-painted furnishings.

Sole al Pantheon

Piazza della Rotonda 63 (06 678 0441/ www.hotelsolealpantheon.com). €€€.
Dating back to the 15th century, the Sole al Pantheon is one of Europe's oldest hotels. Rooms have a fresh feel though, with tiles and pretty frescoes. Bathrooms are not luxurious but they do, however, have whirlpool baths. Rooms at the front have superb views over the Pantheon.

Hotel Teatro di Pompeo

Largo del Pallaro 8 (06 6830 0170/ www.hotelteatrodipompeo.it). €€.
This small, friendly hotel occupies a palazzo that was built on the site of the ancient Teatro di Pompeo; its *pièce de résistance* is its cave-like breakfast room, tucked away inside the ancient ruins. The guest rooms are simply decorated in neutral tones, with terracotta floors and high, wood-beamed ceilings. Opt for one of the rooms in the main hotel building rather than those in the more basic annexe a few streets away.

Teatro Pace 33

Via del Teatro Pace 33 (06 687 9075/ www.hotelteatropace.com). €€.
Hidden away on a cobbled alley near busy piazza Navona, this 17th-century former cardinal's residence has a Baroque spiral staircase that winds up four floors (there's no lift, but chairs are provided every couple of floors for the out-of-breath). Rooms are spacious and elegantly decorated with wood floors, heavy drapes and marble bathrooms; all have their original beamed ceilings. Breakfast is served in the rooms.

Cool pools

Exedra

Cooling off in the Eternal City during the long hot summer is no easy feat. Public pools are dedicated almost exclusively to swimming classes for local *bambini*; few hotels are able to offer anything more refreshing than a lukewarm shower.

The exceptions to this rule are at the very top of the accommodation pile. Some allow non-residents to use their watery facilities – but even this comes at a price.

Space constraints in the centre of Rome mean that to swim, you have to leave the ground.

At the **Radisson SAS es. Hotel** (p177), acres of decking around a designer rooftop pool and chic cocktail bar afford glorious views over the cityscape. In theory, it's open (June-Sept) to clients only, though if you happen to phone ahead when the pool isn't too crowded, you may be admitted; it costs €40 per day for use of the pool and wellness centre.

The view from the rooftop pool of the **Exedra** (p175) is rather more typically Roman, stretching from the Baths of Diocletian (p101) right across the *centro storico*. Again, this facility is for residents only… though with a phone call and payment of around €50 (the fee varies), you can take the waters too.

Management plans to keep the pool at the new-for-2007 **155 Via Veneto** (p171) for clients only. So if you want to soak while admiring a swathe of city from verdant Villa Borghese across to the Vatican, you'll have to book a room.

On Monte Mario, with a dramatic view over the whole of Rome, the **Cavalieri Hilton** (via Cadlolo 101, 06 35 091, www.cavalieri-hilton.it, €45 Mon-Fri, €65 Sat, Sun) has a near-Olympic-sized pool where serious swimmers mix with lounger-bound sun-worshippers clad in designer swimwear.

On the fringes of Villa Borghese, the pool at the **Parco dei Principi** (via Frescobaldi 5, 06 854 421, €45 Mon-Fri, €60 Sat, Sun) is a magnet at weekends for the well-dressed, well-heeled residents of the exclusive Parioli district.

ESSENTIALS

**OUR CLIMATE NEEDS
A HELPING HAND TODAY**

Be a smart traveller. Help to offset your carbon emissions
from your trip by pledging Carbon Trees with Trees for Cities.

All the Carbon Trees that you donate through Trees for Cities
are genuinely planted as additional trees in our projects.

Trees for Cities is an independent charity working with local
communities on tree planting projects.

www.treesforcities.org   Tel 020 7587 1320

Trees for Cities
Charity registration number 1002154

Tridente & Borghese

155 Via Veneto

NEW *Via Veneto 155 (06 322 0404/ www.155viaveneto.com).* €€€€.
New for spring 2007, this boutique hotel towards the top of via Veneto offers 80 doubles and 40 suites done up in art deco style, with bathrooms in marble and teak, and luxurious touches such as cashmere blankets and Bang & Olufsen sound systems in some rooms. The ambitious design incorporates a rooftop pool and, by the end of 2007, a 600 sq m spa.

Aleph

Via di San Basilio 15 (06 422 901/ www.boscolohotels.com). €€€€.
This Adam Tihany-designed flight of fancy comes with a theme – heaven and hell – with common areas in various intensities of devil-red, and bright, 'heavenly' bedrooms. It's a world away from the luxe-but-dull decor of many of via Veneto's megahotels, making it a favourite of the fashion set. A top-floor terrace bar and restaurant operate in warmer months; there's a subterranean spa in white and icy blue. Rooms are modern and luxurious.

Casa Howard

Via Capo le Case 18 (06 6992 4555/ www.casahoward.com). €€.
All rooms in this beautiful *residenza* near piazza di Spagna have been individually designed with an emphasis on quality. Some rooms have (private) bathrooms along the hall. There's a Turkish bath too. The five new (and slightly more expensive) rooms added around the corner at 149 via Sistina have en-suite bathrooms. Massages can be arranged at both properties.

Daphne Inn

Via degli Avignonesi 20; via di San Basilio 55 (06 8745 0087/www. daphne-rome.com). €€.
The Daphne Inn has two locations: one near the Trevi Fountain, the other off via Veneto. Each has seven rooms – some with en-suite baths and some that

Teatro Pace 33 p168

share – all of which are fitted out in organic-modern style with terracotta floors, neutral tones and simple framed leaf prints on the walls.

De Russie

Via del Babuino 9 (06 328 881/ www.hotelderussie.it). €€€€.
The De Russie's modern elegance is a million miles away from the luxury-schmaltz of many hotels on via Veneto. Fabulous gardens and a state-of-the-art health centre make it a star-magnet, though occasionally abrupt service can fall short of what you might expect.

Eden

Via Ludovisi 49 (06 478 121/ www.starwood.com). €€€€.
Elegantly understated, the Eden offers the attentiveness and attention to detail of a top-notch hotel without the stuffiness. Handsome reception rooms, tastefully decorated bedrooms, and a roof terrace with restaurant, piano bar – and truly spectacular views.

ESSENTIALS

Fontanella Borghese

Largo Fontanella Borghese 84 (06 6880 9504/06 6880 9624/www. fontanellaborghese.com). €€€.

This hotel is elegantly done out in relaxing cream and muted colours, brightened by a generous array of potted plants. Shopping meccas via del Corso and via Condotti are just around the corner: it's an ideal bolthole when the credit cards start to melt.

Hassler Villa Medici

Piazza Trinità dei Monti 6 (06 699 340/ www.hotelhasslerroma.com). €€€€.

This is one of Rome's classic hotels, with all the trimmings you might expect: chandeliers everywhere, polished wood and marble, plush fabrics and grand oil paintings, and a garden out back. The attentiveness of the staff distinguishes the Hassler from the impersonal service at Rome's top chain hotels. A few steps away, Il Palazzetto (www.wineacademyroma.com) is an annexe under the same ownership.

Hotel Art

Via Margutta 56 (06 328 711/ www.hotelart.it). €€€€.

Opened in 2002 on a street famed for its art studios, this hotel's lobby has white pods serving as check-in and concierge desks. Hallways are in retina-burning shades, but bedrooms have creamy bed linens and dark wood furniture. There's a small gym.

Inn at the Spanish Steps

Via Condotti 85 (06 6992 5657/ www.atspanishsteps.com). €€€€.

The Inn at the Spanish Steps offers luxury boutique-hotel accommodation smack in the middle of one of the world's most famous shopping streets. Rooms are an extravagant mix of plush fabrics and antiques; some of the deluxe rooms have 17th-century frescoes. Just down the road, its sister establishment – View at the Spanish Steps – has more restrained decor, with sober grey and blue fabrics, dark-wood floors and black-and-white tiled bathrooms. The junior suite boasts a dead-ahead view of the Spanish Steps.

Pensione Panda

Via della Croce 35 (06 678 0179/ www.hotelpanda.it). €.

Panda's location, near the piazza di Spagna, is its main selling point. Its rooms are clean but very basic; newly renovated rooms have high, wood-beamed ceilings and terracotta floors. Air-con is an extra €6 per night. There's no lift and no breakfast, but *centro storico* bargains are hard to come by, and Panda is usually booked solid in high season.

Portrait Suites

NEW *Via Bocca di Leone 23 (06 6938 0742/reservations 055 2726 4000/ www.lungarnohotels.com).* €€€€.

Opened in spring 2006, the stylish Portrait Suites is owned by fashion designer Salvatore Ferragamo. Memorabilia from the designer's archives decorate the hallways; in the bedrooms, a black-and-slate colour scheme is offset with touches of pink and lime. There are spacious marble bathrooms, walk-in wardrobes and – ta dah! – a glamorous kitchenette. Breakfast is served in the rooms or on the spectacular terrace.

Residenza A

Via Veneto 183 (06 486 700/ www.hotelviaveneto.it). €€€.

On the first floor of an imposing palazzo, Residenza A is a boutique hotel with splashy modern art enlivening its grey and black colour scheme. The rooms have been luxuriously finished, with great extras such as flat-screen computers and free internet, roomy showers and Bulgari bath products.

Residenza Cellini

Via Modena 5 (06 4782 5204/ www.residenzacellini.it). €€.

This luminous and spacious *residenza* has huge guest rooms decorated with *faux*-antique wooden furniture. The bathrooms have jacuzzis or showers with hydro-massage. On the floor that opened in January 2007, three rooms have balconies and all are decorated in the same classic style; there's a terrace too. Non-smoking.

Inn at the Roman Forum p177

ESSENTIALS

Radisson SAS es. Hotel p177

Westin Excelsior

Via V Veneto 125 (06 47 081/
www.starwood.com). €€€€.
After its wildly expensive makeover in
2002, the Excelsior's entrance is lavish
and its rooms – with marble bathrooms
– are a Hollywood-style fantasy. The
Villa La Cupola suite is the priciest bed
in Rome at just over €20,000 a night.

Esquilino & Celio

The Beehive

Via Marghera 8 (06 4470 4553/www.
the-beehive.com). €.
American owners Steve and Linda
Brenner mix their penchant for design-
icon furnishings with reasonable rates
and basic amenities to create a 'youth
hostel meets boutique hotel' vibe.
There's a sunny garden, an all-organic
restaurant and a yoga studio, plus free
internet access. Breakfast not included.

Capo d'Africa

Via Capo d'Africa 54 (06 772 801/
www.hotelcapodafrica.com). €€€€.
The Capo d'Africa's lobby may be
somewhat hotel-design-by-numbers
but its location, on a quiet street near
the Colosseum, is great. The rooms are
spacious and comfortable, if bland; the
rooftop breakfast room has knock-out
views of the Colosseum.

Domus Sessoriana

Piazza Santa Croce in Gerusalemme 10
(06 706 151/www.domussessoriana.it).
€€.
Reminders of this hotel's devotional
past – it occupies part of the monastery
attached to the church of Santa Croce
in Gerusalemme – are everywhere,
from the huge religious canvases to the
narrow ex-refectory where breakfast is
served. Tastefully-decorated rooms are
divided into two wings, 'Conventual'
and 'Aurelian'; the rooms in the former,
overlooking the monastery's gorgeous
vegetable garden, are more pleasant.

Exedra

Piazza della Repubblica 47 (06 489 381/
www.boscolohotels.com). €€€€.
From its splendid porticoed exterior to
its opulent lobby, the Exedra is very
glamorous. The rooms run from plush
and utterly comfortable to outrageous.
From May to September, the rooftop
bar/restaurant and pool offer spectacular views. There's a spa too. The only
drawback is the location: it's a little too
close to Termini station for comfort.

To a nunnery

Casa di Santa
Francesca Romana

Once, Rome's religious institutes were solely the resort of penniless pilgrims. These days, the more central, sophisticated religious houses have discovered just how lucrative the tourist trade can be.

Many of these holy hostelries fall into the mid-price range… but offer the decor and facilities of a lowly *pensione*. What they lack in creature comforts, however, they make up for in location. And in some cases, this is breathtaking.

If you fancy staying on stately piazza Farnese, your only option is the **Casa di Santa Brigida** (via Monserrato 54, 06 6889 2596, www.brigidine.org, €€), which offers spectacular views across the *centro storico* from its terrace. But rooms in this 15th-century palazzo are somewhat spartan for doubles priced at €190 and the nuns are famously abrupt.

Rather more sumptuous, the **Residenza Paolo VI** (via Paolo VI 29, 06 684 870, www.residenza paolovi.com, €€€) is owned by the Augustinian order; its jaw-dropping

roof terrace brings you eye to eye with the dome of St Peter's. It's under the same management as, and slightly more comfortable than, the **Palazzo Cardinale Cesi** (via della Conciliazione 51, 06 6819 3222, www.palazzocesi.it, €€€). From this hotel, in the mother house of the Salvatorian order, you step out the front door and into piazza San Pietro.

A little further down the avenue leading to the basilica, the **Hotel Columbus** (via della Conciliazione 33, 06 686 5435, www.hotel columbus.net, €€€) occupies a splendid palazzo with a glorious central courtyard, owned by the Equestrian Order of the Knights of the Holy Sepulchre. For a four-star, it's a trifle austere.

In picturesque Trastevere, the **Casa di Santa Francesca Romana** (p179) is wonderfully quiet and perfectly situated for sightseeing. But with narrow, creaky beds, the Pio Opera dei Santi Esercizi Spirituali that runs the place seems bent on ensuring that your visit to the heart of Christendom remains a spiritual experience. You'll be hard pressed, however, to find cheaper family rooms in this part of town.

At the **Domus Sessoriana** (p175), in the monastery attached to the church of Santa Croce in Gerusalemme, guests' footsteps echo along high-ceilinged corridors like those of monks.

To get bargain-basement prices you'll have to settle for something a little less central. The following websites will help you choose:
- www.monasterystays.com
- www.santasusanna.org
- www.hospites.it

Inn at the Roman Forum

NEW *Via degli Ibernesi 30 (06 6919 0970/www.theinnattheromanforum. com).* €€€€.
Opened in 2006, this boutique hotel's location, on a quiet, picturesque street near the Forum, gives it an exclusive feel. The rooms are an elegant mix of rich fabrics and antiques; the spacious deluxe rooms have canopied beds and marble bathrooms. Breakfast is served on the roof terrace, or in a cosy room with open fire. The two executive suites can be booked together as the Master Garden Suite, an exclusive apartment with a walled garden.

Lancelot

Via Capo d'Africa 47 (06 7045 0615/ www.lancelothotel.com). €€.
This beautifully kept and attractive family-run hotel has elegant mixes of linen, wood and tiles in the bedrooms, some of which have terraces facing the Palatine and the Colosseum. The reception has been given a personal touch with tiled floors and antique furniture, along with some unusual *objets*.

Nerva

Via Tor de' Conti 3 (06 678 1835/ www.hotelnerva.com). €€.
The family-run Nerva is handy for the Forum, and the rather old-fashioned rooms have all been refurbished. The staff are a friendly bunch.

Radisson SAS es. Hotel

Via F Turati 171 (06 444 841/www. rome.radissonsas.com). €€€€.
Built on the site of an ancient cemetery (digs are on show by the entrance), this 'concept' hotel caters for business clients – who don't balk at the location, by the train station – and diehard design fans. The vast rooftop has a bar and pool. In the all-white rooms, the bed is on a low platform, divided from the bathroom by a glass screen; the only splash of colour is the turf-effect rugs. The hotel's minimalism is starting to feel a little dated.

St Regis Grand

Via VE Orlando 3 (06 47 091/www. starwood.com/stregis.com. €€€€.

The hotel's original chandeliers dazzle in massive marbled reception rooms, decorated in opulent gold, beige and red. Rooms have been individually designed using rich fabrics, and are filled with silk-covered Empire and Regency-style furnishings. There's a gym and a sauna.

Aventine & Testaccio

Sant'Anselmo, Villa Pio & Aventino

Piazza di Sant'Anselmo 2/via di Santa Melania 19 (06 570 057/www. aventinohotels.com). €€€.
The three hotels in this group are within a stone's throw of one another in a leafy residential area. The more ornate Sant'Anselmo has recently reopened after refurbishment. The Villa San Pio consists of three separate buildings that share the same pretty gardens and an airy breakfast room; it has a light feel, making it a pleasant place to stay. The Aventino is less manicured. Some rooms have jacuzzis.

Trastevere & the Gianicolo

Antico Borgo Trastevere

Vicolo del Buco 7 (06 588 3774/www. hotelanticoborgo.it). €€.
Down a quiet side street on the quaint eastern side of viale Trastevere, Antico Borgo has small rooms with minuscule bathrooms, but there are wood-beamed ceilings and all the basic amenities. Breakfast is served in the rooms or at the owners' other property, the Domus Tiberina, in a nearby piazza.

Arco del Lauro

NEW *Via dell'Arco de' Tolomei 27 (06 9784 0350/www.arcodellauro.it).* €€.
On a picturesque back-street, Arco del Lauro has four tastefully rooms decorated in modern, fresh neutrals. Budget *residenze* are few and far between in chichi Trastevere: this one is airy and spotlessly clean. Breakfast is taken in a bar in a nearby piazza.

Residenza Arco de' Tolomei

Buonanotte Garibaldi

Via Garibaldi 83 (06 5833 0733/
www.buonanottegaribaldi.com). €€.
Artist Luisa Longo's three rooms
around a courtyard garden act as a
showcase for her distinctive creations:
wall panels, bedcovers and curtains in
hand-painted silk, organza and velvet.
Guests are greeted after a day's sightseeing with a restorative glass of wine.

Casa di Santa Francesca Romana

Via dei Vascellari 61 (06 5812 1252/
www.sfromana.com). €.
This ex-convent, tucked away on a
tranquil side-street, is now a hotel with
a predictably churchy feel. It's popular
with businessmen on a budget and with
families (the quad rooms are spacious
and simply but pleasantly decorated).
The tree-lined central courtyard makes
a pleasant spot for breakfast.

Foresteria Orsa Maggiore

Via San Francesco di Sales 1A (06 689
3753/www.casainternazionaledelle
donne.org). €.
Inside a 16th-century convent that for
many years has been home to a hopping
feminist cultural centre, this women-
only hostel offers B&B accommodation
in bright, clean, recently redecorated
single, double and dorm rooms at rock-
bottom prices. The convent complex
also has eateries, exhibition spaces, a
book shop and a fair-trade store.

Hotel San Francesco

Via Jacopa de' Settesoli 7 (06 5830
0051/www.hotelsanfrancesco.net). €€.
On the quieter eastern side of viale
Trastevere, the San Francesco has an
attractive marble-floored entrance hall
and a lovely roof terrace where breakfast is served when the weather's
warm. Rooms are well-equipped and
reasonably big, though they have a
slightly corporate feel.

Hotel Santa Maria

Vicolo del Piede 2 (06 589 4626/06 589
5474/www.hllsantamaria.com). €€.
On the site of a 16th-century convent,
the Santa Maria has rooms with cool

tiled floors, slightly anonymous peach
decor and spacious bathrooms. They all
open on to a sunny central courtyard
planted with orange trees.

Residenza Arco de' Tolomei

NEW *Via dell'Arco de' Tolomei 26C*
(06 5832 0819/www.inrome.info). €€.
This bijou *residenza* projects a cosy,
welcoming feel. There's beautiful wood
flooring, plentiful antiques and a sunny
breakfast room. All of the bedrooms are
individually designed in a whimsical,
English country-house style; the three
on the upper floor have terraces, the
two below are slightly larger.

Vatican & Prati

Bramante

Vicolo delle Palline 24 (06 6880 6426/
www.hotelbramante.com). €€.
Once home to 16th-century architect
Domenico Fontana, this became an inn
in 1873. It has a large, pleasant reception and a little patio for the summer.
The 16 rooms of varying sizes are simple yet elegant; most have high-beamed
ceilings, some have wrought-iron beds.

Colors Hotel & Hostel

Via Boezio 31 (06 687 4030/
www.colorshotel.com). €.
A short walk from St Peter's, Colors
has bright, clean dorm and hotel
accommodation, plus self-catering
kitchen and laundry facilities, and a
terrace. A new floor opened in 2005; its
superior rooms have air-conditioning,
LCD satellite TVs and breakfast
included. Credit cards accepted for
superior rooms only.

Pensione Paradise

Viale Giulio Cesare 47 (06 3600 4331/
www.pensioneparadise.com). €.
Rooms in this budget hotel are on the
poky side, but friendly staff and a
decent location not far from the
Vatican ensure that backpackers keep
on coming. There's no breakfast and no
air-con, but if you're willing to rough it
a little, you could do far worse.

ESSENTIALS

Getting Around

Arriving & leaving

Airports

Aeroporto Leonardo da Vinci, Fiumicino

Via dell'Aeroporto di Fiumicino 320 (06 65 951/information 06 6595 3640/ www.adr.it). **Open** 24hrs daily.
There's an express **rail** service between Fiumicino airport and Termini railway station, which takes 31mins and runs every 30mins from 6.37am until 11.37pm daily (5.52am-10.52pm to Fiumicino). A one-way ticket costs €9.50.

The regular service from Fiumicino takes 25-40mins, and stops at Trastevere, Ostiense, Tuscolana and Tiburtina stations. Trains leave about every 15mins (less often on Sun) between 5.57am and 11.27pm (5.06am-10.36pm to Fiumicino). Tickets cost €5.

Tickets for either service can be bought with cash or credit card from ticket booths or self-ticketing machines. Stamp your ticket in the machines at the head of the platform before boarding, or you risk a fine.

Terravision (06 6595 8646, www.terravision.it) runs a coach service from Fiumicino to Termini, which also makes stops in the northern suburbs (along via Aurelia) and at Lepanto (journey time to Termini: 70mins). Departures are about every two hours between 8.30am and 8.30pm daily. Coaches from Termini to Fiumicino leave from via Marsala 7 (opposite the multi-storey car park) from 6.30am to 6.30pm. Tickets cost €7 one way, €12 return (€3.50/€6 reductions), and can either be booked in advance online (all major credit cards are accepted), or paid for in cash at the Terravision desk or on the bus.

During the night, a **bus** service runs between Fiumicino (outside Terminal C) and Tiburtina railway station in Rome. Tickets cost €4 from machines, €5 on the bus. Buses leave Tiburtina at 12.30am, 1.15am, 2.30am and 3.45am, stopping at Termini railway station 10mins later. Departures from Fiumicino are at 1.15am, 2.15am, 3.30am and 5am. Neither Termini nor Tiburtina are attractive places at night, so it's advisable to get a taxi from there to your final destination. Buses are infrequent; metro line B at Termini and Tiburtina closes at 11.30pm (12.30am Sat); for the time being, metro line A closes at 9pm daily, with shuttle buses replacing the service at night (see also p182).

Aeroporto GB Pastine, Ciampino

Via Appia Nuova 1650 (06 794 941/ www.adr.it). **Open** 24hrs daily.
The most hassle-free way to get into town from Ciampino is to take the reliable **Terravision** coach service (06 7949 4572/4621, www.terravision.it) to Termini station (journey time: 40mins). Buses leave from outside the arrivals hall after each arrival. Buses from Termini to Ciampino leave from via Marsala 7, opposite the multi-storey car park. This is a dedicated service for the low-cost lines, so you'll need to show your ticket or boarding pass to buy a ticket (€8 single, €14 return; €4/€7 reductions), which can be booked online, or bought (cash only) in the arrivals hall at Ciampino or at the Terravision office in the Termini Forecourt (next to Benetton) or on the bus.

A rival company, **Bus Shuttle** (06 591 7844, www.sitbusshuttle.it), has recently begun a frequent service from Termini (via Marsala) to Ciampino (€6, 4.30am-11.15pm), and Ciampino to Termini (€5, 8.30am-00.30am). Tickets can be bought on the bus or online.

Schiaffini buses (800 700 805, www.schiaffini.it) runs a service between Ciampino and Anagnina metro station every 30-40mins (6am-10.40pm daily), and to Ciampino station (where frequent trains depart for Rome Termini) 5.45am-23.25pm daily; both cost €1. It also runs a direct service (€5) from the airport to Termini station at 00.15am and 00.45am; from Termini to Ciampino at 4.45am. Buy tickets on board.

After the last Terravision bus has departed, getting into the city is well-nigh impossible, as taxis don't bother to pass by.

By bus

There is no central long-distance bus station in Rome. Most coach services terminate outside the following metro stations: Cornelia, Ponte Mammolo and Tiburtina (routes north); Anagnina and EUR Fermi (routes south).

By train

Most long-distance trains arrive at Termini station, also the hub of Rome's transport network. Beware of pickpockets. Night trains may arrive at Tiburtina or Ostiense.

For bookings and information on mainline rail services anywhere in Italy, phone the **Trenitalia** call centre (7am-9pm daily) on 892 021 – 199 166 177 from mobile phones – or consult the official website (www. trenitalia.it). Tickets can be bought at stations (over the counter or from machines, both of which accept credit cards) or online. Under-12s pay half fare; under-4s travel free.

Slower trains (*diretti, espressi, regionali* and *interregionali*) are

very cheap; faster services – InterCity (IC), EuroCity (EC), Eurostar Italia (ES) – are closer to the European norm.

You must stamp your ticket in the yellow machines at the head of the platform before boarding. You risk being fined if you don't.

Rome's main stations are **Ostiense** (piazzale dei Partigiani), **Termini** (piazza dei Cinquecento, customer services 06 4730 6599), **Tiburtina** (circonvallazione Nomentana) and **Trastevere** (piazzale Biondo).

Public transport

Rome's transport system is co-ordinated by **ATAC** (06 46 951, toll-free 800 431 784, www.atac. roma.it). You can download maps of the transport network from the website (click on *percorsi e mappe*), which also has a journey planner.

City-centre and inner-suburb routes are served by the buses and trams of the **Trambus** transport authority. The system is relatively easy to use and as efficient as the traffic-choked streets allow.

Pickpocketing is a problem on buses and metros, particularly on major tourist routes, notoriously the 64 and 40 Express between Termini station and the Vatican.

Tickets

The same tickets are valid on all city bus, tram and metro lines, whether operated by **Trambus**, **MetRo** or regional transport authority **COTRAL**. They are not valid on services to Fiumicino airport. Tickets must be bought before boarding, and are available from ATAC automatic ticket machines, information centres, some bars and newsstands and all *tabacchi*. The latest generation of buses have ticket dispensers on board. Before purchasing a

ESSENTIALS

three-day ticket, consider whether the three-day **Roma Pass** (p13) might not be better value.

BIT valid for 75mins, during which you can take an unlimited number of city buses, plus one metro trip; €1.

BIG valid for one day, until midnight; covers the whole urban network; €4.

BTI three-day pass, covering all bus and metro routes, and local mainline trains to Ostia; €11.

CIS valid for seven days; it covers all bus routes and the metro system, including the lines to Ostia; €16.

You must stamp tickets on board.

Under-10s travel free; older kids have to pay the adult fare, as must pensioners. If you are caught without a validated ticket, you'll be fined €51 on the spot, or €101 if you opt to pay later at a post office.

Buses

Bus is the best way to get around Rome. Once you get the hang of it, the system is easy to use; a sign at each bus stop tells you the routes each line stopping there takes.

Most services run 5.30am-midnight daily, every 10-45mins. The doors for boarding (usually front and rear) and alighting (usually centre) are clearly marked. Note that 'Express' buses make few stops along their route: check before boarding so you don't get whisked past your stop.

Trams

Tram routes mainly serve suburban areas. An express tram service – No.8 – links largo Argentina to Trastevere and the western suburbs. Tram 3 had been replaced by a bus as this guide went to press.

Metro

MetRo is responsible for Rome's two metro lines, which cross beneath Termini train station. Line A runs from south-east to north-west; line B from EUR to the north-eastern suburbs. Line B is open

5.30am to 11.30pm (until 12.30am Sat & Sun). Line A also opens at 5.30am but closes at 9pm daily for work on the long-awaited line C (due in 2011). Shuttle bus services replace metro line A from 9 to 11.30pm (until 12.30am Sat & Sun).

Taxis

Licensed taxis are painted white and have a meter. Touts are rife at Termini and other major tourist magnets; ignore them if you don't want to risk an extortionate fare.

When you pick up a taxi at a rank or hail one in the street, the meter should read zero. As you set off, it will indicate the minimum fare – currently €2.33 (€3.36 on Sundays and public holidays), or €4.91 if you board 10pm-7am. After the first 200m (700ft), the charge goes up according to time, distance and route. There's a €1.04 charge for each item of luggage placed in the boot. Tariffs outside the GRA, Rome's major ring road, are much higher.

Fixed airport tariffs were recently introduced: €40 to/from Fiumicino; €30 to/from Ciampino.

Most of Rome's taxi drivers are honest; if you do suspect you're being fleeced, take down the driver's name and number from the metal plaque inside the car's rear door. The more ostentatiously you do this, the more likely you are to find the fare returning to its proper level. Report complaints to the drivers' co-operative (phone number on the outside of each car) or, in serious cases, the police.

When you phone for a taxi, you'll be given the taxi code-name (always a location followed by a number) and a time, as in *Bahama 69, in tre minuti* ('Bahamas 69, in three minutes'). Radio taxis start the meter from the moment your phone call is answered.

Cooperativa Samarcanda *06 5551/*
www.samarcanda.it.
Cosmos Radio Taxi *06 88 177/*
06 8822.
**Società Cooperativa Autoradio
Taxi Roma** *06 3570/www.3570.it.*
Società la Capitale Radio Taxi
06 49 94.

Driving

Much of central Rome is off-limits
for most of the day for anyone
without a permit. Police and video
cameras guard these ZTL (*zone a
traffico limitato*) areas; any vehicle
without the required pass will be
fined €68.25 if it enters at restricted
times. A strictly enforced no-car
policy applies in the city centre
on some Sundays as well; check
www.comune.roma.it or www.
atac.roma.it for information.

Most motoring associations have
break-down service agreements
with either **Automobile Club
d'Italia** (ACI, 24hr information and
emergency 06 49 981, www.aci.it)
or **Touring Club Italiano** (TCI,
06 3600 5281, www.touringclub.it).

Remember:

■ You are required to wear a seatbelt
at all times, in front and back seats,
and to carry a warning triangle and
reflective jacket in your car.
■ You must keep your driving
licence, vehicle registration and
ID documents on you at all times.
■ Traffic lights flashing amber mean
stop and give way to the right.

Parking

A system in which residents park
for free and visitors pay applies in
many areas. It's efficiently policed,
so watch out for the telltale blue
lines. Buy parking tickets (€1/hr) at
pay-and-display ticket dispensers
or from *tabacchi*. In some areas you
can park for free at certain times,
so check the instructions on the
machine first. €1 parking cards

(*scheda per il parcheggio*), available
from *tabacchi*, save you the bother
of scrabbling for small change.

In zones with no blue lines,
anything resembling a parking
place is up for grabs, with some
exceptions: watch out for signs
saying *Passo carrabile* ('access
at all times') or *Sosta vietata* ('no
parking'), and disabled parking
spaces (marked by yellow stripes
on the road). The sign *Zona
rimozione* ('tow-away area') means
no parking, and is valid for the
length of the street or until the sign
is repeated with a red line through
it. If a street or square has no cars
parked in it, assume it's a strictly
enforced no-parking zone.

In some areas, self-appointed
parcheggiatori will 'look after' your
car for a small fee; it may be illegal
and an absurd imposition, but
it's probably worth paying up to
ensure your tyres remain intact.

Cars are fairly safe in most
central areas, but you may prefer
the hefty rates charged by
underground car parks to keep
your vehicle off the street. The
following are centrally located:
ParkSì Villa Borghese *viale del
Galoppatoio 33 (06 322 5934/7972/
www.sabait.it).* **Rates** €1.30/hr for
up to 3hrs, cheaper thereafter.
Valentino *via Sistina 75E (06 678
2597).* **Rates** €3/hr for up to six hours.

Vehicle removal

If your car is not where you left it,
it may have been towed. Phone the
municipal police (*Vigili urbani*) on
06 67 691 and quote your number
plate to find out which pound it's in.

Vehicle hire

Avis *06 4282 4728/
www.avisautonoleggio.it.*
Europcar *199 307 030/
www.europcar.it.*
Hertz *199 112 211/www.hertz.it.*
Maggiore *06 6501 0678/toll-free
848 867 067/www.maggiore.it.*

Resources A-Z

Accident & emergency

To call an **ambulance**, dial 118; for the **fire brigade** dial 115; for **police**, see p185.

The hospitals listed below offer 24hr casualty services. If your child needs emergency treatment, head for the Ospedale Bambino Gesù.

Ospedale Fatebenefratelli
Isola Tiberina (06 68 371).

Ospedale Pediatrico Bambino Gesù *Piazza Sant'Onofrio 4 (06 68 591/www.opbg.net).*

Ospedale San Camillo-Forlanini *Via Portuense 332 (06 55 551/06 58 701/www.scamilloforlanini.rm.it).*

Ospedale San Giacomo
Via Canova 29 (06 36 261/ www.aslromaa.it/ospedali/osg.htm).

Ospedale San Giovanni
Via Amba Aradam 8 (06 7705 3444/www.hsangiovanni.roma.it).

Policlinico Umberto I
Viale Policlinico 155 (06 49 971/ www.policlinicoumberto1.it).

Pharmacies

Normal pharmacy opening hours are 8.30am-1pm, 4-8pm Mon-Sat. Outside these hours, a duty rota system operates. A list by the door of any pharmacy (and in local papers) indicates the nearest ones.

Farmacia della Stazione *Piazza dei Cinquecento 49-51 (06 488 0019).* **Open** 24hrs daily.

Piram *Via Nazionale 228 (06 488 0754).* **Open** 24hrs daily.

Credit card loss

The following are open 24hrs.
American Express *06 7290 0347/06 7228 0371/US cardholders 800 874 333*
Diner's Club *800 864 064*
MasterCard *800 870 866*
Visa *800 877 232*

Customs

Travellers arriving from EU countries are not required to declare goods imported into or exported from Italy if they are for personal use, up to the following limits:
- 800 cigarettes or 400 cigarillos or 200 cigars or 1kg of tobacco
- ten litres of spirits (over 22% alcohol) or 20 litres of fortified wine (under 22% alcohol).

For people arriving from non-EU countries the following limits apply:
- 200 cigarettes or 100 cigarillos or 50 cigars or 250g of tobacco
- one litre of spirits or two litres of wine; one bottle of perfume (50g)
- 250ml of eau de toilette or various merchandise not exceeding €175.

Anything above will be subject to taxation at the port of entry.

There are no restrictions on the importation of cameras, watches or electrical goods. For information call Italian customs (*dogana*) on 041 269 9311 or check their website (www.agenziadogane.it).

Dental emergency

For serious dental emergencies, use hospital casualty departments (see above). Children should be taken to the Ospedale Bambino Gesù.

Disabled

With its cobbled streets, narrow pavements and inaccessible facilities in old buildings, Rome is a difficult city for disabled people. That said, many city centre buses are now wheelchair accessible and most museums and larger hotels have suitable facilities.

The non-profit **CO.IN** (06 5717 7001, www.coinsociale.it) gives information on disabled facilities at museums, restaurants, shops, theatres, stations and hotels. The group also organises transport for disabled people (up to eight places), which must be booked several days in advance. It runs a phone service in Italian and English (toll-free 800 271 027, from within Italy only).

Roma per Tutti (06 5717 7094, www.romapertutti.it) is an info line run by CO.IN and the city council. English-speaking staff answer questions on accessibility in hotels, buildings and monuments.

Information for disabled people is also available from Enjoy Rome and the APT tourist office (p187).

Electricity

Italy uses 220V – compatible with British-bought appliances (with a plug adaptor); US 110V equipment requires a current transformer.

Embassies & consulates

For a full list of embassies, see *Ambasciate* in the phone book.
Australia *Via Antonio Bosio 5 (06 852 721/www.italy.embassy.gov.au).*
Britain *Via XX Settembre 80A (06 4220 0001/www.britain.it).*
Canada *Via Zara 30 (06 854 441/ 06 8544 43937/www.canada.it).*
Ireland *Piazza Campitelli (06 697 9121/www.ambasciata-irlanda.it).*
New Zealand *Via Zara 28 (06 441 7171/www.nzembassy.com).*
South Africa *Via Tanaro 14 (06 852 541/www.sudafrica.it).*
US *Via Vittorio Veneto 119 (06 46 741/www.usembassy.it).*

Internet

Much of central Rome, plus major parks (*ville* Borghese, Pamphili, Ada, Torlonia) and the Auditorium – Parco della Musica zone, has free wireless hotspots sponsored by the city council. As soon as you open your browser in one of the hotspots, you'll be asked to log on. Initially you'll need to register, giving a mobile phone number when you do so. For information, including a map, see www.romawireless.com.
EasyEverything *Via Barberini 2 (www.easyeverything.com).* **Open** 8am-2am daily. No credit cards.

Opening hours

For shopping hours, see p21; for pharmacies, see p184.

Most banks open 8.30am-1.30pm, 2.45-4.30pm Mon-Fri. Some central branches also open until 6pm Thur and 8.30am-12.30pm Sat. All banks work reduced hours the day before a holiday (many close by 11am).

Police

For emergencies, call one of the following helplines:
Carabinieri *(English-speaking helpline)* 112
Polizia di stato 113
The principal *Polizia di Stato* station, the Questura Centrale, is at via San Vitale 15 (06 46 861, www.poliziadistato.it). Others, and the Carabinieri's *Commissariati*, are listed in the phone directory under *Polizia* and *Carabinieri*. Incidents can be reported to either.

Post

The once-notorious Italian postal service is now generally efficient (try the Vatican Post Office, run in association with the Swiss postal service, if in doubt). For postal information, call 803 160 (8am-8pm Mon-Sat) or visit www.poste.it.

There are local post offices (*ufficio postale*) in each district; opening hours are generally 8.30am-6pm Mon-Fri (8.30am-2pm

ESSENTIALS

Aug), 8.30am-1.30pm Sat and any day preceding a public holiday. They close two hours earlier than normal on the last day of each month. Main post offices in the centre have longer opening hours. Some services are available via the website (www.poste.it); check it first to avoid the queues.

Posta Centrale *Piazza San Silvestro 19 (06 6973 7232/info 803 160).*
Vatican Post Office *Piazza San Pietro (06 6988 3406).*

Smoking

A law introduced in January 2005 prohibits smoking in all public places in Italy except for those that provide a distinct, ventilated smokers' room. Possible fines of between €27.50 and €275 (or up to €550 if you smoke in the presence of children or pregnant women) are the reason why you'll find small groups puffing away *outside* most restaurants, pubs and clubs.

Tabacchi

Tabacchi, identified by signs with a white T on a black background, are the only places where you can buy tobacco products. They also sell stamps, phone cards, tickets for public transport and lottery tickets.

Telephones

Dialling & codes

▪ Land-lines have the area code 06, which must be used whether calling from within or outside the city. When phoning Rome from abroad, do *not* omit the initial 0.
▪ Numbers beginning 800 are toll-free. Numbers beginning 840 and 848 are charged at low set rates but can only be called within Italy.
▪ Mobile numbers begin with a 3. GSM phones can be used on both 900 and 1800 bands; British, Australian and New Zealand mobiles work fine, but US phones (unless they're tri-band) don't work.
▪ For international calls, dial 00, followed by the country code, area code (omitting the initial zero, if applicable) and number. Codes include: Australia 61; Canada 1; Irish Republic 353; New Zealand 64; United Kingdom 44; United States 1.

Directory enquiries

This is a jungle, and charges for information given over the phone are steep. The major services are 1254 (Italian and international numbers, in Italian) and 892 412 (international numbers, in Italian and English, from mobile phones). Italian directory information can be accessed for free at www.1254.it and www.paginebianche.it.

Operator services

To reverse the charges (make a collect call), dial 170 for the international operator. If you are reversing the charges from a phone box, insert a 10¢ coin (refunded after your call).

Public phones

Rome has no shortage of public phone boxes, and many bars have payphones, which are rarely busy as locals are addicted to mobiles. Most only accept phone cards (*schede telefoniche*); a few also accept major credit cards. Phone cards cost €5, €15 and €30 and are available from *tabacchi*, some newsstands and some bars.

Tickets

For pre-booking tickets for sights, galleries and exhibitions, see p11.
Expect to pay *diritti di prevendita* (booking fees) on tickets bought

anywhere except at the venue on the night. **Ricordi** (via del Corso 506, 06 361 2370) sells tickets for classical concerts and for many rock, jazz and other events.

Hello Ticket (800 907 080, 06 4782 5710, www.helloticket.it), by platform 25 in Termini station, takes bookings over the phone and online for most concerts, plays and sporting events.

Time

Italy is on Central European Time, making it one hour ahead of GMT and six hours ahead of Eastern Standard Time. In all EU countries clocks are moved forward one hour in early spring and back again in late autumn.

Tipping

Foreigners are generally expected to tip more than Italians, but the ten or more per cent that is usual in many countries is seen as generous even for the richest-looking tourist in most eateries, where anything between €1 and €5 is normal; some smarter places now include a 10-15% service charge. For drinks, leave 10¢-20¢ on the counter when ordering at a bar. Taxi drivers will be happy if you round the fare up to the nearest whole euro.

Tourist information

The offices of Rome's tourist board, **APT**, have English-speaking staff. For more personal service, the private **Enjoy Rome** agency is highly recommended. Rome's city council has well-stocked, green tourist information kiosks (**PIT**), open 9.30am-7/7.30pm daily; the most central are in piazza Pia (by Castel Sant'Angelo), piazza delle Cinque Lune (by piazza Navona), piazza Sonnini (in Trastevere)

and piazza del Tempio della Pace (off via dei Fori Imperiali).
APT (Azienda per il Turismo di Roma) *Via Parigi 5 (06 4889 9200/ infoline 06 8205 9127/www.roma turismo.com).* **Open** *Phoneline* 9am-6pm daily. *Office* 9.30am-1pm, 2.30-4.30pm Mon, Thur.
Enjoy Rome *Via Marghera 8A (06 445 1843/www.enjoyrome.com).* **Open** *Nov-Mar* 9am-6.30pm Mon-Fri; 8.30am-2pm Sat. *Apr-Oct* 8.30am-7pm Mon-Fri; 8.30am-2pm Sat. No credit cards.
Ufficio Pellegrini e Turisti (Vatican Tourist Office) *Piazza San Pietro (06 6988 1662/www.vaticano.va).* **Open** 8.30am-6.30pm Mon-Sat.

Visas

EU nationals and citizens of the US, Canada, Australia and New Zealand do not need visas for stays of up to three months. For EU citizens a passport or national ID card valid for travel abroad is sufficient; non-EU citizens must have full passports. In theory, all visitors must declare their presence to the local police within eight days of arrival. If you're staying in a hotel, this will be done for you.

What's on

Listings mags *Rome C'è* (www. romace.it, out Wed) and *Trovaroma* (free with *La Repubblica* on Thur) are the best sources of information about shows, concerts and nightlife. The latter has an English section.

Major cultural events are listed on the city of Rome's website (www.romaturismo.it). For an alternative look at Rome's nightlife, check out www.romastyle.info and www.musicaroma.it.

For information on Rome's gay scene, contact **Arcigay Roma** (06 6450 1102, www.arcigayroma.it) or **Arci-Lesbica Roma** (06 418 0211, www.arcilesbica.it/roma). For other gay organisations, see p27.

ESSENTIALS

Vocabulary

Pronunciation

a – like a in ask
e – like a in age or e in sell
i – like ea in east
o – like o in hotel or hot
u – like oo in boot
c – as in cat before a, o and u;
otherwise like ch in cheat
g – as in good before a, o and u;
otherwise like g in giraffe; gl – like
lli in million; gn – like ny in canyon
h – after any consonant makes it
hard (ch – cat; gh – good)
sc – like sh in shame; sch – like
sc in scout

Useful phrases

hello/goodbye (informal) ciao, salve;
good morning buon giorno; good
evening buona sera; good night
buona notte
please per favore, per piacere; thank
you grazie; you're welcome prego;
excuse me, sorry pardon, (formal)
mi scusi, (informal) scusa
I don't speak Italian (very well)
non parlo (molto bene) l'italiano
do you speak English?
parla inglese?
can I use/where's the toilet?
posso usare/dov'è il bagno?
open aperto; closed chiuso;
entrance entrata; exit uscita

Transport

bus autobus, auto; car macchina;
coach pullman; plane aereo; taxi
tassi, taxi; train treno; tram tram;
bus stop fermata (dell'autobus);
platform binario; station stazione;
ticket biglietto; one-way solo andata;
return andata e ritorno

Directions

where is? dov'è?; (turn) left (giri a)
sinistra; (it's on the) right (è a/sulla)
destra; straight on sempre dritto;
is it near/far? è vicino/lontano?

Communications

attacco per il computer dataport;
broadband ADSL (adiesselle);
cellphone telefonino; courier
corriere, pony; fax fax; letter lettera;
phone telefono; postcard cartolina;
stamp francobollo; a stamp for
England/the US un francobollo
per l'Inghilterra/gli Stati Uniti

Days

Monday lunedì; Tuesday martedì;
Wednesday mercoledì; Thursday
giovedì; Friday venerdì; Saturday
sabato; Sunday domenica
yesterday ieri; today oggi;
tomorrow domani; weekend
fine settimana, weekend

Numbers, weights & sizes

0 zero; 1 uno; 2 due; 3 tre; 4 quattro;
5 cinque; 6 sei; 7 sette; 8 otto; 9 nove;
10 dieci; 11 undici; 12 dodici;
13 tredici; 14 quattordici; 15 quindici;
16 seidici; 17 diciasette; 18 diciotto;
19 dicianove; 20 venti; 30 trenta;
40 quaranta; 50 cinquanta;
60 sessanta; 70 settanta; 80 ottanta;
90 novanta; 100 cento; 200 duecento;
1,000 mille; 2,000 duemila
I take (shoe/dress) size porto il
numero/la taglia…; 100 grams of…
un'etto di…; 300 grams of…
tre etti di…; a kilo of… un kilo di…;
five kilos of… cinque chili di…

Booking & paying

booking, reservation prenotazione
I'd like to book… vorrei prenotare…
…a table for four at eight un tavolo
per quattro alle otto
…a single/twin/double room una
camera singola/doppia/matrimoniale
how much is it? quanto costa?
do you take credit cards?
si accettano le carte di credito?

ESSENTIALS

Menu Glossary

Sauces & toppings

aglio, olio e peperoncino *garlic, oil and chilli*; **alle vongole** *clams*; **al pomodoro fresco** *fresh/raw tomatoes*; **al ragù** *'bolognese' (a term that doesn't exist in Italian!)*; **al sugo** *puréed cooked tomatoes*; **all'amatriciana** *tomato, chilli, sausage and onion*; **alla gricia** *as above without tomato*; **all'arrabbiata** *tomato and chilli*; **alla carbonara** *egg, bacon and parmesan*; **alla puttanesca** *olives, capers and garlic*; **cacio e pepe** *cheese and black pepper*; **in bianco** *with oil or butter and parmesan*; **(ravioli) ricotta e spinaci** *filled with curd cheese and spinach*.

Meat & meat dishes

abbacchio, agnello *lamb*; **animelle** *fried pancreas and thymus glands*; **bresaola** *thinly-sliced cured beef*; **coda alla vaccinara** *oxtail in celery broth*; **coniglio** *rabbit*; **lardo** *fatty bacon*; **lingua** *tongue*; **maiale** *pork*; **manzo** *beef*; **ossobuco** *beef shins with marrow jelly inside*; **pajata** *veal/lamb intestines*; **pancetta** *bacon*; **pollo** *chicken*; **porchetta** *roast suckling pig*; **prosciutto cotto** *ham*; **prosciutto crudo** *Parma ham*; **trippa** *tripe*; **vitello** *veal*.

Fish & seafood

alici, acciughe *anchovies*; **aragosta, astice** *lobster*; **arzilla, razza** *skate*; **baccalà** *salt cod*; **branzino, spigola** *sea bass*; **calamari** *squid*; **cernia** *grouper*; **dentice, fragolino, marmora, orata, sarago** *various forms of bream*; **cozze** *mussels*; **gamberi** *prawns*; **mazzancolle** *king prawns*; **merluzzo** *cod*; **moscardini** *baby octopus*; **ostriche** *oysters*; **pesce sanpietro** *john dory*; **pesce spada** *swordfish*; **polpo, polipo** *octopus*; **rombo** *turbot*; **salmone** *salmon*; **seppie** *cuttlefish*; **sogliola** *sole*; **tonno** *tuna*; **vongole** *clams*.

Vegetables

asparagi *asparagus*; **broccoli siciliani** *broccoli*; **broccolo** *green cauliflower*; **broccoletti** *turnip tops*; **carciofo** *artichoke*; **cavolfiore** *cauliflower*; **cicoria** *green leaf vegetable, like dandelion*; **cipolla** *onion*; **fagioli** *beans*; **fagiolini** *green beans*; **fave** *broad beans*; **funghi** *mushrooms*; **insalata verde/mista** *green/mixed salad*; **melanzana** *aubergine, eggplant*; **patate** *potatoes*; **patatine fritte** *french fries*; **piselli** *peas*; **puntarelle** *bitter salad vegetable usually served with anchovy sauce*; **rughetta** *rocket*; **sedano** *celery*; **spinaci** *spinach*; **zucchine** *courgettes*.

Fruit

ananas *pineapple*; **anguria, cocomero** *watermelon*; **arance** *oranges*; **ciliegi** *cherries*; **fichi** *figs*; **fragole** *strawberries*; **mele** *apples*; **nespole** *loquats*; **pere** *pears*; **pesche** *peaches*; **uva** *grapes*.

Desserts

gelato *ice-cream*; **pannacotta** *'cooked cream', a thick blancmange-like cream*; **sorbetto** *water ice*; **tiramisù** *mascarpone and coffee sponge*; **torta della nonna** *flan of pâtisserie cream and pinenuts*; **millefoglie** *flaky pastry cake*.

Miscellaneous

antipasto *hors d'oeuvre*; **primo** *first course*; **secondo** *main course*; **contorno** *side dish, vegetable*; **dessert, dolce** *dessert*; **fritto** *fried*; **arrosta** *roast*; **alla griglia** *grilled*; **all'agro** *with oil and lemon*; **ripassato in padella** *(of vegetables) cooked then tossed in a pan with oil, garlic and chilli*; **formaggio** *cheese*; **parmigiano** *parmesan*; **pane** *bread*; **sale** *salt*; **pepe** *pepper*; **aceto** *vinegar*; **olio** *oil*.

Index

Sights & Areas

a

Abbazia delle Tre Fontane p156
Accademia di San Luca p95
Appian Way p152
Ara Pacis Museum p84
Auditorium – Parco della Musica p99
Aventine p117

b

Baths of Caracalla p120
Baths of Diocletian p101
Bioparco-Zoo p90
Borgo p139
Botanical Gardens p129

c

Campo de' Fiori p60
Capitoline Museums p54
Caracalla p117
Castel Sant'Angelo p142
Catacombs p153
Celio p108
Centrale Montemartini p121
Centro, Il p52
Chiesa Nuova p72
Circus Maximus p55
Circus of Maxentius p155
Colosseum p55
Crypta Balbi p61

d

Domus Aurea p101

e

Esquilino p100
EUR p155
Explora – Museo dei Bambini di Roma p90

g

Galleria Borghese p92
Galleria Colonna p95
Galleria Doria Pamphilj p72
Galleria Nazionale d'Arte Moderna e Contemporanea p92
Galleria Spada p61
Gesù, Il p66
Ghetto p60
Gianicolo p138

h

Hadrian's Villa p158

i

Imperial Fora p56

k

Keats-Shelley Memorial House p84

m

MACRO p99
Mamertine Prison p57
MAXXI p99
Monteverde p138
Monti p100
Museo Barracco p66
Museo Carlo Bilotti p92
Museo della Civiltà Romana p156
Museo dell'Alto Medioevo p156
Museo delle Anime dei Defunti p149
Museo delle Arti e Tradizioni Popolari p156
Museo di Palazzo Venezia p57
Museo di Roma p72
Museo di Roma in Trastevere p129
Museo Ebraica di Roma p66
Museo Nazionale d'Arte Orientale p101
Museo Nazionale delle Paste Alimentari p95
Museo Nazionale di Villa Giulia p92
Museo Preistorico ed Etnografico L Pigorini p156
Museo Storico Nazionale dell'Arte Sanitaria p142
Museum of Via Ostiense p121

o

Orto botanico p129
Ostia Antica p157
Ostiense p120

p

Palatine p58
Palazzo Altemps p72
Palazzo Barberini p95
Palazzo Corsini p129
Palazzo delle Esposizioni p104
Palazzo del Quirinale p96
Palazzo Massimo alle Terme p104
Palazzo Ruspoli-Fondazione Memmo p85
Pantheon p72
Piazza di Spagna p85

Piazza Navona p73
Ponte Rotto p67
Portico d'Ottavia p67
Prati p148
Protestant Cemetery p121

q

Quirinale p94

r

Roman Forum p58

s

St Peter's p143
San Carlino alle Quattro Fontane p96
San Clemente p110
Sancta Sanctorum p113
San Francesco a Ripa p129
San Giorgio in Velabro p58
San Giovanni p108
San Giovanni in Laterano p110
San Gregorio Magno p111
San Lorenzo p114
San Lorenzo fuori le Mura p114
San Lorenzo in Lucina p85
San Luigi dei Francesi p73
San Marco p58
San Nicola in Carcere p59
San Paolo fuori le Mura p122
San Pietro in Montorio p138
San Pietro in Vincoli p104
Santa Cecilia in Trastevere p129
Santa Croce in Gerusalemme p111
Sant'Agnese in Agone p75
Sant'Agostino p75
Santa Maria
  della Concezione p94
  della Pace p75
  della Vittoria p96
  del Popolo p85
  in Aracoeli p59
  in Cosmedin p59
  in Domnica p111
  in Trastevere p132
  in Vallicella p72
  Maggiore p105
  sopra Minerva p75
Sant'Andrea al Quirinale p96
Sant'Andrea della Valle p67
Santa Prassede p105
Santa Pudenziana p106
Santa Sabina p120
Santi Giovanni e Paolo p112

ESSENTIALS

ESSENTIALS

INDULGE YOURSELF IN A

GUILT-FREE

SHOPPING TOUR

Castel Romano

Designer Outlet

TM

Castel Romano Designer Outlet

More than 100 shops of top brands at prices reduced from 30% to 70% all year round.

Book your shopping shuttle from your hotel! For information and booking please contact hotel reception desk within the day before departure and in any case not later than 11.00 AM of the visit date.

Ask your concierge to phone to 06 37350810; 329 4317686.

The cost of the shuttle is 25€
(deposit at the moment of reservation for the service: 5 €)

If you don't feel like driving there is a **shuttle bus** from Central Rome Piazza della Repubblica to the Castel Romano Designer Outlet on Tuesday, Friday Saturday and Sunday.

Vat Refund point: until 30 June 2007, inside Castel Romano Designer Outlet there is a space where you can claim back Vat immediately. If you made purchases using Tax Free Global Refund, also outside of Castel Romano for example in Rome downtown or other cities in Italy, you are eligible to receive vouchers for an additional 10% value that can be used at all of the shops at Castel Romano Designer Outlet.
(These vouchers are valid only on the same day of purchase).

Via Pontina SS 148 Castel Romano (Rome)

Infoline: 0039 06 5050050
tourism@mcarthurglen.com